A Philosophy of Healing and Spirituality

A Philosophy of Healing and Spirituality

A MIND ADVENTURE

Hugh Drummond Fulcher

Disclaimer: This book is intended to inspire innovative thinking about the mind, life, and spirituality and is not intended to be a substitute for professional medical services. Neither the author nor the publisher is responsible for consequences experienced, or not experienced, if using the author's alternative mind healing processes. Practicing alternative healing exercises, given herein, are at the discretion, risk, and responsibility of the reader. Bold processes and exercises have only been practiced by and proven beneficial for the author.

Cover: Jesus inspired spiritual models. Plato inspired philosophy models. Albert Einstein's brilliance showed how imaginative the mind can be inspiring physics based models. Sigmund Freud's psychoanalysis, and mind models, inspired psychiatric models. Lewis Page Fulcher, Sr., and Frances Drummond Fulcher, my parents, fought for me with love and concern, and saved my life, when I was "expecting death" and unlovable.

Copyright © 2015 Hugh Drummond Fulcher
All Rights Reserved

ISBN: 0979071070
ISBN13: 9780979071072
Library of Congress Control Number: 2015900132
H. Fulcher Publishers, Lynchburg, VA
Published by: H Fulcher Publishers

Earlier books by Hugh Drummond Fulcher:

Emotional Mind Modeling (1995)
The Clear Mind Procedure (2007)
Bipolar Blessings & Mind Expansion (2008)
God, the Universe, & You! (2008)
Bipolar Blessings & Mind Expansion 2nd Ed. (2009)
God, the Universe, & You! 2nd Ed. (2009)
Mental Reconstruction Log (To Be Published)

Vita

HUGH DRUMMOND FULCHER RESIDES IN Forest, Virginia, and has two children: Keston Hugh Fulcher, PhD, and Kara Fulcher Hawkins, M.D.

He graduated from Virginia Tech, B.S. in Physics (minor in math), and M.S., in Nuclear Engineering. His thesis was on nuclear reactor modeling and design. He was a licensed operator of the Virginia Tech experimental nuclear reactor, and studied at Argonne National Laboratory.

He was a University physics and engineering instructor for Virginia Tech and Danville Community College. He designed nuclear reactor core models, developed nuclear software monitoring systems, performed nuclear safety analysis, and tested and implemented engineering design systems. He has written six earlier books.

Mr. Fulcher worked with nuclear reactor design and consulting companies, nuclear utilities, and National Laboratories.

Conversations on neurosurgery with O. Hugh Fulcher, MD, an uncle and former Head of the Georgetown University Neurosurgery Department, "expected death," and experience modeling complex nuclear reactors, inspired Mr. Fulcher to model the brain, mind, and God, for adding science and spiritual meaning to the human experiment.

Mr. Fulcher has developed alternative mind healing and spiritual models over a thirty year period and founded a leasing company in 2004. He is a member of *Who's Who in America*.

Table of Contents

Vita · vii
Table of Contents · ix
List of Figures · xiii
Acknowledgements · xv
Dedications · xvii

INTRODUCTION SECTION · xix

    Introduction · xxi

MODELING SECTION · 1

    Modeling Experience · 3
    Early Life · 9
    Siblings · 13
    Feelings · 19
    Emotions · 23
    Emotional Relationships · 27
    Smile and Frown · 37

Love and Sharing · 43
Being Selfish · 47
Conflict · 51
Creative Thinking · 55
Predicting · 61
Psychology · 65
Psychiatry · 75
Philosophy · 81
Adventure · 87
Evaluations · 91
Discrete and Holistic · 97

SCIENCE SECTION · **103**

Bumblebee and ESP! · 105
The Heisenberg Uncertainty Principle · · · · · · · · · · · 107
Neuroscience · 113
Physics of the Brain · 123
Spiritual Physics · 131
Philosophy of Perfect · 141

BRAIN SECTION · **145**

Brain · 147
Healing the Body · 157
Subconscious Processes · 161
Dreams · 167
The Flash · 177
Miracles · 181
Operating the Brain · 185

MIND SECTION · **191**

    Mind ·193
    Memory ·201
    Trauma · 205
    Depression ·211
    Bipolar Disorder ·219
    Episodes and Insanities · 225
    Mental Limits · 233
    Mental Holograms · 239
    Alternative Mind Healing ·243
    Healing Vertigo and Arthritis ·245
    Psychiatric Exercises ·249
    Inner Trauma · 265
    Mental Reconstruction · 269
    Inner Sensations · 277
    Consciousness Model · 279
    The Clear Mind · 283
    Evil and Evil Minds · 287
    Serenity Prayer · 289

SPIRITUAL SECTION · **295**

    Nothing before Time · 297
    Creation · 305
    Soul · 309
    Mind, Heart, Soul ·313
    Beliefs ·315
    Thomas Jefferson's Beliefs ·321
    Christianity · 327
    Born Again · 333

Prayer ·337
Religion · 341
Spiritual Model ·351
Spiritual Messages · 359
Spiritual Meditation · 365
Jesus · 369
Future Spiritual Leaders ·375
Omnipresence and Omniscience ·379
Structure of Heaven · 383
Heaven Model · 387
Proof of God's Existence · 395
Quantizing God · 403
Model of God · 407

CONCLUSION SECTION · **425**

Conclusion · 427

List of Figures

Psychiatric Exercises

Figure 1: Head-Down Resistance · 262
Figure 2: Head-Down and Left Resistance · · · · · · · · · · · · · · · · 262
Figure 3: Head-Left Resistance · 262
Figure 4: Wolves Holusion · 263

Acknowledgements

I am eternally grateful to my parents, Lewis Page Fulcher, Sr., and Frances Drummond Fulcher, (both deceased,) for their love and guidance. They remain the love beneath my wings.

My children, Dr. Keston Hugh Fulcher, PhD, and Kara Fulcher Hawkins, M.D., and her husband, Andy Hawkins M.D., have been supportive in many ways.

I thank computer builders and software developers for tools that have made writing and editing easier.

I thank my Savior, Jesus Christ, and God for sharing so many ideas.

Dedications

A Philosophy of Healing & Spirituality, A Mind Adventure, Everybody's Crazy! is dedicated to those who have supported my writing and life, and to those I hope to assist in living healthy, confident, and spiritual lives. Specific dedications are:

My parents, Frances Drummond Fulcher (deceased) for her patience, and Lewis Page Fulcher, Sr. (deceased) for his wisdom, and both for their love; they were the wind beneath my wings.

My Uncle, O. Hugh Fulcher, MD (deceased), former Head of the Georgetown University Neurosurgery Department, who instilled confidence to reason about the brain;
Thomas M. Fulcher MD (deceased) who took such an interest in my writing;
My children, Keston Hugh Fulcher, PhD, and Kara Fulcher Hawkins, MD;
My cousin Barbara Fulcher Mays and her husband Carlton have always been supportive of me, my family, and my endeavors.
All readers coping with abuse, mental pain, disorders, and uncertainties;
Everyone who loves, cares for, and shares with, others.

Introduction Section

Introduction

"Imagination is everything. It is the preview
of life's coming attractions."

"I must be willing to give up what I am in
order to become what I will be."

"Once we accept our limits, we go beyond them."

— Albert Einstein

Life is heaven or hell depending upon health, relationships with those close to us, reflections of those relationships, inner reflections, and successes or failures. Interactions may be positive, supportive, confidence building, or degrading, damaging, and slow murder. Mental health and happiness depend upon accomplishments, marriage, and other important relationships.

Childhood and spousal abuse and uncertainties eventually degraded my mind into depression and bipolar disorder. Spirituality, psychology, psychiatry, and mental exercises and models became my healing tools. In mania, I began work to connect my Christian beliefs with my physics background. My healing and spirituality became a wonderful, epic adventure.

This work has been intentionally separated from and not restricted by recognized mental health or spiritual authorities. Traditional research structures often restrict creativity. This science/philosophical approach will hopefully motivate those with mental difficulties, their caregivers, and researchers to consider alternate healing and spiritual technologies.

Near death, trials, heartbreaks, and successes of a physicist/nuclear engineer have created a rebounding approach to life. Depression and bipolar disorder began in 1977. I felt forced to search for new meaning in life and the need and reason for after life.

Assumptions and reasons of current activities in life became more apparent. Psychology and mental healing extended into spirituality.

Understanding, and writing about, mental difficulties has been instrumental in healing my bipolar disorder. My science and philosophy study has expanded my Christian beliefs. In His era, Jesus was the progressive liberal who has changed spiritual beliefs and lives throughout the world.

Habit, reasoning, emotion, and inner communication perspectives have developed alternative healing processes. Imaginative exercises affect and heal the brain and mind. Muscles are connected to nerves and nerves to the brain. Performing conflicting exercises forces traumatized neural networks to limits, purging energy from repressed memories. Computers and the brain work faster with less energy. Only we can control and heal our emotions, and minds.

Depression reduces abilities to think in words. When depressed or expecting death, the mind may overreact into fast-thinking and then mania with loss of reason. Manic energy and excitement override normal and social thinking boundaries. When exceeding emotional limits, minds go out of control and degrade into insanity. Subconscious processes are no longer able to converge to complete conscious thoughts. Beyond limits, machines and minds spiral out of control.

Nothing makes sense. Uncertainties and fears awaken spiritual processes. God became my only hope. Caretakers, family, and friends do not understand, or believe, this new out of control spiritual excitement. Their disbeliefs cause the afflicted to distrust family and friends. God understands!

The fortunate get help. Psychiatric medications slow the mind into more rational thinking. However, medications did not prevent my manic episodes. I experienced sporadic episodes from 1977 until 1994. One cannot continue the same activities and expect different results. I decided to develop my own cure for my unstable bipolar mind. I experimented to extend my mind to mental, emotional limits to regain control during difficult times. This is mental reconstruction.

After a few months of conflicting exercises in 1994, I made an important prediction that inner sensations were repressed mental energy releases. I predicted that sensations would migrate throughout the brain and that individual energy releases would decrease over time. After four additional months of conflicting neck exercises, predictions proved true.

During and after exercises, inner sensations have slowly become more pleasant and an incentive to continue exercises for 20 years. We feel confident when we can predict important events in our lives. Predicting gives a sense of understanding. The brain and mind is complex and heals very slowly.

After twenty years, my unique healing and spiritual adventure has been an amazing success. I have not experienced a manic episode since 1994. Everyone becomes creative with minds extended beyond normal emotional limits. Bipolar minds can recover from hopeless depths of despair to soar with creative confidence.

Many soldiers returning from Iraq and Afghanistan experience post traumatic syndrome, PTS. Repressed traumatic experiences are reactivated as stressful memories with loss of control. This loss of control has similarities to mania. Reactivated traumatic memories extend beyond emotional limits and override current awareness and reality. This work is meant to help those with difficulties understand and heal overstressed, reactive minds.

A Philosophy of Healing and Spirituality

Babies are conceived perfectly spiritual with inner potentials of promising futures. They know no evil. With nurturing, babies will grow healthy and choose their own adventures and destinies.

Traumas and brainwashing build inner imaginary jails within young minds and bodies. The afflicted may live and work for others', and not their own, goals. Without ingrained brainwashing and trauma effects, we are healthier and smarter.

Life began as an abused child. Everyone seemed to treat me well, except my older and bigger brother. He seemed good to others but a bully to me. I had good parents, but they did not, or were unable to, control or stop sibling bullying. At that time, parents may have thought that was the way siblings acted. As a child, I often experienced uncertainty and fear.

Sibling bullying is worse than school bullying. There is no escape. It is the parent's responsibility to prevent sibling abuse. Effects of childhood abuse last a lifetime without counseling or mental reconstruction. I have worked to overcome childhood bullying for twenty years.

Bullying is catching. If a brother bullies a younger brother, he becomes devalued in the eyes of the older brother's friends. Some of his friends will degrade the younger brother also.

All children can be smart and successful if encouraged and not abused. I made sure my son would not abuse his younger sister. He was the best of brothers. Healthy atmospheres for children depend upon parents' guidance and discipline. Without childhood abuse, both of my children became doctors. A loving, caring childhood is so important for mental health and successful life.

Parents should teach their children to build mutual confidence, early in their lives. There will be less sibling fighting. Parenting will be easier. Siblings will grow with respect for one another and for parents. Parents should also empower each other for building strong close-knit families. The whole becomes greater than the sum of its parts.

Everyone must be taught to recognize, ignore, or respond to put downs. People who put others down have a lack of self-esteem and principles. Not addressing persistent put downs causes inner stress and possibly mental illnesses.

My career began teaching university physics for VA Tech and continued in nuclear reactor design. I felt normal, confident, and productive until 1972. I married an adult child of two alcoholic parents within three months of knowing her. Adult children of alcoholics mimic ingrained alcoholic behaviors observed when young.

My former wife worked hard and was good at things she did. She was also good at manipulating and degrading her husband when we were alone. She learned deceptive controlling from her alcoholic, deranged mother. I had good, positive minded parents in a good country environment and did not know how to counter her conflicting behaviors. I became depressed, bipolar, and near death. We never had marriage counseling or discussed expectations. For marriage, we need to find someone who is confident enough to praise us and not put us down.

Emotional writing began when manic, locked in a psychiatric ward. I recalled and frantically wrote detailed physics equations from memory to prove my sanity. Physics made sense. My former wife's impulsive behaviors made no sense. When I felt near death, she showed no love or concern. Married couples are blessed if they love, and are supportive of, one another.

My former-wife's behavior seemed to control, in fear of being controlled. She was successful in her work but never relaxed and died of a heart attack in 2000. It is difficult to overcome a dysfunctional childhood.

We become experts at daily and work communications. However, most of us are less adept at emotional communications. The same words often mean different things to emotional spouses.

Without established principles and a strong concept of self, emotional interactions distort who we are. Others may control our lives. However, with principles, emotional communications flower.

We must develop principles to keep us, and those we encounter, in perspective when things are going well or negatively. Deep rooted principles prepare us to maintain self worth when others abuse us. We must establish rules to evaluate, respond to, or avoid abusers. If abused in childhood, it is imperative to establish principles to build self-worth. Others recognize and treat us according to perceived self-worth.

Writing is important in healing fragmented minds. I originally wrote as part of my healing process, then documented thoughts and theories in case my children had similar afflictions, and expanded writing to help readers heal their afflictions.

Before 1994, high doses of psychiatric medications had not prevented sporadic manic episodes. Mania is disruptive to normal thinking and activities, lessens inhibitions and awakens creative thinking, and uncovers spiritual awareness.

Inner healing sensations and spiritual feelings are difficult to believe unless having experienced them personally. Inner healing processes and spiritual communications are intuitive, and different from verbal and nonverbal communications.

My psychiatrists said there is no cure for bipolar disorder and that medications only help prevent manic episodes. After years of manic frustration, I decided to invent my own cure. However, I have followed my psychiatrists' advice and continued medications. After many years of taking medications, I felt they were no longer suppressing creative thinking.

Medications had not prevented episodes. I was forced to be creative. Necessity was the mother of my alternative healing invention. Maintaining sanity and building inner confidence has required a long, dedicated effort. Before bipolar disorder, I could have never imagined a spiritual writing destiny.

I have "expected death" on several occasions: in a near automobile crash in 1967, in depression, and with psychiatric medication side effects in 1977. The mind processes differently without hope for tomorrow, and expecting death.

As a nuclear engineer, I spent much of my career modeling and designing nuclear reactors. I have used this experience to construct brain and mind healing, and spiritual, models. Modeling reveals necessary details in complex designs.

The Modeling Section builds background for understanding the brain, mind, and spirituality. Models that encourage holistic thinking about the brain and mind are helpful in healing.

Freud modeled the brain as having two parts: subconscious and conscious. He also developed his id, ego, and superego models. Mind models do not need to be so detailed or completely correct to promote inward thinking and heal minds. The mind is complex and can be modeled in many ways: for example, discrete and holistic.

Humans do not sense or understand reality. Every thought is only a mental model of reality to engage and control environments. Some models refine earlier models. Hopefully, models will inspire science and spiritual research by readers.

The Brain Section includes neuroscience and a unique physics approach. Subconscious and dream models provide insight to inner processes. With inner healing and understanding, thinking improves.

Scientists have not yet developed a significant understanding of consciousness. My Physics of the Brain, and Conscious, Models explain subconscious processes and consciousness.

Essays include normal and unusual consciousness. If we understand more of our normal and emotional mental processes, we can improve inner awareness, mental ability, and mind control. Minds and muscles grow in ability only when "briefly" stressed to limits.

Early philosophers questioned medicine, law, and religious practices with great risk. These areas had powerful influences in early societies. Historically, questioning these practices often resulted in imprisonment or death.

Americans have freedom of speech and human rights. I question medical and religious practices. The brain, mind, soul, and God can be modeled and questioned to improve life.

For thirty years, my laboratory has been my own mind and body. Experiments and exercises have resulted in unusually pleasant feelings, improved mind control, and prevention of manic episodes.

Reconstructing the brain and mind is similar to bodybuilding. Body builders do not become champions overnight. Mental reconstruction takes years. After years of work, both can be astounding.

One cannot simply say to the brain, "Heal your ingrained trauma and brainwashed afflictions!" It does not work. However, creative models of the brain and mind guide psychiatric exercises for stimulating neural networks and subconscious processes to recognize and heal trauma effects. The brain and mind slowly relearn to process as they were designed to do. Healing requires patience.

The brain creates the mind, and recursively, the mind controls the brain. The brain requires stimulation and feedback to recognize and heal its afflictions. Minds are constructed by synchronized neuron activations, and resulting electromagnetic resonances and mental holograms.

Neural network reconstruction sensations are similar to chiropractic adjustments. In chiropractic, joints are returned to their least energetic, best operating positions with a "snap" sensation.

I am unaware of similar mind/body/spirit research promoting healing at mental limits with conflicting exercises. Generally, there is psychiatric benefit in all exercises, if performed correctly. My work focuses on models and exercises that have had the greatest psychiatric effect. Exercising muscles closest to the brain are the most efficient in healing the brain and mind. I have not had depression or manic episodes for twenty years, my monumental success!

I no longer fear depression or mania. Success has been "my cure" of my bipolar disorder, controlled excitement in life, improved writing skills, and dedication in following God's calling. I have continued spirituality, physics, modeling, and unique exercises for my cure and a more complete life.

Introduction

We should distinguish between psychiatric healing sensations and beliefs. Healing sensations are localized. Spiritual sensations are more distributed or holistic throughout the brain.

Writing *A Philosophy of Healing and Spirituality* has improved reasoning and spiritual skills for developing personal beliefs and a spiritual identity. Concepts are intuitive. Only a few equations support spiritual models.

I have worked to recall and document expected death experiences to build my spirituality. Enlightenment is attained only from personal inner thoughts and experiences. Some, including myself, have received demanding words from God that have significantly changed lives. Inner spiritual messages can be as inspirational as studying traditional spiritual books

Traditional religions focus on their dogma and give little importance to current spiritual messages. Current spiritual recipients must have humility and patience to translate God's continuous perfect spiritual waves and resonances into truthful words. Truth is lessened when ego and power corrupt translations. Interpretations of perfect spiritual wave information into words are never perfect. Words and sentences are only symbols of reality and can never totally represent any act or thought. Thoughts are so much more than words. Words have different meanings to different individuals. There are always uncertainties in life and beliefs.

"Perfect spiritual words" brainwash, imprison minds, and destroy creativity. Using the word, "perfect," limits thinking, questioning, and creativity. Humans cannot read or write perfectly. Translations into different languages lose meaning.

Spirituality is communicating to give God praises and receive spiritual guidance, reflections, comfort, and understanding. Religions are structured tools to believe in, praise, and benefit from God and His wisdom.

Christians develop a personal relationship with Jesus. This work supports my personal relationship with God and Jesus, integrated within God. When writing this book, I have received holistic, spiritual feelings of comfort and awe. God is comforting and awesome. I did not discuss my evolving spirituality until developing explanations for my unusual feelings and ideas.

Spiritual feelings, thoughts, and emotions have lifted my spirits and changed my life perspectives. Spiritual feelings usually have arisen as gentle, meaningful words of love and hope.

Frustrated and attempting to complete my first book in 1995, I received unexpected, demanding spiritual words: "Don't Leave God Out!" This inner message seemed to come from all directions. God left it up to me in how to include Him in my writing. I have obeyed and written spiritually for twenty years. These powerful words changed my life.

When hopeless, near death, or in extreme need, we feel God's presence more strongly. Even in need, spiritual communication is enhanced by relaxing the mind, body, and face with eyes closed, and with pleasant, excited expectations of a young child.

After near death experiences and God's powerful message, I felt compelled to question my beliefs and make "simple" models to understand and write about God. The Heisenberg Uncertainty Principle, cosmology, physics, Christianity, and inner spiritual messages have guided my spiritual adventure.

The Heisenberg Uncertainty Principle is a physics law that proves scientists cannot measure very small physical properties more precise than a certain criteria. Atom properties are different than human sensed properties. This law proves there will always be uncertainty in the universe. One model is that God continually integrates physical uncertainties into spiritual certainty.

General relativity and cosmology provide an understanding of the early universe and behaviors of large systems like galaxies. God exists throughout the universe. Will scientists ever model God? We do not fully sense or understand very small and very large systems. We only make models of reality to achieve our purposes.

Indoctrination, by political and religious leaders, intimidates to control. Religion is an escape from daily uncertainties and despair. True religions expand creative thinking and spiritual freedoms. Creative thinking is a path toward understanding God. Memorization without understanding has little spiritual value.

False religions suppress freedom of thought, and narrows reasoning. Families, societies, and religions must protect gentle, loving people from mind predators. Some religious predators are aware that bipolar suffers are vulnerable and more easily influenced, manipulated, and abused. Abusing the vulnerable is the greatest of sins.

Many would-be spiritual leaders have received exciting spiritual messages. However, without humility and patience, excitement, greed, and power corrupt would-be spiritual leaders. Spiritual leaders must have humility and patience to be true to God and their followers.

My models of God begin with science and Christianity and extend into philosophy. God designed, created and engineered the universe. Scientists and engineers design and build machines to explore, understand, and control systems within the universe for Man's benefit.

Traditional Christian writers have made translations without science knowledge and, hopefully, without prejudice and only for reasonable personal gain. Humans do nothing perfectly. My spiritual interpretations are as unbiased as I am able to do.

Several early scientists were judged to be crazy or evil by dogmatic political and spiritual leaders. Scientists continue to be threats to "perfect" religions and brainwashing governments.

In writing the American Constitution, Thomas Jefferson fought for human rights and freedom from religious oppression, allowing America to be the creative leader of the world. American inventions have been responsible for worldwide advances. Traditional religions have suppressed creative ideas to maintain control over followers.

Like an earthly father, God desires for humans to understand and praise Him. We learn about God from science, religions, and inner spiritual messages. God reflects praises back to us. Children are reflections of parents. Humans have free wills to learn of, and reflect, God's wisdom.

We do not truly understand another's difficulties until we have experienced similar difficulties. Difficult, disabling experiences force us to evaluate our vulnerabilities, histories, and futures, and trust in God. After healing, we understand and enjoy daily and spiritual lives more fully.

Spiritual messages feel creative and later feel as if known for a long time. True spiritual leaders will unite humanity through understanding, example, and deeds, not simply words.

Being chosen to write spiritually was due to my experiencing spiritual awareness during manic episodes and believing death was imminent on more than one occasion. We are more aware of God's presence when quiet, relaxed, and surrendering, or when extremely emotional, insecure, on in pain. After my last manic episode in 1994, my awareness and thinking have been normal until unusual creative, spiritual ideas arise with feelings of needing to be included in this book.

Making models of the mind, soul, heaven, and God has been to discover who I must become. Nurturing confidence to believe in oneself is essential for believing in God. The physical and the spiritual blend together. There is no distinct line between the two. Humans often make artificial boundaries to analyze things. After reading this work, readers will no longer think the same about the mind or spirituality.

We can break the mental chains of childhood abuse and false indoctrination. Integrating science, current spiritual messages, and traditional religions is the future of spirituality.

I have been blessed in receiving messages from God, and have felt more spiritual than imagined. I have been asked to write spiritually but have not been asked to be evangelical. I have done the best I could with the skills and time I have had. This adventure is my mental healing and spiritual dream.

Everybody's crazy not believing a physicist/nuclear engineer can experiment, persist, and heal his bipolar mind, and receive life changing spiritual messages. Everybody with mental uncertainties is crazy for not working to heal their minds and strive for spiritual understanding. Everybody is crazy in severe unfamiliar situations.

Modeling Section

Modeling Experience

—m—

SIMPLE MODELS AND ARE IMPORTANT for learning and emotions. Dolls build caring skills. Toys develop study and workplace skills. Without models in our minds for doing or building things, we can do nothing. As we mature we develop theories and models to understand and control our environments and to understand the universe and God.

Models are tools for learning needed details and guiding complex construction. They are necessary for constructing and operating complex nuclear reactors. Models usually represent ideal examples of what can be constructed.

Mind models support development of complex ideas. Spiritual models may help readers question religious dogma to strengthen personal beliefs. Mind models develop detailed and spiritual thought processes.

Physics is based upon precise mathematical models of activities on the earth and throughout the universe. With models, physicists understand, predict, and sometimes control environments for human benefit. Physicists continue research to define new models for understanding nature and providing increased human freedoms.

Human vision does not provide a true picture of reality but provides models of environments allowing pursuit of goals. Vision is sensitive only to a limited electromagnetic radiation spectrum – light. Humans do not sense individual atoms but integrated groups of atoms.

God "sees" with all electromagnetic waves. With very short waves He "sees" atoms. With very long spiritual waves, He "sees" the entire universe. Later essays describe and model spiritual waves. Humans sense and understand a very limited reality. God knows reality.

With insight from nuclear reactor modeling, I construct models of the mind and God for psychiatric healing and spiritual awareness. Science, spirituality, and alternative healing processes expand the mind. Intelligent people look at options and details before making important decisions.

Nuclear engineers mathematically model nuclear reactors to determine if they will work as designed before building them. Computer models are used to determine efficiency and ensure safety criteria before operation is permitted. Nuclear engineers cannot predict behaviors of individual neutrons and fissions they cause, but with statistical and integration models can predict safe control of nuclear reactors. My spiritual models are information integration models.

Brain and mind models construct a complete thinking system. We strive for completeness in thoughts and sentences. However, mental completeness is corrupted by ingrained, erratic, energy from repressed trauma and painful memories. Trauma effects or scars disrupt normal brain activities. The mind may achieve its highest potential when all trauma effects are purged from the brain.

Models of God are integrated throughout the universe and heaven for spiritual wholeness, omnipresence, and omniscience. God is present on earth, on the other side of the universe, and within you. God has awareness of each atom and controls all perfect field forces in the universe. Constant field force laws allow an organized universe, and life on earth.

Models support God's complete awareness of the universe and heaven. With omniscience and omnipresence, God's spiritual information must be updated, integrated, and reflected evenly throughout the universe and heaven at a near infinite speed. Spiritual information must travel much, much faster than the speed of light for God to be omniscient within a big universe.

If healing models are reasonable and truthful enough, they will help readers understand and heal overstressed minds, and feel God's presence. If models allow us to predict activities, we may enjoy or avoid those activities. We must teach our children how to think and not what to think. Great discoveries and organizations are made by people who had learned how to think.

Memorizing suppresses creativeness. Governments and religions require memorization to control societies and believers to greater or lesser extents. Laws protect people's rights; however, less control and greater freedom expand minds and souls.

Some mind models integrate thoughts for understanding the wholeness of God. Other models are specific for supporting human purposes. Words and gestures are integrated models forming communication skills.

A basic mind model is that low-energy thinking is high-level thinking and high-energy thinking, such as anger, is low-level thinking. In anger, we can only think of a few aggressive options. With low-energy, we can take our time and think of many creative options. Briefly stressing the mind to high energy levels followed by calming down promotes mental healing, emotional understanding, and creativity.

Examples of models:

- Subconscious processes are much more complex and faster than conscious processes. The subconscious is continually making comparisons of sensed environments with memories constructing action or reaction options. The same spoken and written words stimulate similar meaning and memories. Memories include subliminal pictures and words that may never rise to conscious levels. Subconscious resonances compete for energy to build consciousness. Routine responses become efficient and confident.

- Mental attitudes should be: never act or feel above or below anyone. You do not have friends who act above you.

- Be good and fair to everyone independent of gender, race, wealth, and social status. Cherish those who are good to you. Feel free to dislike those who abuse you.

Understanding neuroscience models enhances mental healing. Subconscious processes are multi-level reflections of conscious thinking, and culture our thinking to define who we are. Subconscious processes need conscious reflection to understand and heal their inner activities. Subconscious theories or models are listed below:

- Mental problems occur when the conscious mind denies reality and does not reflect the truth to subconscious processes. Psychiatrists and mind models provide feedback for subconscious processes to understand conscious distortions for promoting mental healing.

- While awake, subconscious processes continually iterate to converge to and construct rational, complete conscious thoughts. If subconscious processes do not converge, the mind becomes manic and out of control. Thinking becomes irrational and reactive.

- Sigmund Freud developed a mind model consisting of unconscious and conscious parts. Today we use the word "subconscious" instead of "unconscious." Of course, the mind is more complex than this simple model. However, simple models help us think and reason. Modern psychology has developed complex mental models, for understanding and healing minds.

- Consciousness is a mind model constructed from "limited" senses, awareness, memory, heredity, and cognition. Humans have limited models of reality. Only God knows reality.

Models are to help readers reason about, understand, and heal their minds for health and inner joy. Humans construct models of themselves and their environments to be able to predict future interactions and survive. Spiritual models provide inner confidence and security with hopes of a meaningful life and eternal heavenly bliss.

With limited senses and minds, everybody's crazy believing humans understand reality. We make mental models of limited realities to survive within and engage environments. After receiving a demanding spiritual message, I have been compelled to construct mind and spiritual models to discover who I must become.

Early Life

—⁂—

*"You have to live your story before
being able to write your story."*

— Amy Shearn

Genetics is the blueprint for human life. When a sperm meets an egg, they become integrated to receive the spark of life and complete spiritual wisdom. Parents and environments continue to mold children's behaviors and life. Successful and unsuccessful reactions to challenges develop confidence and lack of confidence.

The embryo is excited about growing faster and bigger as cells divide and grow. The embryo is aware of every cell division and every neuron connection made. It is excited about forming the skeleton and body and plans for, and looks forward to, a strong, exciting future. Neurons are aware of near and far neurons in a growing brain through shared electromagnetic radiation resonances.

Originally embryos do not need to control slow-moving arms and legs or environments. Inner processes are as fast as dreams and are aware of all internal growth. Later mental processes develop senses and a slow consciousness to control slow moving arms and legs for engaging environments.

Pre-consciousness is so fast embryos are aware of more mental activities than adults consciously experience the rest of their lives. Spiritual, genetic, and parental guidance is fundamental in constructing young bodies and minds. Spiritual and subconscious processes are exceedingly fast.

There is a dramatic change in an egg upon conception. Fertilized eggs receive complete spiritual wisdom at conception. They are totally helpless and must depend on God, and their mother and father. Adults are more spiritual when helpless and must depend on God. I think this is true since creative and spiritual ideas and science discoveries, after initially being conceived, feel as having been known for a long time.

Fast-processing little brains must wait for feedback from, and control of, eyes and slow moving arms and legs. Early inner-conscious processes become dominated by a slow, energetic new consciousness for controlling bodies and engaging environments. Environmental consciousness and memory begin at birth. Early inner awareness continues within subconscious processes and sub-memories that become the core of human mental abilities.

Awareness is developed by sensitivities within our bodies for environments. From a consistent womb, babies must learn to survive inconsistent environments and various threats.

Young babies perceive environments with equal importance with dominant right-brains. This is a reason we do not remember early years. Later in life, with right-brain dominance, we do not remember repetitive things such as steps. As a child grows, the detailed left-brain becomes more dominant and develops stronger, detailed memories.

Vision stimulates electromagnetic resonances in the brain for constructing meaningful images, thoughts, actions, and memories, and for understanding and navigating environments. Babies slowly learn to distinguish between things they can and cannot control. However, babies control nursing early on through genetics or instinct.

Babies' right-brains holistically record normal and conflicting activities of the gods, their parents, in awe without understanding. As words and actions become understood later, a young child connects former visions and feelings with emotional words. We should be careful what we say and do around babies and young children. Young minds record everything, and eventually, subconsciously, connect words to earlier experiences.

Loud and threatening words and behaviors brainwash babies and young children. Children both fear and mimic loud, threatening behaviors as they grow up. Mimicking such behavior develops aggression for defense and control. Threatening words and behaviors instill primitive flight or fight mentalities and behaviors.

Babies have extreme reactions to trauma. Their minds go out of control. However, babies are small and weak and not so disruptive to parents. Adults losing control are disruptive to those around them.

Baby's subconscious, iterative processes for constructing conscious thoughts do not initially converge to reasonable inner and environmental awareness. Trauma memories are deeply, emotionally entrenched within baby's overstressed neural networks. Babies' and young children's reactions to trauma and emotional activities construct thinking and reasoning limits that usually last for a lifetime. My work is dedicated to purging and replacing childhood emotional and trauma limits with wider, more organized, creative limits.

Continuing solutions to time changing functions, such as thinking, are iterative. Related repetitive subconscious processes converge to develop reasonable, complete thoughts. When subconscious iterative processes do not converge, the mind goes out of control, with incomplete thinking and unreasonable decisions, as occurs in mania.

From my experience, psychotherapy cannot release even ten percent of the brain's early trauma effects. During early life verbal analytical left-brain functions have little influence relative to right-brain, holistic awareness. Vision is holistic until babies learn to focus on specific details. Psychotherapy has difficulties in purging trauma effects that are not connected with speech. Instigating recall of or reenacting trauma events may help purge energy from trauma memories.

Human growth is organized and integrated. We do not grow only at the end of our feet. Cells divide, integrate, and expand. Integration is important in spiritual models.

In the womb, unborn babies' minds are spiritual. Spiritual thinking has not been eclipsed by higher energy environmental and trauma thinking processes. Unborn babies know no evil. When purging early limiting, ingrained emotions and traumas, humans regain spiritual insight.

Models for prayers are lowering mental energy with humility and bowered heads. With dedication, humans can improve their spiritual communication technology. Left brain dominance controls mental processes for engaging environments. Calming the mind and body engages right brain dominance for nurturing holistic thinking and spiritual communication.

An infinite God created humans for them to learn and reflect human sized knowledge and praises back to Him. With free wills, we may choose to live our lives for ourselves or build an everlasting spiritual purpose.

Everybody's crazy not believing new born babies have spiritual awareness. Interacting with worldly activities overwhelms young minds and eclipses spiritual awareness. Life's goal is to survive physical environments and recover spiritual awareness and wisdom. We must become spiritually reborn to enter spiritual dimensions.

Siblings

PARENTS STRIVE TO GIVE THEIR first born every advantage. Too often the first child learns he is the center of their universe and more important than parents, other adults, and younger siblings. He becomes a spoiled brat. Parents gloat at every new thing the first born learns and accomplishes. He may be the smartest child ever. He will rule. He is their hope for an extraordinary future.

Here comes trouble. The second child is born. Number one no longer receives his massive attention and becomes jealous. How could this happen to him? The first child abuses by taking toys away, pushing, tripping, twisting, lying on, lying about, and so forth.

Later on the spoiled first sibling calls the second degrading names such a dumb, stupid, ugly, and so on. The second sibling feels unwanted and worthless. At some point, younger abused siblings must come out of the closet and tell parents, other adults, and teachers they are being abused. Without speaking up, younger siblings continue to be abused by older siblings, and even by their friends they influence, into and beyond high school. Unfortunately, bullying is catching. Bullies isolate their victims, as unworthy of friends and beyond help.

Parents must teach older children that bullying is a moral weakness. Younger siblings should not feel guilty or inferior. Parents must explain to younger siblings why an older sibling is abusing them. Understanding reasons early on reduces adverse emotional effects and enhances self-worth.

If the younger child is submissive and overpowered, he will be mentally degraded, and may feel helpless, inferior, and second class for life. Unless an abused person receives psychiatric care or practices my mental reconstruction, childhood trauma scars limit creative thinking throughout life. A much larger sibling is more damaging making a young child feel more helpless.

If a younger sibling becomes aggressive and fights back, he may overcome older sibling torture, trauma, and degradation more easily. There is some possibility that a stronger younger sibling may abuse a weaker older sibling. Who knows what happens in families with drugged, drunken, and uncaring parents?

Most parents do not recognize the long-term psychiatric damage first siblings have on younger siblings. They fail to discipline older siblings when they abuse younger siblings. Many parents think second or younger siblings are just slower than their idolized first born. Being slower is mostly due to sibling or other bullying. Parents are responsible if allowing damaging and degrading behavior by any sibling. Aggressive children require aggressive discipline. Bullying is the parents' fault. They should be in control of their children.

Poor parenting promotes "superior" first siblings and "inferior" younger siblings. Parents should not have younger siblings if they cannot protect and nurture them. Early on, the first born must be taught to obey and respect his parents and younger siblings.

Smart parents teach their children to love, nurture, and work to give each other confidence. Each child will have less trauma scars and be confident and smart. Parents may ask questions like, "How have you added confidence to you brothers and sisters today?"

Abuse, and fear of abuse, causes younger siblings persistent worry. Worrying about and fearing trauma from older siblings limits mental and often physical development. Sibling bullying is more damaging than school bullying. There is nowhere to hide. Unfortunately, only severe behavior and mental damage is recognized by families and schools. Other important effects of bullying are not treated.

Americans need to understand the value of psychiatric and psychological counseling. At early ages, counselors can more easily free young minds from limited thinking and behaviors caused by childhood abuse. Everyone needs counseling to discover and recover from repressed limiting trauma memories to like, and believe in, self. Many people do not recall childhood trauma and brainwashing until effects become disruptive later in life. Early healing can prevent so much agony and pain, and expand abilities during life. Healing builds self-confidence and inner joy.

The second child will not be as inquisitive as the first due to constant worry and fear. He will think everyone else's ideas are more important than his own. He may be able to study and concentrate only when alone. Other's voices and opinions are more important to him than his own thoughts. So much of the second sibling's time and life is wasted with worry, fear, and insecurity.

Before the second child comes along, the first must be punished if he disobeys parents or degrades other children or grownups. It is unhealthy for a young child to feel and act more important than parents and grownups. He must learn to respect grownups, others, and pets.

Parents should praise all children to build their confidence and self-worth. Abused children need more praise and confidence building. Parents should train their children to build up each other's confidence, since there are others who will degrade and destroy their confidence.

Good followers learn to care for and respect adults and other children. They make caring leaders. Narrow-minded, prejudiced parents only care that their child is a leader. Dictators are created by dysfunctional parents.

Discipline is difficult today. "Good parents can't spank children." Parents no longer know how to discipline their children. Threats of time out and asking children to apologize for bad behavior are not effective disciplines. Parents cannot spank their children today and many let older siblings severely abuse younger siblings.

Parents should evaluate children behaviors and set appropriate isolation or timeout guidelines. They should define and explain punishment criteria for bad behaviors early on. Children will begin to reason about consequences of bad behaviors. Punishment should inflict psychological pain relative to pain perpetrated on others. Punishments must be worse with repeated offences.

Abusive children should receive punishment that makes them feel confined and uncomfortable for appropriate times, depending upon abuses. They have abused and made others feel uncomfortable, uncertain, and hurt. Many variables should be considered.

While in punishment, children should be made to verbally repeat or write why they are being punished a number of times, or read and report on part of an appropriate article or book. Punishment should be a learning experience. It's for the child's own good! Readers usually don't abuse. Let abusers know they will be free only when they are sorry, and apologize, for their abusive actions. Parents may ask several times, "How sorry are you?" to be sure the offending child understands what being sorry means.

A verbal or writing example might be: "I shall not hit or abuse my younger brother, etc." some number of times before gaining freedom to play or watch favorite TV programs. Lack of discipline for aggressive children degrades the family unit. If reasonable discipline is not given to limit early abusive behavior, the prison system will execute unreasonable discipline and limits later. Then, families are more seriously degraded.

Children need consistent guidance to learn and obey social customs and limits. Discipline problems grow over time if unchecked. After some time, abused siblings will rebel from abusive older sibling or parents.

Sooner or later, he will blame his parents for letting his older brother abuse him. Too often the second child does quick, unacceptable things to gain mental freedom and attention. "It's his parents fault." Raising children is a huge responsibility.

Rebelling teenagers seldom continue learning accepted vocational and social skills. Too often, rebelling, abused teenagers turn to "fast" illegal and abusive activities they have endured at home. Life becomes fast and furious. Conflicts arise. The abused have not learned to communicate about or resolve abuse or conflicts. "Grab that gun!"

Parents should limit children's fast paced cartoons and video games. These activities are addictive to young minds and lessen attention and respect for "slow moving" parents and others. Parents must learn more, and be alert and smarter than ever to mold children into future well-adjusted adults.

Young children become fearful and brainwashed by parents' yelling, threats, and forceful actions. As they grow and feel the power of becoming adults, yelling and threats begin.

When young, I could not "understand" why my older brother was abusing me. This lack of emotional reasoning and confidence enabled my former wife to abuse me. I did not want conflicts or to make a fuss; I endured. Abuse grows if unchecked. I was living an unreasonable life that nearly cost my life.

We cannot continue nurturing and loving and expect controlling, damaging people to change their behaviors. Their behaviors have been ingrained during childhood. We need to be more assertive, or make plans to avoid them.

There is a difference between normal and emotional confidence and reasoning. In normal thinking, I had good reasoning in physics, engineering and normal interactions. I did not hold true to myself in emotional interactions. I was false to myself.

As a teenager, I had to study while isolated. My thinking and studying was less important than others' words and actions. Ingrained thoughts and behaviors die hard. Good parents must ensure each child understands his thoughts and opinions are important.

Habits of the abused become "comfortable" to some extent. After years of abuse, it is difficult to improve abusive relationships. Behaviors are familiar, and have been accepted for a long time. Separation from an aggressive sibling for some time may be needed to stop abuse. A grown sibling must not let abuse continue. Only develop, and have, friends who treat you well.

After relationship parameters and behaviors are established, they are difficult to change. My former wife's behavior was negative to me but normal to the children and others. After five years of negative impulsive verbal and body language, I became depressed, manic, and with little reason.

Sibling abuse is due to lack of family planning and values. Without defined family values and lack of parental guidance, the oldest increases confidence and "accomplishment" by degrading younger siblings. Younger siblings are not able to compete and "must" develop alternative skills for attention, or they may simply rebel. Often "quick" alternatives do not build good principles and values. If the oldest is good academically, younger siblings feel they cannot compete. Good family principles and values will guide all siblings in developing self-esteem and successful talents.

Parents are crazy for not preventing older siblings from abusing, and bullying, younger siblings. Sibling abuse and bullying affect the abused for a lifetime, without counseling or mental reconstruction. Mental reconstruction and meditation are paths toward inner peace and health. Handed down alcoholic behaviors affect generations, and almost destroyed me. Too much alcohol makes an idiot superior to a genius.

Feelings

> "We've discovered by walking through the uncomfortable feeling of saying no, there is incredible peace and freedom on the other side."
>
> — Kathy Kinney and Cindy Ratzlaff,
> Co-authors, *Queen of Your Own Life*

> "Feelings are semiconscious awareness of stimulated, integrated thoughts."
>
> — H. Fulcher

It is difficult to understand or believe mental healing or spiritual feelings unless experienced. When received, spiritual communications develop deep down feelings of truth and inner joy. In depths of depression without hope for tomorrow, I felt life escaping, an eerie feeling. I was aware of surroundings but had feelings of not being present. In depression and helplessness, spiritual feelings build a higher closeness to God.

As depression and mania lessen, a more normal awareness returned. Spiritual sensitivity lessened but remained higher than earlier sensitivity.

My second near-death experience was caused by side effects from the prescription drug, Haldol. After this experience, I received unusual spiritual feelings and messages. Near, or "expected," death experiences are discussed in later chapters.

Parents influence children's attitudes. Teaching a child to feel and act superior, or calling him a genius develops an entitlement attitude that ruins his and others' lives. "Just be yourself" is too vague to guide a child's attitude and behavior. My philosophy on child rearing and life was and is: "Do not feel or act above or below anyone. Have no friends who act above you."

With different backgrounds and abilities, the same activities and communications produce positive feelings for some and negative feelings for others. Feelings are semiconscious reactions to ideas and actions that stimulate comparisons with core principles. Core principles are developed through genetics and earlier learned experiences.

Feelings relate to levels of pain and pleasure. Core principles relate to healthy and confident living standards.

Feelings assist decision-making by subconsciously integrating meaning from many related memories without requiring the higher-energy or longer times of conscious recall. Intense feelings can elevate into higher-energy conscious thoughts.

"Feelings" are stimulated by senses and integration of related memories. Feelings of arms and fingers being extended, and fingertips touching piano keys enables a concert pianist to play fast, precise music. Arm, hand, and finger positioning is precise and becomes semi-conscious. In concerts, a piano player must have timing and feeling of the keys.

We feel relief, freedom, and accomplishment after completing difficult challenges or solving difficult problems. We should frequently search for and solve small and large challenges to build problem solving skills and mental confidence.

Others may help us build confidence, but working and striving to accomplish important and difficult tasks on our own is the fundamental process to build self-confidence. We must be willing to accept trials and errors. Understanding trials and errors builds confidence for achieving success.

Pain is the only feeling that stops at the thalamus without passing information to the cortex for additional processing. Immediate pain does not require higher level mental processing for avoidance.

Exceeding emotional limits has engrained baby, childhood, and adult brainwashing traumas. Parents, adults, and religious leaders brainwash young children. Everyone needs to uncover and reason through repressed, brainwashed effects to improve decision making. Trauma and brainwashing effects have been ingrained for so long we are not aware of their adverse feelings and effects until they cause significant difficulties. At the right ages, brainwashing is lessened by giving children reasonable options to think on their own.

Depression begins with feelings of hopelessness, and that things can never get better. There appears to be no way out. Decisions become uncertain. The mind slows down and may degrade to the point of not being able to recall or think in words. Hopefully, a reconstructed mind brings inner happiness, agility of thought, and confidence in spiritual beliefs.

In prolonged depression, some may feel God has forsaken them. Feelings of lost self-esteem, confidence, and control increase. Fears of insanity emerge when one cannot believe his own thoughts. Spiritual feelings become stronger during sickness and distress. Many may feel like a helpless child, surrender to God for guidance, and become reborn.

Everybody's crazy to ignore their feelings. We must pay attention to, study, and understand our feelings to improve mental health and lives.

Emotions

Emotion: A complex pattern of psychological changes, including physiological arousal, feelings, cognitive processes, and behavioral reactions, made in response to a situation perceived to be personally significant.

— Gerrig, Richard J. & Philip G. Zimbardo
Psychology and Life

"The best reason in the world to move—perhaps the most difficult exercise of all—is to learn how to push away the emotional obstacles that have been holding you back from accomplishing your personal goals."

— Bob Green

With different backgrounds, the same activities and communications promote positive emotions for some and negative emotions for others. Emotions are reactions to stimuli, ideas, and actions that are related to inner core principles that normally reside below conscious levels. Pain activates emotions to lesser or greater extent. Core principles are founded upon genetics and mostly early life experiences.

Emotions are reactions to significant life experiences and have higher energy than feelings. Reasons for emotions are usually are more apparent than those of feelings. Expressing positive emotions can be fulfilling. Internalizing pleasant or stressful emotions is not good for mental or physical health.

When I was young, my older brother's words and actions kept my self-esteem low. Even though he was cruel to me, my mother always said I should love my brother. These mixed experiences produced uncertainties and confused emotions. It is not healthy to love and trust someone who persistently hurts and degrades you.

Love begins with feelings and requires work to build feelings into emotions. It takes activities or memories of activities to maintain feelings and emotions. Love can be destroyed and rekindled.

If the abused, or sexually abused, suppresses emotions and does not deal with or report abuse, he or she will internalize unfounded self-guilt. Recalling, acknowledging, and reporting abuse to authorities is painful but initiates emotional healing. Recalling abuse for a brief hurtful period is much better than experiencing sporadic uncertainties and negative emotions for a lifetime. Abuse imprisons minds and souls.

Repressed childhood memories and emotions are obstacles to reaching potentials. We must develop ways to release excess mental energy. Muscles should store all the energy they can. The brain and computers should use the least amount of energy to be efficient.

Bipolar disorder is an emotional disorder caused by stress beyond coping limits. The brain and machines go out of control beyond energy limits. In depression, mental energy can become too low for the brain and mind to operate efficiently. With lost mental and physical energy, depressed persons become devoid of emotions. The brain must maintain needed levels of energy.

Persistent degrading behaviors by "significant others" ingrain feelings of worthlessness that do not seem to get better. Emotional losses of loved ones and status or other long-lasting stresses cause depression and bipolar disorder. A depressed person has recurring thoughts that do not converge to solutions or corrective actions. The abused often feels too small or embarrassed to discuss abuse, feelings, and agony.

Overstressed minds may go from slow, low-energy depressed moods to highly emotional fast thinking, and excited moods with erratic thinking. Manic depression is discussed in the "Bipolar Disorder" essay.

After years of sporadic manic episodes and prescribed psychiatric medications, I was still having episodes. In 1994, I concluded I must do something differently. I no longer expected freedom from episodes while continuing the same things. I designed and practiced mental reconstruction exercises to cure my disorder. They have worked for twenty years.

Curing bipolar disorder requires emotional work to recall repressed memories, and purge excess trauma energy and its disruptive effects. Bipolar persons often overreact quickly and forcefully to perceived threats to degraded, unstable egos.

For example, a bipolar teenager having difficulties with math may overact violently when asked to do his math homework. Repressed failures in math may cause tormented, unreasonable emotions. Reducing trauma energy through mental reconstruction improves mental control and may enhance spiritual sensitivities. It is often difficult to describe holistic, spiritual healing.

My work is dedicated to reducing mental and emotional pain, family frustrations, and, possibly, save lives of manic-depressives and those they encounter. The drawback to my alternative healing exercises and processes is that they take years of dedicated effort. Only individuals can control and truly heal their own minds and thinking.

Our minds are genetically designed to analyze potential threats and react emotionally for our protection and well-being. We may feel emotional when seeing someone who is attractive to us.

Emotions are holistic and right brained. They are formed by integrated memories and thoughts that construct our core values and mental limits. The right brain integrates discrete left brain awareness and thoughts into integrated, meaningful directives to guide our lives. Emotions become stronger when activities are near at hand or at limits.

We drive our cars thinking of many things with little awareness of slowly turning the steering wheel left or right. We do not think in discrete words when controlling the steering wheel. Right brain activities are performed semiconsciously such as normal breathing. Smooth slow changing and repetitious activities are controlled by the right brain. Fast things like quick braking causes the left brain to become dominate for discrete control.

"Flashes" during "expected death situations" extend the mind beyond emotional limits. In response, the traumatized mind relives emotional memories at nearly one million times faster than normal awareness to make a life saving decision. "The Flash" essay explains this estimate.

Relationships can be wonderful. They may support elevated emotions for a more active, rewarding life. True lovers build one another's confidence. Caring for and working to help and please others is a higher form of life. We must promote worldly love more than ever.

Emotions are most meaningful when achieving at our best while mutually supporting and loving one another. The key to good relationships is doing more for others than they do for us. This mutual talent builds strong relationships. How great relationships could be if spouses or partners would sincerely praise each other every day! What could be more spiritual?

Psychotherapy and mental reconstruction stimulate trauma memories to emotional limits for releasing disruptive energy. Subconscious activities iterate and integrate trauma memories into rational thoughts and memories. Emotional healing expands in-depth and creative thinking. We become healthier, happier, and smarter.

Everybody's crazy for not working to understand and reduce disruptive emotional and trauma energy. The brain and mind work more efficiently with less energy. We must reduce energy of, negative emotional memories to improve our lives and lives of those close to us.

Emotional Relationships

> "You're either going to live the life chosen or the life assigned. I want you to live the life chosen."
>
> — Dr. Phil McGraw

> "Sadness, happiness, and laughter are reflections of inner principles."
>
> — H. Fulcher

IF WE APPROACH PEOPLE CORDIALLY, most will be receptive and pleasant to us. Others will think we are vulnerable and work to expose our weaknesses and degrade us for their emotional ego or some other advantage. For mental health, we must work to understand the personalities and goals of spouses, those important to us, and those we must endure.

As a naïve teenager, I continued to believe if I was pleasant and good to everyone, everyone would like and be good to me. The world does not work that way. There are prejudices, miscommunications, and evil throughout the world. I muddle along trying to please those I can and avoid those who mean harm. I find pleasure and satisfaction in those who are good to me.

During marriage, I lived two separate lives. My normal life was when I was away from my wife or with my wife and around other people. She showed closeness around others. When alone with my wife, she was distant, avoiding closeness and "busy every minute," My life with her made no sense.

We must develop criteria to evaluate spousal and other important relationships. Developing strong, holistic feelings of unity, while retaining independence of thought, builds strong marriage principles. Different formulas work for different couples. Without communication, understanding, and sacrifice relationships degrade, and fail. A primary responsibility for spouses is to complement each other every day. Spouses must be truthful in complementing. It takes thought and work.

Power-based controllers dominate and brainwash to imprison spouses' minds. More so after marriage, power based spouses vie for emotional control, using money, wit, intelligence, sex, humor, or threats. Never allow a controlling spouse to isolate you from friends and family, or things get worse. Each spouse must preserve their freedom of thought and judgment.

As women attain and exercise greater freedoms and power in America, they will become as self-centered as men. Normally men have greater desire for sex than women. This gives wives opportunities to gain power over good gentle husbands by avoiding or delaying sex. Women seem to be more willing sex partners before marriage.

As males lose dominance, male genetic, physical, and mental capacities will deteriorate. Will America, dominated by women in the future, deteriorate or continue as a world power?

We should make emotional decisions using our own reasoning and backgrounds, but ask for advice when needed. We should not just mimic another's thinking. When observing older couples, it is obvious if one spouse has dominated and controlled the other.

Brainwashing occurs when someone or some group convinces victims to believe that their ideas, control, and demands are more important than victim's ideas, needs and desires. Brainwashed victims think in, and repeat, exact words of brainwashers. They may be parents, military drill instructors, and political or spiritual leaders. Forced memorization is a powerful brainwashing tool.

The brainwashed think and react mostly with their emotional low level, reactive limbic brains. If someone listens to and reasons about conversations or speakers' messages, he integrates new thoughts within his mind and speaks about them in his own words. Cerebral hemispheres perform higher reasoning.

Brainwashed memories do not filter throughout the brain like normal ideas. They remain in localized, high energy compartments that react vigorously when stimulated by related activities.

Many think they have freedom of thought but are restricted by, or "chained to" early brainwashing and trauma experiences. We must purge energy from repressed trauma memories to mentally reconstruct and recover normal, creative abilities. Purging trauma effects is important before engaging in long term relationships. It is difficult to be consistent with ingrained trauma effects.

If seeking romance, be prepared to make his/her happiness your highest priority. Little things can make all the difference. If you find you can't devote top priority to your significant other, get out before marriage or you will hurt him/her. Never be or endure a dominant, degrading spouse. A dominant, deceptive spouse will shorten your life in a slow emotional murder.

Fifty percent of my criteria for loving relationships is how your spouse, partner, or close friend treats, praises, has allegiance to, is truthful with, and nurtures, you. Twenty percent, of my criteria, is on how a spouse takes care of him/herself and your children. Twenty percent is how your spouse engages in work and domestic activities to support the family. These guidelines assumes few financial issues.

Five percent, of marital relationship criteria, is on how your spouse treats her/his relatives and friends. The last five percent of a marital relationship is judged on how your spouse treats your relatives and friends. Obviously, these are rough guidelines but are meant to help readers think about close relationships.

Nurturing needs to be helpful toward individual and joint goals. Developing interactive criteria and responsibilities early on may build happy marriages. Criteria can be updated. It is important to mental health that your spouse treats you well. Degrading spouses cause lost health and early deaths.

Develop general criteria for resolving negative interactions and behaviors early on. Resolve family difficulties together.

Praises must be honest, with greater impact than criticisms, or they lose importance. Emotional evaluations should be separate from reasoning evaluations. Emotions are more sensitive with subconscious dynamics and are different between men and women. Humans are fragile in many ways. We want to make those we love feel important and want to feel important by those we love.

Sinister spouses and others scheme to gain control over loving spouses, partners, and friends. The most ungodly scheme is when one spouse uses their children to gain power over the other spouse. Unfortunately, this tyranny happens in so many relationships. If persistently feeling mentally abused get counseling, mentally reduce the importance of your abuser, become as mentally independent as you can, get out, or prepare to endure your slow murder.

Several factors, including money, security, or children, may require enduring an unhappy marriage, work place, or relationship for some time. See a counselor and psychologically separate your self-worth from your tormentor. Keep in mind the things you are good at and enjoy, irrespective of what your tormentor might say. To remain mentally healthy, be truthful with yourself. Unfortunately, I waited eighteen years for change and love that never happened.

If your significant other or friend treats you as inferior, he/she is too emotionally inferior to be with and controlling you. Emotionally, or at least mentally, consider him as less important. If someone is acting superior to you, he is making you "be" inferior. I have no friends who act superior to me. If someone acts superior to you, he/she is socially and spiritually inferior and dumb as a bed post.

If we remain enablers, controlling, criminal spouses will continue to lessen us, and cause us to question our decisions and sanity. After degrading us, emotion criminals will think we are highly inferior and feel indignant to be with us. He or she has used dumb emotional control to degrade us. The meek need to build and adhere to principles for building self worth, or controllers will make us emotional worms.

Some sense giving as a sign of weakness to abuse others. Some spouses from abusive childhoods may think: "I feel unworthy and my spouse must be unworthy to be with me." These deep down thoughts stem from feeling less than other children when growing up, due to lack of good parenting or money. Parents may have allowed older siblings or older neighborhood children make younger children feel and "be" inferior. Well-adjusted children do not hurt, or make, other children feel inferior.

Loving spouses or partners might say: "I love that you are so willing to please me in so many ways. You have confidence in yourself and in me. In turn, I desire, need, and want to please you as my highest priority. Let's build confidence together each day. We will build a wonderful relationship that will last forever!"

Some ladies I have met emphasize being equal to men in the work place. Men are not good at emotional competitions with women. Uncertainties cause them to feel weakness so they, too often, exert forceful, controlling behavior over their wives to cover up lack of confidence and self-esteem.

Most women are the emotional, nurturing experts. They should skillfully nurture good husbands so they will freely reflect nurturing back to them. For generations, male egos have been more fragile and more easily destroyed than women's egos. Historically and genetically, more has been expected of men. Mutually giving attitudes build confidence, strong relationships, and happy couples. A loving husband cherishes a loving wife.

Many couples are good at supporting and encouraging the psychological growth of their children, but fail to continue giving confidence to each other's social needs and work challenges. Spouses need to be sensitive enough to know when to help and when to let their spouses resolve their own issues.

We cannot rely only on that loving feeling. It does not last unless nurtured. We must evaluate if we and our potential lovers or spouses can give whole heartedly through good and bad times. For long term love to grow, it must be built on logic that builds understanding and emotions that become family principles.

Financial and other important issues should have realistic starting points and predictions. Important discussions should be honest and logical at agreed upon times after both spouses have had time to prepare. There should be no blind siding! Discussions should have defined and reasonable goals. When practical, both spouses should write down and share important ideas. Writing down goals and decisions makes them defined, focused, and achievable.

I was raised in a country community in Central Virginia and learned that husbands and wives always supported one another. There were disagreements but voices were never raised. Families stood up for families and neighbors. I later realized I lived in "Almost Heaven."

My ex-wife had learned from her mother to compete with her husband. Controllers do not love or nurture those they control. I continued to praise my wife. It was all I knew. My former wife never said a nurturing comment to me when we were alone.

Almost everyone in my childhood country environment was gentle and pleasing. My disorder was never learning to say "no." With effort, I have become more comfortable in saying "no." I continued in the marriage hoping things would get better, and then for the benefit of the children. We divorced after eighteen years of an unhappy, stressful marriage.

My former wife's mentality was to always show superiority and be in control when we were alone. It was her emotional sickness. She was dedicated to her work, not her husband. Stress of having to "be superior" caused her heart condition, and death in 2000. Alcoholic behaviors affect generations.

The positive side of our marriage is that we could not have had two more wonderful children. I am so proud of them. I wanted to be proud of my former wife.

I study couples I meet and think there are more controlling wives than controlling husbands. However, drunken men can be more devastating to wives and families. Drunken husbands and wives are devastating to each other and their children. Alcohol abuse promotes false superior feelings and ideas that encourage degrading the "weak" near them. Too many drinks create kings and queens.

Some spouses fear being stigmatized if divorced and stay in abusive marriages for years. They hide dark, emotional secrets.

A self-centered husband dominates a wonderful wife and divorces her because she has become degraded and them below him. He later marries a lesser woman who dominates him. In marital and other relationships spouses must "unlearn" dominating, degrading characteristics for both partners to be happy and feel fulfilled.

Relationships are primarily power, love, or reasoning based. From ancestral genes, we worship and fear power greater than our own. Hitler inspired fear in and power for the German people. With his forceful, emotional speeches he made them feel aggressive and superior. Christians are taught to love, fear, and worship an all-powerful God.

Young children both fear and worship "powerful and yelling" parents. Affected children learn to believe in and respond to power with a mixture of fear and love. As abused children grow, they will eventually avoid or reject degrading power-based parents. Later, they will develop an insatiable need for power over those near them or recoil into a shell of fear.

Relationships may be good or destructive to one, two, or many. Self-respecting and loving people share reasoning, feelings, and emotions to elevate everyone involved. Degrading relationships are based on power, prejudice, hate, jealousy, and self-centeredness.

Language, in emotional relationships, often becomes twisted. A husband may say or do something he thinks is positive for his wife. She may take it as negative or not enough, and becomes emotional.

As we age, repressed trauma memories from different childhood backgrounds gain influence and may cause unexpected difficulties. The husband thinks his actions and words are positive and his wife is being unreasonable. He gets emotional, angry, or quits communicating. The marriage becomes dysfunctional and difficult to save, even with counseling.

It is wonderful when spouses care for one another, communicate well, and neither spouse needs to control. Mutual sharing and building each other's confidence makes heaven on earth. In good marriages, faces shine with each other's reflection. I complement such happy, wonderful couples when I can. They inspire me.

After several years of marriage, it is easy to recognize who is controlling or being controlled. We usually recognize controlling behaviors as having determined, authoritative language and posture. Many of us comply, but feel inferior, violated, and hopeless. Worst yet are the subtle controllers. We are deceived into thinking a controller is helping, or even elevating, us, but is degrading us, sometimes even in front of others. We may crazily hope things will get better for years.

Good emotional relationships take away our worries. What a wonderful life we should live! However, greed, selfishness, and controlling attitudes ruin lives. Even in close relationships, abusers seldom change behaviors unless the abused rebels. Just hoping things will get better is usually futile.

I have experience, on husbands trapped in unhealthy marriages. Manipulating, greedy wives continue asking for more and more without caring if overstressing husbands. Greedy wives degrade husbands and make them feel inadequate financially and socially. Many husbands will feel inadequate and hide abuse. She acts superior, shows no love, makes her husband feel inferior, and withholds sex to manipulate. Greedy wives suck the life out of once loving husbands. As the husband's health suffers, repressed anger builds. A manipulating wife shows no sympathy.

Dominating wives cause persistent stress, heart attacks, bipolar disorder, and slow murders. Husbands are then physically trapped by "caretakers" that caused the loss of health. Pre-marital counseling could have established emotional communications and honest attitudes that could have saved so much pain and so many losses of life.

Before marriage, weeks of counseling must be required. Counselors must have fiancées write down and discuss expected behaviors, life styles, sex, money, security, savings, material possessions, drinking, food, spiritual beliefs and tolerances, emotional sensitivities, and weaknesses. Marriage is the most important health and financial contract couples make. Life is too precious for a spouse or anyone to cause early death. People live longer in supportive marriages.

From a philosophical viewpoint, I have wondered why God made two sexes. Not feeling complete creates emotional uncertainties. Wouldn't life be easier if humans felt emotionally complete without needing to rely on someone of the opposite sex? However, God made Adam with emotions. He was lonely without Eve. And the trouble began.

Humans experience uncertainties. Some levels of uncertainty make life interesting. Emotions arise from uncertainties and accomplishments over uncertainties. Loving couples complete one another and their children continue their spirits on earth genetically and by parental training. Ancestor and parent activities and memories build offspring genetic blueprints.

God loves and is emotional. He created the universe with physical uncertainties and certainties. Atoms have uncertainties. Light and gravity have certain, constant characteristics. God integrates physical and mental uncertainties into spiritual certainties. Humans do not have certainty of everlasting life.

Emotions often accelerate good and bad actions, reactions, and behaviors. We must learn to control emotions. Either emotions overpower reason, or reason overpowers emotions.

We never know what happens between two people when they are alone. My former wife acted like a normal wife when we were around other people. I was ashamed to admit I was in such a horrible marriage. My parents thought divorce was a failure. We divorced after eighteen years.

Hell-bound school bullies mentally degrade victims. Bullies feel good about themselves, only briefly. Twisted minds need to repeat abuse or find other victims.

Everybody's crazy continuing abusive relationships. So many people do not feel good about themselves unless they control and degrade those close to them. This behavior stems from childhood uncertainties and survival instincts. Many of us have been degraded into submissive, low self-esteem behaviors. Coping, with sibling abuse when young, enabled spousal abuse later.

Smile and Frown

—⚍—

FACIAL MUSCLES ARE STRONGLY CONNECTED to the brain, mind, and emotions. The mind consciously and subconsciously controls the face. Faces give insight into long term thinking and attitude. Facial expressions reveal current thoughts and emotions. Relaxing the face is the easiest ways to reduce stress within the brain and mind. Pleasant feelings in the face and brain increase as the brain and mind heal. Never underestimate the healing power of a persistent smile.

The face strongly affects the brain and mind. When meditating on the face's contours and muscles, reflections from the face integrate more fully with subconscious processes.

We increase facial awareness by gently rubbing and stretching the forehead, cheeks, and chin. Overall or holistic awareness is constructed by reflections between the face, selected areas of the brain, hands, and body. The face, body, brain, and mind construct an integrated consciousness. Consciousness is spiritual. Different facial and brain awareness becomes prominent if a bee stings a foot.

What does smiling and broadening the face do for us? When smiling the brain broadens, relaxes, and uses less energy. Smiling faces show we are ready to accept a broad range of ideas, activities, and environments, while anticipating pleasant, interesting things.

Smiling and broadening the face releases childhood, and later, trauma effects. Excess energy is released from traumatized neural networks more readily when keeping the brain relaxed and energy efficient. We become more comfortable with who we are. Smiling is our Fountain of Youth!

Smiling, relaxing, and broadening the face sensitizes the mind to be receptive to others and God. An innocent childlike mind expecting good news is helpful during prayer.

Frowning indicates to others that our minds are tense and unreceptive. Focus is on self and inner concerns. Listening skills are lessened.

Frowning activates hurtful memories and prepares mental and physical resources to attack. It also shows we are hiding who we really are.

Persistent frowning lets repressed trauma and negative memories fester, possibly for life. My work is intended to lessen inner tensions and stress. Intentionally smiling relaxes and heals the brain and mind. Smile for mental health.

Faces show greater influence of trauma effects later in life. Sunken upper cheeks usually relate to extreme abuse and repressed anger. Persistent emotional thoughts mold facial contours. Some lives are dominated by reactive survival thinking. These poor souls threaten to annihilate anyone challenging their "imaginary" superiority and revealing their insecurities. They dare anyone to make eye contact.

Practicing "smile" healing requires patience. One has to gently smile and broaden the face for twenty or so seconds to sense the brain relaxing. The brain has a delayed reaction from facial exercises.

Most people sense that a broadened, smiling face is a positive, sign of an outgoing and caring person. We are drawn to people who we think would like and care about us. We love those who share our joy. The brain processes differently when the face and brain are broadened and relaxed. Thinking is less self-centered and protective of ego and intellectual abilities.

Smiling promotes caring, holistic right-brain dominance. Frowning promotes left-brain dominance, up-close and short term thinking, and restricts creative thinking. Smiling and broadening the

Smile and Frown

face may be an area of study for increasing mind control, healing, and expansion.

Some skill is needed in broadening the face. There is more healing effect when relaxing and reclining. Flush healing feelings around the crown of the head become prominent after nearly twenty years of mental reconstruction and a few years of smiling exercises. Unusual feelings are promoted when using the tongue to create a slight vacuum in the throat, and to some smaller extent, in the brain. I experienced unexpected control over the face and brain. Yes, I am an engineer.

If rubbing horizontally between the eyebrows with some pressure and there is pain, these muscles and related areas within the brain are tense. Rubbing releases muscle tensions and mild pain, and releases tensions within the brain. When facial muscles are relaxed, related areas of the brain are relaxed. Periodic exercise keeps muscles between the eyebrows smooth and relaxed. Feel the difference.

Stressed nerves and muscles near the spinal column are connected to motion degradation in the arm and are painful with chiropractic vibrations. Similar to the rubbing exercises above, repressed energy is released and pain lessens with vibrations. Muscle and motion abilities are restored when there is no longer pain with vibrations. This chiropractic process is referred to as opening up the nerves. Likewise, rubbing between the eyebrows is opening up the nerves. Smiling becomes easier and fuller.

Recline so all muscles are relaxed. Rub horizontally between eyebrows and across the bridge of the nose to relax muscles. Close eyes focusing long distance. Broaden the forehead and gently smile. Relax and repeat broadening until discovering the most relaxed position. After this, my heartbeat is sensed within the brain. I feel the flushness of increased blood flow to the brain and around the crown of the forehead. Increased blood flow heals the brain.

On my back facing straight up, with a slight smile, a relaxed broadened forehead, and meditating, I often experience a tightening around the sides of my forehead. Sensations change as mental reconstruction continues throughout the years.

On the other hand, tensing frown muscles tenses the brain and promotes selfish, protective thoughts for maintaining self-esteem, self-preservation, or control. With faces of an amazed child, minds are open to learn from parents, others, and God.

When listening to, and accepting, interesting ideas we open our eyes wide, raise our foreheads, and broaden our faces, naturally broadening our brains and opening our minds. These physical and mental connections are so ingrained and common that they are seldom thought about. Mirror brain cells are activated when viewing faces. Mirror cells allow us to interpret faces quickly to engage, fight, or flee. They activate quick responses.

In physics, a basic principle is: for every action, there is an equal and opposite reaction. This holds somewhat true for the brain and face. When the mind has pleasant thoughts, it is a natural reaction for the face to smile and broaden. Gently smiling for a minute or so may promote unexpected positive thoughts, or possibly even prevent a depression.

I frequently smile when seeing people on the street and sincerely care for them for a brief time. I think about what their lives might be like. This practice helps me to be more caring. Like most people, I have a general caring for others.

The basics of humor and laughter are building up someone or something as important, followed by unexpected uncertainty, nonsense, or failure. Laughter is enhanced by anticipation of unexpected disconnects or uncertainties in stories. Laughter often continues easily when related to earlier humor. It is important to laugh every day. When laughing our minds are relaxed and forgetting troubles of the day. Laughter is the best medicine for a long life.

Never confuse humor with putdowns. Humor among friends should always be so far out that everyone involved recognizes the nonsense. I abhor false humor, and putdowns, that make listeners question intent and their wellbeing. These perpetrators are psychological worms. They think their deranged humor makes them appear superior.

Inner reflections and principles develop well-adjusted individuals. Subconscious processes continually iterate to converge to complete thoughts, and consistent feelings and emotions.

If the mind is happy, the face is happy. If the mind is sad, the face is sad. If the body is hurting, or the mind is stressed, the face shows the pain. However, some individuals learn to hide their emotions with false faces. Deception is not healthy for individuals or those observing their faces. The brain and face are meant to work together. However, poker faces deceive.

Perform reflective exercises in front of the mirror. Facial mirror exercises need to be practiced for 15 seconds. Hold your happiest face for 15 seconds and then reflect on your thinking. How has your face affected your feelings, emotions, and attitude? The holistic right-brain reacts slowly to practiced facial expressions. At times, practice various facial expressions: sadness, anger, hurt, excitement, joy, envy, greed, humbleness, comfort, confident, fear, and love in front of a mirror to learn who you are. Hold each facial exercise for 10 seconds for the brain to react. Take your time, do various exercises now and then. Evaluate emotions with each facial contour.

We spent our young lives learning to be what parents and others wanted us to be. As mature adults we should study our inner thoughts and behaviors to remold our lives into who we want to become mentally, socially, and spiritually. It requires bold, psychiatric practice. When knowing and feeling comfortable with whom we are, our minds and faces relax. Appearances improve.

In performing facial exercises, we improve, who we are, and increase our value to others. As we get older, our facial lines show persistent inner thinking, stress patterns, and reactions to interactions and challenges.

I was depressed in 1977 to the point it hurt to think in words. Words felt as if embedded in molasses. At the worst of times I could not think of a single word. I existed in a thoughtless haze and would freeze in place since I had no reason to do anything or go anywhere.

I would look in a mirror and try to smile. My smile muscles would not work. My frozen face disclosed a hurting, uncertain mind. If one becomes so depressed that he does not care about his own well being, he still might care about others, but he may not feel worthy of bothering others.

After years of mental reconstruction and not thinking of anything in particular and glancing in a mirror, I realized I was smiling inside and outside. Life had become so different than depressed times. Thoughts come easy, are pleasant, and feel ready to fly.

I credit my happy disposition to mental reconstruction, my spiritual beliefs, practicing smiling, and appreciating the small things in life. When appropriate, I smile and speak to people I meet when out and about.

Is a smile ever wasted? Not if we are confident. The important thought when smiling is we have briefly cared for someone. It is spiritual showing someone we care for and wish others well. If ignored, we have still been spiritual. We should feel good about ourselves.

Keep your mind free to graciously accept or if needed reject other's ideas. Be your own person but respect your boss, family, those hurting, and all who are good to you. Without mental freedom, we are not free. Expand and appreciate your mental freedoms. Relax your brain to feel free and smarter. Smile.

Everybody is crazy for not smiling when meeting others. Smiling is healthy for the brain, mind, and body. A smile shows openness to, and acceptance of, others. Ladies can also give a quick smile, be busy, and go on about their business.

Love and Sharing

"Love one another, but make not a bond of love."

— Kahlil Gibran, *The Prophet*, 1994, NY, A Knopf

"Love grows by giving. The love we give away is the only love we keep. The only way to retain love is to give it away."

— Elbert Hubbard

"Most of us feel the need to do good things. Petting my cat gives feelings of love and sharing. We receive positive responses."

— H. Fulcher

LOVE IS AN INTERNAL SUBJECTIVE state of unselfish loyal and benevolent concern for the good of another: A perfect love is complete giving of ourselves to one another. Perfect love is nurturing our newborn baby expecting nothing back except a reflection of ourselves.

Spiritual parents love their baby and increase love for each other through their baby's reflections of themselves. True love grants freedom but needs reflection from loved ones.

Before we begin close or intimate relationships, we should ask ourselves if we are willing and able to please that person. Secondly, we should ask if that person is willing and able to please us. Together, we should discuss things we both need to feel fulfilled. Avoid those who say they need a high level of security or material treasures. Good relationships are spiritual.

True love means surrendering to one another. Love is honestly.

God has love and concern for us and needs our spiritual successes. He patiently waits for our reflections of His love returned to Him.

Christians believe we should love Jesus more than we love our spouses and children. We will be able to love our spouses and children even more.

Controlling behavior is void of true love, builds false self-esteem, and causes inner guilt. Only caring, and giving and receiving love, develop true, lasting self-esteem.

With more opportunities and complex lifestyles, love is difficult. One spouse may need to work away from home. Spouses may seldom see one another. Distance over time is challenging to maintain love and unity.

If you are degrading or controlling your spouse for emotional or other gain, get psychiatric help immediately. Controlling people cannot even love themselves. Love is spiritual.

Love and caring are learned by observing loving and caring parents. Heredity also plays some role in love and sharing. If we had loving childhoods, it is easier to love and care. Some can even love the unlovable.

If we grow up observing uncaring, selfish parents, we will be fundamentally selfish and uncaring, unless having received psychiatric unlearning or having practiced mental reconstruction. There may be many other ways to mentally reconstruct.

True sexual love builds warm emotions with feelings of being wanted and cared for, and willingness to surrender to one another. It is spiritual when sexual partners communicate and share needs, likes, dislikes, love, caring, creativity, and encouragement. Love is gentle.

Sex can be the most important time to build closeness and share reflections with one another. Show eagerness to share love but have patience when needed. Sharing love creatively and consistency builds joy in souls.

Work to maintain feelings of closeness but do not make a bond of love. Encourage individuality in interests and goals. Well rounded spouses build mutual and individual personalities.

I met a lady, on an airplane, who managed 4000 employees. She told me, "Success in management is sharing the joy of others' (employees') successes." Sharing joy of others requires a high level of love and caring. It is easier to revel in the joy of one's own successes. Good parents revel in their children's successes.

It is natural to distrust people who look and talk differently until interactions build similar reflections. Hopefully, with modern communication technologies throughout the world, we will receive friendly reflections from all peoples.

Everybody's crazy to continue loving, and giving to damaging, selfish takers. Continuing to give to takers without positive reflections causes depression and insanity. Can psychiatry heal damaging, distorted minds? From my experience, those who have had "expected" death situations have become more loving and spiritual. Love is imaginary, spiritual, and beyond the physical world.

Being Selfish

—⦿—

"Everybody has a personal truth. A personal truth is what you believe about yourself when nobody's listening and nobody's watching."

— Dr. Phil McGraw

"A strong sense of self is the foundation of personal power. If you define yourself by what someone else thinks, you've already lost the battle. Assert the right to be who you want to be."

— Dr. Phil McGraw

We need to think selfishly, at times, to understand and evaluate ourselves and our actions to enhance our lives. Self is always in the equation in everything we do.

We must strive to accept and improve ourselves. Faults should be evaluated and addressed. No one is perfect. Our thoughts and actions should first be acceptable to ourselves, and we should present our true selves to others. It is important to evaluate ourselves relative to those important to us. We should evaluate how we are treating others, and how others are treating us. There are many levels of good and poor interactions.

We must unlearn false beliefs, values, and fears others have ingrained in our minds when young, and even later in life. We should be skeptical of those diminishing us, and minimize importance of their influences in our lives. Those who are negative to us have selfish purposes. If allowed to continue, negative influences and behaviors may cause depression, lost health, and other disasters.

We should never putdown or degrade others. It lessens us. Conversations should be flowing without abrupt cutoffs, redirections, or controlling statements. Promote others' freedoms when possible. Positive mindfulness is a powerful force.

A forceful tone of voice is meant to control and degrade others. In the beginning of close relationships, we should speak up to end degrading voices and actions. Stop controlling, degrading behavior early, or it increases over time.

Without speaking up, we continue to internalize anger, which degrades our self-worth. At some point we may lose control, and emotionally explode. Sinister perpetrators expose our loss of control, but do not escape God's judgment.

We must evaluate and understand our hurtful histories to learn to become more comfortable in the present. Connect brain, mind, and body with the now. Unite present awareness, senses, feelings, and emotions. Evaluating histories helps us predict and look forward to fulfilling futures.

Connecting memories with sensations and emotions builds future thoughts. Thinking integrates memories with dreams of the future. Without thinking about the future, we can do nothing.

In earlier centuries, religious leaders held followers accountable for "evil" dreams. Today, we believe we have little control over dreams. Dreaming minds should be selfish toward understanding our histories and abilities for planning futures.

Being Selfish

Everybody's crazy not believing dreams should be selfish processes. We must learn about ourselves from dreams to improve our lives and then the lives of others.

Conflict

—⚡︎—

CONFLICT ARISES WHEN THERE ARE competitive or opposing thoughts or actions, and there is a state of divergent interests, activities, or goals. Conflict includes inner struggles from incompatible or opposing ideas, drives, and wishes stemming from internal or external needs or expectations.

Long standing conflicts cause stress throughout the brain and body with a possible myriad of physical and mental symptoms. Stress is caused by poor health, hurtful relationships, and believing one's life is out of control. With inner conflict, one may not be able to accept circumstances or think life can get better through his or others' efforts.

We need to address conflicts and develop resolutions to maintain mental health and achieve life's goals. Addressing appropriate levels of conflict and finding solutions at emotional highs and lows develops a versatile mind. We are healthier experiencing brief periods of uncertainty and conflict for developing creative solutions than letting conflicts fester for a long time.

Experiencing and surviving difficult, conflicting times makes us appreciate normal and enjoyable times. Strong, creative, and versatile brain structures are developed with controlled conflict exercises near, or at, emotional limits. The mind heals.

Don't let childhood traumas limit your IQ for life. Become aware of emotional limits. Trauma ingrained emotions limit how we think and love. Mentally reconstruct to expand mental abilities out to genetic limits.

At emotional limits, we feel uncertain, possibly with fears of insanity. Beyond emotional limits, we become self-centered and out of control. Recovering from, and pondering, limiting experiences makes us more aware of our inner principles. We must let go of who we are to become who we want to be. We must integrate our new behaviors and selves with our histories and with those we care about and who care for us.

Nothing happens within the universe or brain without conflict. We must think or do something, or do nothing. When resolving conflict, the brain re-grows, and becomes smarter. Every day we have challenges, sometimes at limits. At limits, muscles re-grow and become stronger.

Traumas challenge who we are and can become. Threats may be immediate or slowly evolving. Security is primary to life. Trauma causes guilt, even without fault, instilling inadequacy, weakness, and fear.

Humans do not have awareness without conflict. Awareness is activated by the brain's reactions to sensed energy. There is always conflict in the brain on prioritizing signals from senses and activated memories. The brain is conditioned to give security threats high priority.

We increase knowledge and abilities by accepting, understanding, and controlling conflict. Manic-depressives experience more conflict than most. I had conflict and feelings of inadequacy when God ask me: not to leave Him out of my first book. I thought, who am I to write spiritually? I decided that I could only write with the skills and knowledge I had, and requested God's guidance.

Even though bipolar disorder amplifies emotions and conflicts, manic-depressives have an unusual opportunity to improve their lives through spiritual communication. Surrendering free will by lowering energy of the brain invites God's blessings.

Practicing my psychiatric exercises and processes may prevent, or cure, bipolar disorder for others. Much of this book is dedicated to my alternative healing exercises and processes. Mental healing practices may reduce probability of mania and going out of control. My "Psychiatric Exercises" essay gives details. I have written truthfully but my work is so different that readers may have difficulty accepting it. Many things in life are difficult to believe unless experienced.

I have had conflict in writing for helping readers with such a different healing and spiritual model. The main conflict was whether readers would have the patience for such a long challenging program. Also, a question is that only manic depressives may be able to benefit fully from this work.

I am grateful for having, and having been cured of, bipolar disorder and having received spiritual blessings. I have presented ideas as truthfully as I understood them and will continue improving healing processes and spiritual communication skills. It has been conflicting to determine the best way to write and conclude an unusual work and truth.

I have not had manic episodes for twenty years. However, under severe situations, absolutely anyone might go out of control and become irrational. If a criminal repeatedly breaks in our house, steals, and deceitfully hides or damages valuables, we have conflict on how to protect ourselves and respond.

Twisted spouses and individuals use conflicting body and verbal languages to confuse and control innocent spouses and others they meet. Without understanding conflicting body and spoken languages, the innocent may suffer trauma effects. The damage is incurred in the victim's split second of insanity in not understanding the conflict between the two languages. Body language is processed with the right-brain and verbal language is processed with the left-brain. Opposing messages from the two brains cause uncertainty, confusion, and stress.

I wish to help readers understand the conflict in the two impulsive mixed messages and not be adversely affected. Understanding and acting upon knowledge is power. Some offenders may not be fully aware of their conflicting messages. If we observe someone close to us sending mixed messages, point out the conflict early. Perpetrators may recognize their confusing actions and stop, or they know we understand, and stop. Men show conflict and control with physical and verbal threats. Women are usually more subtle. Conflicting behaviors (skills?) may have been passed down through generations.

Prolonged conflict and stress is unhealthy. From heredity, our brains and minds are cultured to react to conflict by preparing to fight or flee. Adverse to our health, we subconsciously hide or internalize emotional memories ingrained by conflict. Early generations either fought, or fled avoiding long term stress. Learning to handle conflict and release tensions stimulates brains and minds to be more creative.

In living our lives we develop fundamental principles. Human are either love or power based. It takes nurturing, training, and sophistication to be love based. Without training children will become power based. Conflicting psychiatric exercises can help us become less stressed for loving ourselves more, and then to become love based in interacting with others.

Everybody is crazy to live with long term conflict and stress. Get counseling or get out, if possible. Resolving short and long term conflicts build confidence, improves mental health, makes us smarter, and enables us to be more successful. Parents should introduce children to appropriate challenges as they grow to teach them the art of resolving conflicts.

Creative Thinking

—ɯ—

WHAT DOES "CREATIVE" MEAN? It means thinking of ideas or making something that has never existed before, something new, different, and useful. Humans have the ability to create new ideas. We can construct images or ideas of things we have never seen or heard of before. Some of us are more successful at developing creative thoughts than others. We become more creative with practice! Repeating the same old tasks, ideas, and slogans stifles creativity but gives confidence in doing routine things.

Brains are much like muscles. They do only what they need to do with some small additional ability for emergencies. Muscles and brains increase in ability when stressed to limits. When meeting mental challenges at limits or practicing my mental reconstruction methods, minds increase in ability and creativity. Academic tests and athletic competitions increase mental and physical skills and expand abilities and limits.

For individuals who stay in their comfort zones, their minds perform "ho-hum" tasks day in and day out. Resolving challenges develops creative minds. Mind models help develop reasoning and creative skills.

Mental holograms, the images and scenarios we are sometimes aware of in our dreams and, at times, with our eyes closed, are building blocks for thought. Subconscious processes compare and integrate mental holograms from memory to construct new holograms for developing new creative thoughts. Mental holograms consist of three and higher dimensional images and scenarios that include emotions and reaction potentials for creating new memories. The brain and mind need building blocks to create ideas. My creative thinking model is that subconscious manipulating of mental (dream) holograms is the basis of human thought.

Every complete and creative thought is constructed with subconscious building blocks or sub-thoughts. Through heredity and life experiences, subconscious process and comparison rules integrate sub-thoughts to create conscious thoughts, as images or words.

Sub-thoughts are stored within the brain as low-energy mental hologram images and scenarios. Dream and subconscious hologram scenario processes construct memories including emotions. Integrating dream holograms and sub-thoughts creates new three dimensional memory images and scenarios that can be recalled when stimulated internally or externally.

Coherent light, electromagnetic radiation (EMR,) sources from two angles integrate within a surface to construct three-dimensional commercial holograms. Mental holograms are constructed on neural membranes from many firing neuron EMR sources from many directions.

Firing neurons, throughout the brain, emit EMR, in all directions, which are partially absorbed by neural membranes at various locations and angles. From billions of neuron activations, some EMR is coherent. Coherent EMR is absorbed within a complex configuration of neural membranes at many angles constructing higher dimensional mental holograms throughout the brain. The brain is complex. Mental holograms are much more detailed than commercial holograms since they reside on a complex three dimensional neural membrane structures rather than on a two dimensional plane.

Dreaming is important to creativity. Dreaming processes are mostly subconscious but can become conscious during the awakening process. Dreams have animated three dimensional perspectives of dream characters and scenarios. Dream images may include sensed realities or imaginative integrations of sensed realities. Some images are creative fabrications.

Dream image and scenario expression depends upon life and heredity experiences. In the beginning of dreams, we question the impossible but then accept and experience it with excitement, or fear.

Subconscious and dreaming minds compare holograms, from memory, at various angles using subconscious hereditary and learned processing rules to create new holographic images as part of the reasoning process. We have some control over imagination and reasoning processes. At other times, creative ideas emerge with little conscious thought.

In my mental creative model, subconscious processes rotate mental hologram images on many axes for analyzing and integrating their resonances with other memory resonances. Subconscious processes recognize faces from many angles, even angles not viewed. The subconscious mind rotates and integrates memory images to recognize visual images at different angles. Mental or spiritual holograms reside within virtual or spiritual dimensions.

EMR, from neuron activations, travels at the speed of light in the brain. Light travels in matter slower than in vacuum. Subconscious minds process like lightning.

The brain is physical. We should not limit the mind to physical dimensions. In my creative model, spiritual waves have too little physical energy and too long waves for man's devices to detect and measure. Detecting and measuring devices can only measure differences. Spiritual wave lengths may be longer than the diameter of the Milky Way.

Spiritual waves are reflected between the origin and the edges of the universe and are absorbed and emitted by light throughout the universe at very fast rates. We can only make models of spiritual waves that give God His omnipresent and omniscient properties over a great big universe.

Humans are sensitive to around 10^{-7} meter light wavelengths. We do not see long radio waves but our radios allow us to "hear" radio waves, which extend from about .01 to about 10,000 meters. Humans do not see, and human devices do not detect spiritual waves. Light, gravity, and spiritual waves consistently transmit perfect information throughout the universe.

Neuron activities produce and integrate synchronized, resonating electromagnetic waves that create consciousness. Thousands of subconscious and higher dimension hologram processes create conscious streams of thought. Some electromagnetic waves from subsets of 85 billion neurons become synchronized allowing us to focus on one idea at a time. Wow!

Successful mental challenges increase versatility for synchronizing, integrating, and extrapolating memory holograms to create new meaningful mental holograms. Processes become more refined, as memory holograms are compared at wider angles to create new ideas. If two mental holograms have similar resonances, they integrate to form a new mental hologram or sub-idea. If this new mental hologram resonance is stimulated long and strong enough, the sub-idea is elevated to a full blown creative, conscious idea. Thinking, memory, and life advance.

If a bullet passes across our line of vision, its image occurs too fast for us to see it but it is real. We see very little of reality. If we look at a tree long enough, our eyes and brains develop a conscious image in our minds.

If ideas are truly creative, they seem like having been known for a long time! Spiritual messages, received, feel as if known for a long time. Writing dreams and spiritual ideas down is wise as they have very low energy and are quickly forgotten. We must learn from others but maintain our creative ability.

An integrated theory of the universe should accurately predict behaviors of small, intermediate, large, and very large physical systems. Cosmology requires additional dimensions to model the universe.

Spiritual dimensions must exist to create the human mind and God's omnipresence and omniscience.

I develop models and theories to understand the mind, universe, and God. Over a century ago Louis Pasteur was mocked when he discovered that microbes cause human diseases. In the past, people have been very slow to accept new creative ideas. Today, many are still slow to accept new ideas.

Awareness is different from consciousness. For example, we may be aware of knowing someone's name but are not conscious of that name. We may have awareness of knowledge but not be conscious of that knowledge at a specific time.

We may recall forgotten names and knowledge later on. There are creative exercises we can do to improve memory. We might visualize images of a new acquaintance with two people we know, one with the same first name and the other with the same last name. It is a simple integration skill. It takes practice. Often it is easier to recall images than names.

Pondering in-depth thoughts over long periods of time develops strong, thick neural networks for specific ideas in chosen areas. Einstein pondered for long periods of time on difficult concepts resulting in his prestigious discoveries and models of the universe. Studying about, and making models of, the universe helps us understand God. God is the original scientist and engineer. He designed and built the universe. We understand artists by studying their work.

The mind records perceived vision and words perfectly. The difficulty is in recalling memories. Stimulated by an old friend, we may recall events long forgotten, and thought impossible to remember.

An artist creates a work of art. His subconscious mind remembers each stroke and stage in creating the artwork. The artwork is physical. Memories of painting processes are spiritual.

The universe is God's artwork. He remembers the instant of Creation and evolves His design. We learn about artists by studying their art and about God by studying His universe.

A broadened face and open mind increase the probability of having creative ideas. Studying in selected fields and occasionally elevating emotions followed by calming down, as in prayer, promotes creativity. The healed, reconstructed mind can be very creative in overcoming difficulties. Extending the mind to emotional or mental limits promotes creative thinking. We must surrender who we have been, to become who we need to be.

People who have experienced little uncertainty in their lives are rarely creative. Uncertainty promotes creativity and survival thinking. Writers are creative. They must decide to use this or that word. Once creative mental processes are developed, creativity usually continues.

A young child becomes awe struck when seeing exciting things. His eyes and mind open wide. Experience has taught adults not to be in awe of new things but to reason about or ignore them. Some adults relearn to be creative.

Everybody's crazy for simply memorizing others' ideas and teachings. We must develop creative ideas of our own or others will brainwash us and control our lives. If we don't take control of our lives others will.

Predicting

We like people who, and things that, are predictable. We generally know what to expect from our friends. It is heartwarming when someone does something better for us than predicted. Surprises, beyond the expected, warm the hearts of givers and receivers. Scientists develop theories to predict laws that govern activities throughout the universe for human benefit.

We predict routine and difficult activities, and sometimes astounding occurrences. We use current knowledge and intelligent guesses to predict success, love, failure, or danger. Routine predictions have become mostly subconscious. Here are some routine predictions we make:

Routine predictions:
1. Our legs will function and support walking as remembered.
2. We will be able to drink water.
3. We will be able to balance and ride our bicycles.
4. We will recognize and enjoy our friends.
5. We will swim as practiced and remembered.

Difficult predictions:
1. Completing tasks requiring stamina - running long distances.
2. Completing efforts that require skills. Software development, engineering design, winning a professional tennis tournament,

and successful physics research that requires complex training, memory, application, and, of course, patience.
3. Being understood using a little known language.
4. Successfully giving a presentation on solving or managing a complex problem.
5. Before manufacturing products, companies must predict that customers will need and buy those products.

Limiting predictions:
1. Stretching out and catching a football beyond expected limits, ignoring possible injury.
2. Risking health and life for victory in war.
3. Predicting that inner sounds within the neck, brainstem, and throat were energy releases from localized overstressed neural networks and that sensed energy releases would lessen with exercises and migrate throughout the neck, throat, and brain over time
4. Conflicting psychiatric exercises would briefly stimulate traumatized neural networks to limits speeding up releases of their repressed energy for them to become resynchronized with normal brain activities.
5. In designing complex nuclear reactor cores, nuclear engineers must predict neuron behaviors and neuron percentages absorbed by uranium, water, support structures, or poisons: used to control neuron levels. Predictions, experiments, and testing must be precise to safely control reactors at designed power levels.

I had one life saving event that I could have never predicted. Miraculously, I received a spiritual "flash" of emotional life events that controlled my arm, jerking my steering wheel to the left, and saving me from "an expected fatal car crash." I momentarily predicted I would die. I did not predict a life saving miracle.

Predicting

    Predicting daily, long-range, and complex outcomes depends upon our senses, memory, cognitive skills, and educated guesses. Sometimes we make decisions on feelings or instincts we are unable to explain. Without abilities to remember and predict, we can do nothing.

    Everybody's crazy and can do nothing if not able to predict future short and long term activities. Routine predictions are mostly performed subconsciously. The better we can predict; the smarter and more successful we will become.

Psychology

—⚏—

"The truth is the kindest thing we can give..."

— Harriet Beecher Stowe

"It is an overwhelming thought to realize that as we degenerate in morality, we increase in force."

— Dr. David Jeremiah, *The Handwriting on the Wall, Secrets from the Prophecies of DANIEL*, 1992.

Psychology is the science of the mind which includes behavioral characteristics of individuals and behaviors related to fields of knowledge, organizations, and specific activities. There are various theories or systems of psychology, such as *Freudian Psychology*. In this essay, I write mostly about psychology relating to mind healing and spiritual models.

Without counseling, most of us continue to repeat unhealthy thoughts, actions, and habits that have become engrained in our brains and minds, mostly during childhood. Mental healing processes stimulate repressed memories to become more conscious allowing reasoning about, not mimicking, ingrained brainwashed ideas and actions. We become free to learn and practice healthier, productive activities.

Words and body language communicate ideas between humans with positive and negative purposes. However, when thinking to ourselves, we should not limit thinking to word processes. Manipulating images within scenarios and other wordless processes improve creative thinking. We anticipate and visualize known roads, turns, and signals as we drive toward destinations.

Subconscious wordless resonances and processes are foundations of inner thought development. When writing we often have to culture words many times to best represent our inner analog or flowing thoughts. Culturing or making complete sense of initial rough ideas gives feelings of completion.

Memorizing and brainwashing ingrains rigid ideas and strong emotions. Brainwashed ideas are not easily changed. The background enrichment of normal memories is lacking. Ingrained memories are stored in localized reactive brain components differently from normal developed memories stored holistically throughout the brain. Tyrants brainwash to control. Brainwashing is not in any one's best interests. The military brainwashes recruits so they will obey and follow the chain of command in threatening situations. This is necessary for successful missions and the security of the country.

The left brain is more constrained by physical time. The right brain has spiritual freedoms. Practicing right-brain, left-brain dominance control improves thinking. Spiritual books were written to control but build spiritual lives of believers. However, being forced to memorize scripture, brainwashes followers allowing control by corrupt spiritual leaders.

True spiritual leaders empower by building up followers' wellbeing and confidence. Leaders set known goals and promise to achieve those goals. Managing must follow.

Mental structures and values are molded by choices and decisions we have made. Personal mission statements should be based upon stated principles. Committing to accomplish goals builds character and successful organizations. In leadership positions, we must be sure our criticism is not worse than the behaviors we are attempting to correct. We must acknowledge, learn from, and correct our and subordinates' mistakes early on. Most of us hold on to early learned spiritual beliefs until we experience a significant emotional event and become bold enough to think on our own. A significant emotional event may be a near death experience, relationship with Jesus, another spiritual leader, or directly with God.

We lose sense abilities when not used. Skin sensing abilities are being lost by wearing clothes. Outside, the air feels alive to the skin. I have feelings of acquiring knowledge when skin is exposed in natural environments. The breeze through the trees breaks the air into refined pressure fabric that speaks to the skin and stimulates nerves and brains.

People tend to think most people think similarly until someone develops a noted reputation. Einstein was slow at learning languages. Thinking in images or pictures longer when young may have helped Einstein develop his impressive discoveries and models.

Suppose you had never heard of Einstein and relativity, and he began talking to you about his theories. Of course, you would think he was as crazy as a fish. However, you were the limited one, and not knowing him, you would be reluctant to admit his thinking was vastly superior to your own.

Practice and repetition ahead of time give confidence to perform tasks in real life situations. We must evaluate progress to improve repetitive thoughts and actions. We practice important tasks many times to ensure we perform well. Some of us work twelve hours a day to become experts not to fear failure or layoff.

Before building, we mentally visualize task and details. It is important to begin work with the end product in mind so you know where you are and where you are going. Keeping the end product in mind makes work seem easier and go faster with less error.

We find comfort in repeating uplifting rhymes and spiritual rituals. Recitals provide more comfort and confidence as we get older.

We like to be part of important ideas by repeating them with like-minded believers. We want to fit in and need to believe in something greater than self to give strength to overcome weaknesses, and fears of death. When young, we received comfort in our parents' nurturing and protection.

Unfortunately, cruel, controlling people use the power of repetition for evil. Remember Hitler! False superior psychology builds false self-esteems. We must understand and defend ourselves against false emotional, repetitious words and slogans.

From hereditary, we have been engrained with "flight or fight" in threatening and emotional circumstances. However, our brains and minds have not been genetically prepared for persistent, long-term frustration, abuse, and stress that we cannot escape.

What could build confidence more than spouses smart enough to know when to give help and when to allow their spouses to resolve their own challenges? Long term relationships are difficult. We should evaluate whether we and potential spouses are able to give whole heartedly through good and bad times.

Some characteristics of good mental health are:

- never abuse anyone physically, mentally, or financially
- build self-confidence in achieving truthful, honorable goals
- like yourself, inspire confidence in others
- evaluate who does and does not build confidence in you and others
- do not feel or act above or below anyone
- evaluate and avoid those acting superior to you,
- develop an art for disagreeing and building friendships
- encourage good and discourage bad behaviors
- help the needy to relieve hunger and suffering and to become self-sustaining when possible
- accept suggestions and criticism, evaluate intensions
- be respectful when providing positive or negative suggestions

- choose friends wisely for natural give and take, and for longer lives

Leadership characteristics are:

- good listening and communication skills
- organize, train, and build confident employees
- be creative in achieving goals and rewarding achievers
- acknowledge subordinate achievements and share their joy
- if necessary, correct or discipline poor performers early

Mental reconstruction releases trauma energy, restoring abilities and spiritual sensitivities. Christians reduce mental energy and surrender as we pray. Spiritual communication is more effective with either very low or very high energy. Normal mental energy levels are for everyday thinking, interactions, and activities. Relaxed attitudes and spirituality are important for mental health.

Newborn healthy babies have complete, holistic minds. Young babies think and learn as fast as adults dream. They do not think in words. Early and later traumas ingrained memories in brain compartments. Reasoning and thinking become distorted and incomplete.

Some people have experienced severe trauma that have caused split personalities within different brain "compartments." In an extreme case, a 1957 movie: *Three Faces of Eve* portrayed the schizophrenic disorder of a lady with three different and separate personalities.

We all have experienced trauma in our lives. Our brains and minds are compartmentalized to lesser or greater extents. We think within narrow-minded, emotional compartments when abused. Many divorces are caused by compartmentalized emotional miss-communications.

Strong emotions during confrontations deepen mental compartmentalization and downgrade understanding between spouses and others. When a spouse is angry with the other, his/her mind thinks selfishly. Language becomes emotional and repetitive, communication is deteriorated. The brain and mind are healthier and smarter when working as a whole rather than within emotional compartments.

Subconscious minds compartmentalize memories in several ways. Examples of learning sources:

1. from observations without reacting (including baby observations,)
2. from observations initiating actions;
3. from authorities, parents, teachers, others;
4. from required books;
5. from selected books;
6. from own initiatives including social interactions;
7. from others' initiatives;
8. from the media;
9. from traumas, mixed messages, and impulsive controllers;
10. from intellectual traumas (embarrassing intellectual performances – speaking, tests, mental mistakes;)
11. and from successful or failed environmental interactions.

From ancestor emotional trials and errors, heredity has constructed our brains and minds to understand and navigate our worlds. Will human heredity changes advance faster as we explore and reason about our universe through science and communication advances? Or will easier lives make future generations dumber?

As we get older, most of us do not remember recent things as well, but remember early experiences easier. This loss of ability is ingrained in human genetics for the next generation to learn history from the previous generation.

At a luncheon with two gentlemen I had worked with 30 years ago, we discussed old times. I recalled events and people after either of the two gentlemen had brought them up. I would have never recalled some of those memories on my own. Our minds never forget anything. We can recall long forgotten events and people when stimulated.

Younger folks switch from one idea to another faster than older folks do. However, older folks often develop patience for in-depth concentration in selected areas.

Recalling hurtful emotional losses, conflicts, or traumas are easier than recalling positive emotions. Positive emotions are felt more holistic and less focused than negative emotions. Negative events and actions are more difficult to forget. Psychologists and psychiatrists are learning more about helping victims unlearn traumatic emotions and events. Unlearning is important for soldiers with post-traumatic syndrome. Unlearning is purging energy from ingrained, trauma memories.

Being yourself means knowing, and letting others know, the real you. Deception and lies may attempt to make others think we are greater than we are. If caught, we are less than worms. The best thing we can say about ourselves and others is the truth.

True love gives unselfishly to loved ones. We judge lovers through our feelings, and their words and body language. Love should never be one way. Relationship criteria must be more definitive than feelings. We need to distinguish between givers and takers and between nurturing and degrading. We need to question those who negatively affect us. We need and deserve a response from an offending person if we have been open, truthful, and pleasant. In emotional relationships, we must evaluate who has had good intentions toward us.

We must evaluate influences books have had on our thinking. Books are independent of time, giving them a spiritual aspect. When read, books can change our future. They can promote positive and spiritual, or negative and evil, changes in our lives.

Spiritual messages give feelings similar to just solving a difficult problem after having pondered on it for some time. At the moment of solution, we burst with excited feelings of relief, freedom, and accomplishment. Solving difficult problems and spiritual feelings give certainty of understanding an unchanging truth.

On the negative side, dictators and false spiritual leaders believe that they have a God given right to do the evil they do. Brainwashed followers become arrogant in aggrandizing their dictators. Some believe their spiritual leader is perfect and they have the right to kill others to evangelize their misguided beliefs. I cannot believe our parents and God gave us life to be killed by misguided followers of misguided religions. Babies and the innocent are easily brainwashed. We must understand the influence of negative, controlling psychology!

We must distinguish between things we can influence and things we cannot. We should spend the most time on influencing things we can positively influence. Accept or avoid things we have concerns about but cannot change. We cannot change yesterday's history.

The womb is the closest thing to heaven humans ever experience on earth, and we can't recall it! Children grow up and find that parents are not all powerful and perfect. Human souls yearn for perfection and security once experienced in the womb.

As we grow, we strive to accomplish in different ways. In competitions, we want to excel at our best. Emotions aroused from unexpected accomplishments are the most meaningful. However, losing a game to a child for him to experience the feeling of winning can be good if not overdone. Children need to win and accept loss.

Even though we may speak and understand the same language, we develop unique personal inner emotional languages. Activation of our inner emotional and hereditary languages constructs inner happiness, self-esteem, self-confidence, or lack thereof. When people are emotionally attached, emotional languages dominate and meaning sometimes diverges. This language diversion keeps psychiatrists in business.

People that commit evil lack caring. After the end of the Civil War, southern soldiers and families suffered severely. Appomattox sheriff, Billy Hicks, hired about twenty bullies. Instead of distributing food and supplies donated by the North to local families, he kept much of the donations for himself and made money by selling food and supplies to outsiders.

Power and opportunity led to corruption and lack of caring for needy people in Hick's own community, from the *Civil War Handbook*, National Park Commemorative Series, Copyright 2011. Hicks must have had a lack of parenting. "A child who is allowed to be disrespectful to his parents will not have true respect for anyone," quote by Billy Graham.

There are caring people in the world. Visionary, Steve Jobs, of Apple died in October 20011. He dreamed of a future beyond current ideas, technologies, and lifestyles. When in college he had to sleep on the floor in dorm rooms of friends. As CEO of Apple, He gave himself a salary of $1. Experiencing rough times awakens the creative, spiritual mind. Apple has become one of the world's richest companies.

Jesus was a spiritual visionary enhancing millions of lives for two thousand years. Visionaries do not accept the way things are. Jesus changed the world and His teaching has guided souls to heaven.

There are few visionaries that truly improve society's ways of thinking and living. We should give credit to those who initially test, verify, and then promote innovative science discoveries and technologies. The rest of us are like cattle blindly following the leader. No one achieves greatness by following "every day, normal paths."

Religion is part of psychology and healthy societies. Are we bold enough to study and evaluate traditional religions? Opposition will be fierce, from the brainwashed. Thomas Jefferson was bold, innovative, and did so. See my essay on "Thomas Jefferson's Beliefs." The more truth we learn about the universe and God; the more spiritual we can become. Knowing the truth and being truthful is good psychology. With technologies advancing, the human race has just begun to think!

Everybody's crazy not studying and using positive psychology. We need to know ourselves before interacting with and evaluating others to be happy, purposeful, and help build an intelligent, spiritual society. Everybody's crazy acting superior to anyone. They become morally inferior to everyone.

Psychiatry

In 1977 and manic, I had my first encounter with an older psychiatrist. I was emotional, unsure of my thoughts, reactive, and beyond mental limits. I was skeptical of everyone else's words and actions, but expected miracles from psychiatrists.

I cannot recall this psychiatrist asking me questions. Possibly, he sensed I was beyond rational responses. However, my senses were acute, and at a distance, I overheard him tell my dad that he could not do anything with me. In my state of mental pain, I expected death, shortly.

This psychiatrist prescribed Haldol and the next appointment in two weeks. In over a week, muscles all over my body were cramping. In my mental pain, I thought it was the dying process. Feelings of death engulfed my mind and soul. In the emergency room, I saw a doctor I knew and liked. His brief attention gave me hope. He had been a tennis friend. I had had a severe reaction to, and was taken off of, Haldol. I quickly improved. My next psychiatrist, Dr. Gene Goode, was encouraging and helpful. I developed confidence that he was working to help me.

In career travels, I have had six or seven psychiatrists for medication maintenance. All seemed to be for my best interest, except one. I had not had mania for years and felt this doctor was not honest or helpful. I left him after two or three visits. If unable to look out for yourself, even some psychiatrists may take advantage of you.

From my perspective, psychiatry is the study, understanding, and guidance of patient moods, thinking and behaviors within, at, and beyond emotional limits. Psychiatrists nurture patient thinking and behaviors through psychotherapy and medications. Psychiatric medications are intended to restore neurotransmitter, or brain chemical, levels to normal levels. Normal levels had been adversely affected by severe stress, depression, and mania.

Minds and machines go out of control when stressed beyond limits. Often unusual, erratic, and fast thoughts occur when mental limits are breached. Established mental limits remain over a lifetime unless overridden by trauma, illegal drugs, persistent negative encounters, mental reconstruction, psychotherapy, or loss of loved ones or health.

Some mental limits need to be more restrictive, and others need to be expanded. Adjustments, needed, depend upon principles, health, interactions, and conflicts.

Normally, we spend little time thinking about our moods until events occur that make us unusually happy, sick, sad, or afraid. If negative events happen, we may become depressed and even suicidal. If positive events occur often, we may develop a twisted ego and feel above, and abuse, others. After near death experiences, many are more appreciative of life and become more caring.

Loss of self-esteem, caused by loss of a loved one, job, and so on, may cause depression. Self-image becomes confused and even devastated. Relationships are adversely affected. If depression and uncertainties sink below negative thinking limits, bipolar disorder may explode into a once depressed mind. In this case, the mind rebounds from depression quickly. Positive emotional limits are sporadically exceeded in manic episodes. Exciting new, but irrational thinking begins. At the heights of mania, a manic-depressive may think he can think through any problem or difficulty.

Emotional limits establish thinking, behavior, and interaction boundaries. Under certain circumstances, we become aware of our mental and physical limits. Without thinking we continually know we cannot fly. Most behavior characteristics and limits are subconscious as we perform routine activities. Psychiatry is needed if we cannot control our thoughts and behaviors within mentally healthy, and socially acceptable, limits.

We must value our own lives to be able to value the lives of those who love and depend upon us. We have social responsibilities. We must respect the well-being and freedoms of others. Psychiatry helps us define and build acceptable thinking and behavior limits for our and others' well-being.

From my own and others' mental challenges, those who have helped heal, mental suffering, or prevented suicide, have become personal saints. These gifted, people are brave, patient, and caring enough to understand and gently guide us when our thinking is scattered. Healing self and others is spiritual. Jesus healed.

Too often, when there is a senseless mass killing in America, officials and the news media report that the perpetrator has had psychiatric disorders and had quit taking medications. Psychiatrists must heal patients before thinking and actions become desperate. Unfortunately, the psychiatric community does not get involved until patients are overstressed and out of control.

Anyone feeling justified in harming, killing, or inciting cohorts to harm or kill those who have never harmed or threatened to harm anyone has a mental disorder. Each of us has levels of mental imbalances and prejudices. Some abuse and others enable their own abuse for years. We have been brainwashed and have ingrained prejudices by parents, neighborhoods, societies, and religions early in life.

Christians believe they are spiritually superior to other religions. Muslims believe they are spiritually superior to other religions. Can religions be different and still perfect? We should be careful describing religions or anything as perfect. It is dangerous to us, and others, who think differently.

Psychiatry must advance and practices broaden to cure individuals, societies, and countries of dreadful beliefs, fears, and prejudices to prevent senseless religious wars and destruction. America has matured and continues to nurture by integrating people with different backgrounds to live together with love in peace. Religious leaders need to consider psychiatry and philosophy to reason about, not memorize, their religious books and practices, and to consider the effects of preaching "perfection." Perfect religions have caused wars and false spiritual superiority since man began to worship God. Perfect cannot change or get better. We must use "perfection" cautiously.

Psychiatry and psychology must play an important role in framing the world's future thinking as they are the best hope in reducing brainwashing that occurs in childhood and later on. Brainwashed beliefs can be detected by victims not remembering sources of beliefs, by recalling forced ingrained ideas, or by recognizing absolute, perfect, and unquestionable beliefs. In the future, Psychiatrists will be able to cure brainwashed or highly emotional irrational beliefs by analyzing energy release sensations from psychiatric exercises and processes. Adults demanding behaviors of a child in emphatic ways brainwash.

Psychiatrists and psychologists should gently question emotional beliefs and ask if ideas could be slightly different in several ways to detect brainwashing. World leaders need more reason and less emotional thinking. God was and is absolutely reasonable in constructing the universe and in integrating information throughout the universe. Light and gravity communicate their information perfectly throughout the universe.

However, humans never have perfect knowledge or write perfectly. If we are humble and surrendering to God, we receive greater spiritual communication, guidance, and blessings.

Rigid religious interpretations and practices, meant to give followers "certain" lives, have made the world an uncertain, scary, and dangerous place. For humans to continue living for the next thousand years, religions must teach love, honor, and respect of all peoples in a relaxed atmosphere, with choices, to promote world peace. Religious leaders and psychiatrists must work to convert prejudices, hate, superiority, and desperation into love and peace so even the unlovable can be nurtured, trusted, and loved.

The highly brainwashed only regurgitate memorized, hackneyed ideas and phrases with absolute certainty of their validity and application. My goal is for children and adults to learn at their own speed with reason and options, and not to be brainwashed with forceful ideas and unquestioning beliefs. Rigid, brainwashed thinking leads to violent emotions against anyone believing or being different.

Psychotherapists uncover and question emotional and brainwashed ideas. They stimulate patients' minds to recall brainwashed idea origins. Recalling repressed memories and reducing their energy heals the brain and mind. Each of us needs to reduce the energy of emotional and brainwashed ideas to lesser or greater extents.

Freud believed various teenage and adult dysfunctions were caused by sexual frustrations. They ingrain trauma scars in the brain. I defer sex discussion to the experts. However, imagination helps. Our thoughts are imprisoned by engrained trauma effects. Most of us do not achieve our potentials.

Everybody's crazy if not recognizing their need for psychiatry. Reducing pain and uncertainties of trauma effects frees the mind to be creative. Before manic depression, I was easy going but inwardly angry from my former wife's deception and abuse. My alternative mental reconstruction processes were critical in reducing trauma effects and preventing manic episodes for over twenty years. What could be better proof of success than that?

Philosophy

—ɷ—

"The whole problem with the world is that fools and fanatics are always so certain of themselves and wiser people so full of doubts."

— Bertrand Russell, Philosopher

From: www.thefreedictionary.comphilosophy:

Philosophy covers study of the following aspects of life:

1. Love and pursuit of wisdom by intellectual means and moral self-discipline.
2. Investigation of nature, causes, or principles of reality, knowledge, or values, based on logical reasoning rather than empirical methods.
3. A system of thought based on or involving such inquiry: the philosophy of Hume.
4. The critical analysis of fundamental assumptions or beliefs.
5. The disciplines presented in university curriculums of science and the liberal arts, except medicine, law, and theology.
6. The discipline comprising logic, ethics, aesthetics, metaphysics, and epistemology.

7. A set of ideas or beliefs relating to a particular field or activity; an underlying theory: an original philosophy of advertising.
8. A system of values by which one lives: an unusual philosophy of life.

PHILOSOPHY COVERS A WIDE VARIETY of thought and disciplines. My work expands philosophical and critical thinking into spirituality. Philosophy, science, and spirituality are integrated to promote creative thinking for encouraging readers to think beyond their normal limits. Research and mind expansion does not need to be limited by ancient categories.

Historically, philosophy did not include law, medicine, and religion. In earlier times, religious leaders were government leaders. Powerful religious leaders did not want philosophers interfering with their beliefs and power. This was also true for medicine and law. However, it is reasonable that philosophers question religious teachings relative to science, spiritual truths, consistency, and human rights.

A responsibility for scientists and philosophers is to distinguish between facts and beliefs. The best thing we can do for anyone or any group of society is to tell the truth.

Philosophical theories arouse the mind for understanding and advancing human reality. They guide new and useful thinking processes to enhance human quality of life.

Take time to reflect upon your thinking and life. Are you satisfied how others view and treat you? Are you presenting your true inner self to others? Building a principled inner self makes a person whole. People recognize honesty in people.

Philosophy, science, and religion must include assumptions, limits, or model the entire universe and God. Everything in the universe and heaven are connected. God is holy and integrates heaven, the earth and the universe. In science, we must define assumptions in our theories explaining some truth about life or the universe for them to be believable.

Philosophy

Philosophers search for questions that need to be answered. Their questioning current knowledge and practices often precedes science exploration.

On the other hand, religions teach followers their beliefs are above questioning. Fundamental Christian leaders teach that every word and sentence in the Bible is perfect and cannot be challenged, changed, or added to. Religions often have conflicts between science advances and freedoms, and their "perfect beliefs." Political and religious leaders work to retain, and add, power over their citizens and followers.

Scientists must work to prove their predictions and theories with repeated successful experiments. Religious leaders declare their spiritual books are ultimate sources of God's truth; no proof is needed.

Must philosophy and religion be separated into ancient branches of study or can we integrate them to unite and expand human knowledge and abilities to assist God in advancing souls for His and human enrichment in heaven? Holy means God integrates all ideas and events into oneness with His unified purpose.

We should learn from historical and current teachers but make our own important life and spiritual decisions. The more we learn; the more choices we have. When thinking of loving and helping others, and praising God, we are weaving the fabric of our souls. Without souls, minds are terrible things to lose upon physical death.

Physicists and cosmologists work to discover God's design and engineering of the universe. The more we learn about the universe the more we learn about God.

Physicists have proven the universe is built upon physical certainty, probability and uncertainty. God integrates His awareness of all activities in the universe to create His spiritual certainty and wisdom. There are physical occurrences and thoughts in the universe that appear negative and non-spiritual, but when they are integrated over the entire universe create God's complete and perfect wisdom. Being spiritual also means understanding and overcoming evil.

As the universe evolves, God's spiritual awareness and wisdom increase. We learn. God learns. At the end of the universe, God will have complete knowledge and no longer needs a physical universe.

Christians believe God is Light, will always be perfect, and will do what is best for us. People who have survived severe sickness or trauma seem to believe more strongly in God. When referring to God as all Light, I capitalize "Light."

If God knew the entire future of the universe, He and humans would be predestined and could not make real decisions. God would only be a recorder of universal activities. My God is greater than that. His decisions influence the universe and our lives for His and our futures. A gracious God would not deceive humans by allowing them to make only imaginary decisions.

My philosophy reasons about life, environments, and spirituality. I attempt to ask questions that have not been answered. We must challenge current thinking to learn more about nature, methods of questioning, and logic to understand and resolve intellectual conflicts. On the other hand, religions teach followers they have answers beyond questioning. There are moral differences between advancing and controlling.

Some philosophers conclude that man has no purpose. We may have shallow mini-purposes throughout life, but at the end of lives, what integrated goals have we accomplished? Future generations must continue to seek answers. How should we serve God?

During our lives, spiritual thoughts and activities nurture our souls for integration within God's infinite resonances upon death. Records of our truthful lives, our souls, become integrated resonances within God. Humans have a purpose; otherwise, God would not have given us life. Humans have free will. God has a purpose for giving humans free will.

Traditionally, humans have learned from and been molded by previous generations. Future generations will learn more and more from the internet and guide parents in new technologies and concepts. Will the internet include moral games for children to learn about and play? Online games should not glorify killing. Teaching morality online should be part of the internet and made fun.

Will the last generation achieve heaven on earth?. Is this one of God's purposes?

Our minds are our most important gifts. We are responsible for nurturing our minds for our and others' benefits. Psychiatric drugs hide our minds from who we are and should be. Psychiatric drugs often make our minds and us less than we have been.

Psychiatric exercises purge disruptive trauma effects from the brain and mind to reveal our real selves. The mind is complex and takes a long time to heal and discover who we are. Philosophy begins with established facts and reasons to make the unknown known.

Hopefully, my theories will inspire readers to ponder life, philosophy, and science in greater depth. Possibly, some theories or ideas may be proven as science.

Everybody's crazy thinking philosophy and its questioning cannot improve creative, in-depth thinking. Studying great philosophers improves imaginations and creativity.

Adventure

—⚎—

"It is confidence in our bodies, minds and spirits that allows us to keep looking for new adventures, new directions to grow in and new lessons to learn."

— Oprah, January 12, 2011

Adventure: an enthusiastic undertaking with uncertainties and unknown risks, while searching for and expecting a positive outcome.

We should treat every opportunity as an adventure. Daily interactions and journeys should be adventures, looking for positive social and spiritual outcomes. Say or do something that will add to another's day, or possibly, life. Personally, I try to begin with something uplifting or funny. I often listen and briefly mention a healing or spiritual idea from my books. Everyone's time is valuable. I use a gentle, brief approach in trying to help. Listening is critical.

Spiritual need has its timing. Many good churches provide a spiritual adventure when the time is right. For me, communicating with Jesus and God is an adventure. I search for and need affirmation for inner peace. God gives us creative ideas and purpose along our adventures.

A Philosophy of Healing and Spirituality

We were born with an inner drive to search for physical, social, spiritual support. We search in promising directions for benefits and truth. Human truth is unique and different from other species. My cat's truth is different than mine. He enjoys playing cat and mouse.

Humans are not complete without receiving social and spiritual support. We should seek and record our spiritual adventures. After writing is refined, we should briefly share our best ideas with others, at receptive times.

So many people are overstressed needing psychiatric healing and strong belief systems to be happy, confident, and productive. I experienced sporadic, disruptive manic episodes from 1977 to 1994. One adventure has been to search for and develop an alternative, physics based cure for my bipolar disorder. My cure has been a blessing and a monumental success. I know what it's like not to be able to trust one's own thoughts and mind.

My mental reconstruction healing process has been my greatest adventure. In my manic episode of 1993, I became aware of localized energy release sensations in my neck, throat, and brainstem during neck exercises. Unusual sensations have become more exciting. I did not initially know what to expect but knew sensations were important toward healing my disorder.

I sensed inner sensations as tiny localized energy releases from overstressed, traumatized neural network segments. I feared my mental adventure might lead to insanity. However, I felt I must try something different to cure my disruptive bipolar episodes. It was degrading and scary being out of control.

After a few weeks I decided I could not stop energy release sensations so I continued to exercise my neck to purge all repressed energy from my neck, throat, and brainstem. I thought trauma energy could be purged in a few months and was unsure whether results would be positive.

After a few months of exercises, sensations became increasingly pleasant. At that time, I felt energy releases must be for my benefit! I worried less about negative effects and insanity. Later on, I developed conflicting, resistant neck exercises that increased releases.

I have released repressed trauma energy for twenty years. The brain is complex. Sensations have changed significantly over the years. Generally, individual sensation energy has become less over time. Quantities have become greater. Pleasant sensations inspired continuing exercises. Over time exercises and sensations have become routine. I never dreamed my adventure would last over twenty years. The brain and mind contain so many inner stresses and conflicts.

Exercising muscles closest to the brain has the greatest effect in healing the brain. Muscles are connected to nerves and nerves are connected to neural networks.

9. Conflicting exercises stimulate overstressed neural networks to emotional limits. At limits, traumatized neural networks release repressed energy, to become more normal, and re-synchronize with normal brain activities. My healing adventure has achieved a goal of preventing manic episodes for twenty years – my cure.

To greater or lesser degrees, everyone needs to purge disruptive, repressed trauma effects from the brain for mental stability and creative thinking. Computers and minds process better and faster with less energy. Less energy is easier to control.

Everybody's crazy not planning adventures for accomplishing long-term goals. We must take risks to achieve important long-term successes.

Evaluations

SCOPE OF EVALUATIONS

HUMANS EVALUATE THEMSELVES, THEIR BABIES, children, spouses, others, environments, engineered devices (such as cars,) and religions. We should evaluate God's influence in our lives. What are we doing for God to influence our lives?

Subconsciously, environments are continually evaluated and compared to hereditary and earlier developed threat and survival limits. Today, we are often aware of threats when driving.

Are our evaluations shallow, narrow, detailed, or holistic? Are they truthful and complete? Evaluations should consider important parameters. We often hear: "Why did I stay in an abusive relationship so long?" Many of us have continued hoping abusive relationships would get better without making adjustments. We should not expect different results if we continue to accept degrading behaviors.

Aggressive individuals have experienced poor parenting and have learned that the weak deserve to be abused. Aggressive people have little care or concern for others' wellbeing.

Unless two beautiful giving people marry, the abusive spouse will scheme to gain power and control over the loving spouse. Many women tend to assert more control after marriage.

Husbands or wives may be good to all others but abusive to their spouses. Aggressive spouses work for psychological advantage over milder spouses to "prove" their superiority. Anyone acting superior to anyone is morally inferior.

After degrading a wonderful spouse into depression, the uncaring aggressive spouse then thinks he/she is too good for her/him. Unless there is change or counseling, the abused spouse accepts a slow murder. He or she may be too embarrassed to admit that he or she made a poor marriage decision and is being abused by an immoral spouse. Controllers lie and deceive.

When young, we were programmed, or brainwashed, by parents, teachers, spiritual leaders, and later by the military. Repressed memories have impact on how we act, react, evaluate, and live. As adults we me must recognize and cherish the good we have received and convert non-spiritual teachings into spiritual thoughts and behaviors.

Some are lucky. Their parents taught them to think and evaluate options when they were young. We must learn to think for ourselves. Reacting to conflicting situations and controlling emotions is difficult. We must evaluate to trust others, or experiment to discover the truth.

Social

Psychology and psychiatry help us become less biased, less selfish, and more reasonable in evaluating ourselves and others. We must prepare for positive and negative interactions. Social evaluations should have detailed and also holistic criteria. Evaluate current and long range goals and goals of those we interact with for mutual achievement.

Some men and women make marriage evaluations mostly on appearance. Others make evaluations on money or stardom. Most young folks do not commit to mutual confidence building and the importance of relaxing when together as being of vital importance. It can be stressful and even deadly if one spouse always needs to act superior to the other spouse. Both spouses' health and happiness degrade.

Everyone should evaluate themselves before evaluating others before entering into relationships. They should first determine if they can meet realistic expectations of potential spouses or friends. Potential spouses should discuss each other's core values and principles. Social relationships should benefit everyone involved.

We must establish our inner values and principles before making long term commitments. An important principle for building relationships is showing others they are important enough to be listened to.

We should give priority to pleasing those close to us in good and in difficult times. Evaluate relationships when there are emotional or significant occurrences. If dedication is slipping, plan calm mutual discussions and, if needed, have counseling to evaluate options. Reduce emotional importance of relationships when interactions no longer meet both person's needs and goals, and cannot be improved. If physical or mental abuse continues, get counseling or leave when possible. Continued abuse is slow murder.

If mental and physical abuse increases, discuss reasons. Negative words and activities degrade and control. Calmly discuss interactions and activities not helpful to the relationship. Praise pleasing interactions as they occur. A well-adjusted person might say: "Let's take time and consider positive and negative things to improve our relationship. What are we giving to one another?"

We must evaluate if difficulties can be resolved. Make simple tests and evaluations to determine value of relationships. If there is little value in a relationship, lessen emotional involvement. Value your life more. We cannot continue giving to a taker. It is dangerous to our health and causes our slow murder.

CAREER

Most people want to earn their security, importance, and achievements. Some believe being dependent on others or the government is acceptable, and develop an attitude of entitlement. Some spouses who do not work develop attitudes of entitlement and control working spouses. They have time to focus on controlling their working spouses.

Rewards in the work place are often evaluated unfairly. Some workers degrade and intimidate. Others take credit for co-worker successes. Some work hard to please the boss, help others, and promote workplace ethics. Creativeness, hard work, helpfulness, and honesty are good traits for success at work. We should positively evaluate co-workers who are truthful, dependable, and help others.

Humor is helpful in social environments and in getting along at work. A pleasant atmosphere increases work efficiency.

Spiritual

Christian songs espouse the belief that God is Holy and interacts with humans through prayer in a complete way. We may be able to improve the way we pray to become more receptive to God's guidance. Through God, our prayers become holistic and affect the entire universe to some very small extent. God only reflects spiritual information to us that we are able to understand, with the mental and spiritual abilities we have.

We must lower our mental energy to receive God's constantly present spiritual information we are able to understand. Sometimes, when thinking of possible activities, we receive affirmative or negative feelings from God to guide our thoughts.

We can only interpret God's perfect truths we receive, with fragile, imprecise human made words. We should evaluate our beliefs, environments, and ourselves frequently for continuing a full, spiritual life. We receive spiritual guidance, only when we have open spiritual free wills. Usually, God's guidance for us is of a general nature, holistic, or Holy. God does not tell us why He chooses us to bear His burdens, but if we follow His guidance we receive His blessings.

Evaluations

In attempting to finish my first healing book, I received an unexpected, astounding message from God: "Don't leave God out!" This message was so impressive, that I immediately evaluated it as true. I have written spiritually for twenty years guided by that strong spiritual message and its continuing harmonics. God asks us to do tasks but gives us freedom in doing them.

Everybody's crazy for not evaluating our and others social and spiritual goals and accomplishments. Evaluate successes and failures to adjust goals for improving social and spiritual successes.

Discrete and Holistic

—⟵m⟶—

DISCRETE MEANS FOCUSING ON SOMETHING that is detailed or distinct - for example, discrete is focusing on hitting a tennis ball. In this case, holistic means analyzing a tennis player's entire approach to the game.

Holistic means physical and spiritual completeness. God and His Reactions are always complete or holy. We do not pray to part of God. Relaxing and lowering mental energy allows the right-brain to become dominant to construct long range, holistic awareness and thoughts. Practicing switching between left- and right-brain dominance assists mental and spiritual skills. We must maintain holistic right-brain dominance for improving imagination and creative thinking.

Dancing appears, and is, awkward when the detailed left-brain is dominant. The left-brain focuses on individual physical details and movements. When relaxed with holistic right-brain dominance, the entire body becomes coordinated and flows smoothly as a whole. The rhythmic right-brain holistically coordinates integrated dance movements.

Discrete thinking may be thought of as a member of a choir singing solo. This singer may make wonderful musical vibrations in the air, for us to hear and enjoy. If her voice is on key with rhythm, she may inspire love, faith, or other great things. We may lose ourselves in her world.

Holistic may be thought of as a 500-member choir singing in perfect harmony. Some sing tenor, some sing base, and others sing in different parts. Individuals sing differently but with no individual standout. All voices are equally important and fill the air with beautifully integrated, holistic air vibrations. Each discrete voice constructs an important part of the enriched integrated vibrations in the air we enjoy. Singing can bring everyone together with a united spirit.

The holistic right-brain integrates thoughts similar to 500 integrated voices filling the air. When the brain is relaxed, synchronized firings of billions of neurons, throughout the brain, integrate to construct a symphony for creating a single conscious thought and purpose.

Normally, the right-brain is more relaxed than the left-brain. It analyzes more distant views and environments for completeness and future response. The left-brain reacts more to up-close threats and fast responses.

When manic, the right-brain becomes persistently dominant. Manic-depressives tend to concentrate on the "big picture" and think more spiritual. They lose detailed left-brain reasoning and generalize that even different things have equal importance. In higher levels of mania, right-brain thinking may blend into irrational dream characteristics and insanity with loss of reality.

The left-brain is dominant during normal mental energy levels. The right-brain dominates during very low and very high mental energies, or moods, with increased ability for spiritual awareness.

Psychiatrists prescribe lithium to bipolar patients to prevent moods from becoming too high or low. The left-brain is dominant during normal moods and everyday detailed thinking and control. However, medications may distort brain processes to the point of feeling, thinking, and acting like a zombie. Thinking is slowed and may become irrational. The body becomes awkward.

We need detailed left-brained thinking most of the time to work our jobs, care for our families, and for sanity. During manic episodes, the afflicted may lose everyday detailed reasoning skills but become more spiritual with holistic thinking. Practicing switching from right-brain to left-brain dominance recovers left-brain reasoning skills, reduces mania, and increases mind control. We can influence left- or right-brain dominance. We must decide if we want to think about physical details and relationships or think holistically and spiritually about the Big Picture. We can help manic-depressives come back down to earth and be more reasonable by having them concentrate of various details while exaggerating frowning. Also, we may exaggerate broadening of the face to ensure right brain dominance and improve relaxation.

Consider electromagnetic, EMR, spikes from firings of one neuron. It fires with its frequency and unique EMR wave contour. Its activation frequency and wave characteristics relate to one choir member's voice.

Synchronized firing of billions of neurons produce integrated EMR resonances forming higher dimensional mental holograms for developing conscious images and ideas. The right-brain is affected by and controls greater numbers of synchronized neuron firings. It is more difficult to synchronize and control greater numbers of neurons firing. It is easier for the dominant right-brain to go out of control.

Mental holograms are higher dimensional subconscious images and scenarios created by integration of neuron firings and other brain activities. They are building blocks of cognition. At times, they become conscious as in dreams.

Let's relate mental holograms to commercial holograms. The firings of one neuron produce a weak hologram throughout the entire brain. Firings of all synchronized neurons construct an integrated bright, detailed higher dimensional hologram. Bright integrated holograms are the brain's tools for constructing vision, consciousness, and imagination.

When hologram resonances are strong enough and last long enough, they produce consciousness. There are millions, maybe billions, of resonances in the brain at any one time. As an example, one EMR resonance is promoted by each cone within the eyes, and so on.

Let's consider the eyes' and brain's integrations for tracking fast moving vision. If individual cone or rod size vision sensitivity varies from cone to cone or rod to rod so fast, we sense a blurred continuous flowing vision. Spokes on a fast turning wheel appear as quickly moving and slightly varying circles. Image variations may be caused by slight wheel vibrations and even brain structure variations. Images vary too fast for the eyes and brain to construct individual images of spokes. Images are integrated as rather continuous circles. A main function of the brain is to integrate images, sensations, and memories. Subconscious sub-thoughts are integrated to construct thoughts and emotions.

When we see a ball, we do not see individual atoms on the surface of that ball. Our eyes have integrated atom images to form the ball image we recognize.

The brain is electrical and processes very fast. EMR from synchronized neuron activations construct very fast subconscious resonances and processes. Harmonic resonances integrate to create slower varying "standing" waves, which if lasting long enough and change slow enough, construct consciousness.

Conscious resonances have distinct energy levels. Slow, low energy resonances communicate more easily with the soul for spiritual communication. Depression slows EMR resonances, improving spiritual sensitivities.

EMR from neuron activations are shared with other neurons at the speed of light. Neuro-chemicals passed along axons and dendrites between neurons are much slower but fundamental for synchronizing neuron activations and creating subconscious and conscious resonances.

Mental holograms exist within or as higher dimensions. If a thin near two-dimensional photographic film can store three-dimensional holographic images, spatially complex three-dimensional arrays of thin neural membranes can store higher-dimensional information and images. Higher dimensional mental holograms give the mind its spiritual dimension.

Additional visual dimensions may represent emotions and truthfulness, which are not easily visualized. An entire mental hologram may have levels of red tinting if the mental hologram includes negative emotions. A gold tinted hologram may express great truths, and so on for various levels of emotions and truths. Holistic emotional colors may be the most important information passed on to the soul.

Let's continue holistic thought integration. We have a telephone number with seven discrete numbers – 266-7883. Initially we have to remember seven numbers. We can use the telephone keypad to construct the word, "compute." We now have only one concept to remember. We can use our spelling skills and the telephone keypad as our integration tool to recall the number.

Another integration tool is using acronyms. IBM is all we need to know to find and address the company, International Business Machines. We have integrated three longer words into a short acronym. After some advertising they both mean the same to potential customers. The acronym is easier to remember, speak, and makes the company's advertising more efficient.

Holusions are excellent tools for left- and right-brain dominance switching exercises. Holusions are detailed two-dimensional art works the mind can integrate into three-dimensional images if focusing long distance "through" the two dimensional detailed images. The right brain becomes dominant as the three-dimensional image appears. See the "Psychiatric Exercises" essay to learn more about Holusions.

We are vaguely aware of the assumptions and decisions our subconscious processes make to construct our conscious processes and thoughts allowing us some control over our lives. Working to understand, normally subconscious, or inner mental processes during mania became a process to improve mind control levels of sanity.

Babies learn the mechanics of walking using the detailed left-brain. Adult walking is a repetitive activity no longer needing conscious thought for individual steps. The right-brain controls semiconscious repetitive walking and long distance vision. The left brain becomes dominant for detailed thoughts needed to change stride or direction.

Coordinating numerous nerves and leg muscles is necessary for raising a leg. This process has become subconscious and so routine that we have developed wordless, holistic thoughts to lift and control that leg. We do not need to worry about complex details of each nerve and muscle.

Words are only discrete symbols for building and expressing ideas. Reading engages the detailed left brain for interpreting words. When reading, eyes and subconscious minds convert words and sentences into images of people, environments, actions, and so on. Converting abstract words to mental images and actions is an imaginary task of the subconscious mind. Reading increases imagination. However, images and actions readers envision are different from the writer's thoughts and visions while writing. Words are never perfect. People's minds, actions, visions, abilities, and imaginations are different.

Well chosen words and well constructed sentences can activate the right brain to imagine flowing and holistic images and thoughts. Reading can inspire wonderful imaginations to build exciting lives.

Everybody's crazy for not evaluating and understanding differences between left- and right-brain thinking. Relaxing into right-brain holistic thinking allows synchronized whole body dancing and big picture thinking. The same words stimulate different imaginations in individual readers. Words have a constant, unchanging spiritual quality.

Science Section

Bumblebee and ESP!

SCIENTISTS HAVE DISCOVERED THE LANGUAGE bumblebees use to communicate with one another. With orientations between short flights, bumblebees communicate directions to nectar, and so on. I communicate with bumblebees.

Let's begin with a simple brain wave communication experiment with bumblebees. Watch a bumblebee flying in place and occasionally flitting back and forth claiming his territory. This happens often in the spring around my farmhouse and barn. I observed one bumblebee's actions until I could predict his behavior.

I slowly moved within eight feet of the bumblebee and stayed still with a constant facial expression. He ignored me. While slowly increasing emotional energy and thoughts, I mentally threatened to harm this bee. He turned his stinger toward me and backed up uncomfortably close to my face. His mode was to attack perceived threats.

Emotional electromagnetic frequencies in my brain had become faster and stronger. The bumblebee sensed my threat and displayed a counter threatening posture. When the bumblebee was within six inches of my face, chill bumps engulfed my body. I kept the same facial expression but quickly reduced aggressive thoughts. Without my moving, the bee then went about his bumblebee business. I do not recommend this bumblebee experiment. One might get stung!

Bees threaten humans with movement and body language. Humans threaten humans with body language and words. Body language during verbal communication is extremely important. It can negate positive words.

Sometimes it is good to speak and sometimes body language says it all. A loving hug, slow dance, and even watching a ballet can be more meaningful than a thousand words.

This experiment proved that bees can sense high-energy, emotional brain waves. Thoughts and emotions are not entirely our own. Humans communicate with words, body language, and also emotional brain waves.

When my cat wants to go out, his language is rubbing at my feet and walking toward the door. I understand. I know he is happy when he purrs and rubs against me. When I talk to him he thinks I "purr" erratically.

As an example of ESP or human spiritual wave communication, my son was in a car accident 25 miles from my home. I immediately sensed he was in trouble as I stepped out of my front door. He called me so quickly, before I could call him, to let me know he had had a car accident. He was not injured. His emotional long distance communication was transmitted through brain waves, ESP in spiritual communications. I was as certain he had had some kind of trauma as if I had seen it.

Many of us pray believing we share thoughts with God through ESP or higher spiritual dimensions. Spiritual dimensions, beyond human understanding, allow God to be everywhere and "hear" our prayers from wherever we are. God senses and understands our brain waves. It is important to "listen" for God. He is everywhere in this big universe, which is 28 billion light years in diameter. God is "big or infinite" but "hears," and pays attention to, human prayers.

Everybody's crazy not believing in ESP, and electromagnetic and spiritual brain waves. God interprets our prayers into his everlasting perfect spiritual wave awareness.

The Heisenberg Uncertainty Principle

―∞―

THIS SCIENCE ESSAY IS PRESENTED to support my imaginative, philosophical "Nothing before Time" model. It also supports my model of Creation and spiritual concepts such as God's omnipresence and omniscience. Philosophers construct models and theories to give them something to reason about and to see where they might lead.

I model the moment before the Big Bang as an integrated primordial certainty. Existence was completely organized. Entropy was zero. It was certain the universe was going to exist. Philosophy extends beyond science give direction to research.

The Heisenberg Uncertainty Principle has proven there will always be uncertainty in measurements of very small atoms and subatomic matter. Here are the science accepted Heisenberg Uncertainty Principle equations:

1) $\Delta E \Delta t \geq h/(2\pi)$

2) $\Delta p \Delta x \geq h/(2\pi)$

These two equations limit the precision scientists will ever be able to measure atom and elementary particle properties. In equation 1) the change in energy of an elementary particle when multiplied by the time for that change to occur must be equal to $h/(2\pi)$ or some exact multiple of that value. The above product cannot be less than $h/(2\pi)$. Very small elementary particle characteristics are very different from everyday human observations.

From equation 2) the change in momentum of an elementary particle multiplied by the distance for that momentum change to take place must be equal to $h/(2\pi)$ or be some exact multiple of that small value.

Let's define $h/(2\pi)$: h is Planks Constant, 6.626076×10^{-34} joules-seconds. When divided by (2π), it is the exact lowest quantum value of orbital angular momentum of any elementary particle. Elementary particles can also have exact multiples of this orbital angular momentum. $nh/(2\pi)$ are fundamental physics constants and part of God's deep structure language.

We must make assumptions in everything we do. In science research, we make assumptions and work to prove or disprove our hypotheses. Before time, I assumed primordial quantum existence vibrated between the point of the Big Bang and an infinite evenly distributed primordial existence. This is the simplest quantum model of "Nothing before Time" I could develop that could have characteristics and potential to create God and the universe. Space as we know it did not exist.

I have assumed primordial quantum energy, ΔE, between primordial iterations, Δt, when multiplied together was always <u>less</u> than $h/(2\pi)$. In this model, I hypothesized that <u>reverse</u> Heisenberg Uncertainty equations held true in primordial existence. It was uncertain if "nothing" existed before time and the Big Bang.

The Reverse Heisenberg Uncertainty Principle equations were modeled as less than, rather than greater than $h/(2\pi,)$ for modeling primordial existence. There is some scientific basis for this reversal since cosmologists have concluded that unified field forces, including gravity, were repulsive at the moment of the Big Bang singularity.

This must be true for the universe to explode outward with such force. An extremely compact explosion, from repulsion forces, occurred as energy, space, time, and God were created. Confined quantum energy was created at discrete locations in space as elementary particles and then atoms in a fraction of a second after the beginning of the Big Bang. Energy and time were created from "Nothing." Space and time were created to allow physical changes and an expanding universe. Primordial energy and time, $\Delta E \times \Delta t$, became greater than $h/(2\pi)$ and it was *certain* that a new universe was going to be created.

Einstein proved mass and energy are interchangeable, $E = mc^2$. When primordial vibrations became very fast, they essentially <u>had</u> the "same" energy within uncertainties and were perfectly reflected or multiplied at an explosive rate creating the Big Bang. Primordial dimensions were more closely related to spiritual dimensions than physical dimensions. God was created as the "mind" within unified field force activities. Then He designed and engineered the physical universe.

The concept of an additional iteration of primordial energy making no difference is similar to the definition of infinity. We can add to or multiply infinity and we still get infinity. From this reasoning, "Nothing before Time" had infinite energy, and, therefore, in most respects we can consider God and the universe to have infinite energy.

My model of God is somewhat similar to EMR activities integrating within the brain to develop conscious ideas. The mind is constructed by integrated electromagnetic and spiritual waves. The mind is greater than its brain activities.

Time and energy integrated together was too great and violated the Reverse Heisenberg Uncertainty Principle forcing *nothing* to explode into spiritual wave energy as all of existence, God. As God began creation of the universe, time was created allowing physical changes and measurements of physical differences and changes. Before time, primordial changes affected all of existence equally.

For changes to occur in the universe there must be potentials for uncertainties, otherwise everything would stay the same. God created an expanding physical universe with increasing, diverse uncertainties allowing complex differences and changes within the universe and increasing spiritual awareness to record those changes. Humans have abilities to think of or imagine diverse thoughts about the universe and its origin, Nothing before Time.

In 10^{-35} seconds after the beginning of the Big Bang, God, the Unified Field Force, created all 10^{82} hydrogen atoms of an expanding universe. At this time, the Unified Field Force separated into gravity, electromagnetic, strong and weak-nuclear, and electroweak Higgs field forces and God's constant spiritual dimensions. God's spiritual wave dimensions retained integration characteristics of "Nothing before Time." Spiritual wisdom is constant throughout a constant spiritual space.

Spiritual integration dimensions must exist if God is omniscient and omnipresent. His awareness of all information throughout the universe must be shared and integrated within each point in the universe very rapidly for God to be up to date. Christians believe in God's omnipresent and omniscient abilities.

Interaction of spiritual and physical dimensions is not modeled by known physics equations. However, Light, electromagnetic radiation, is certainly an intermediate medium between spiritual and physical dimensions. God is much more than light. In spiritual dimensions, which are independent of space, God is constantly aware of the entire universe, which is 28 billion light years in diameter. Spiritual awareness of a great big universe requires communication speeds much, much faster than the speed of light.

Primordial waves exceeded primordial laws, including the Reverse Heisenberg Uncertainty Principle, causing a mathematical singularity and creating spiritual existence, God. Some change had to occur in "Nothing before Time" for God, the first Awareness, and spiritual space - heaven, to be created. God initially created 10^{82} hydrogen atoms (the simplest mass structure – with potentials,) and time and physical space, in 10^{-35} seconds after His existence. Before this time only spiritual space existed. Residual 10^{82} primordial reflections of primordial existence created God and His potential to integrate all atoms through field forces and space.

God was and is the symmetric reflection of 'Nothing before Time.' He then created the universe as an asymmetric and symmetric physical system of space, time, and matter. Gravity is the residual effect of God emotionally desiring to return the universe and Himself back to the original perfect order at the moment of Creation.

Let's develop a model of the frequency of the primordial vibration at the end of primordial existence just before Creation. The energy of the universe can be roughly calculated as the rest masses of all hydrogen atoms in the universe:

$$E = n \times MC^2$$

E = energy of the universe
n = number of hydrogen atoms in the universe - 1E+82
M = mass of a hydrogen atom - 1.7E-27 kg
C = the speed of light - 3E+8 m/sec

E = 1E+82 x 1.7E-27 x 3E+8 x 3E+8 = 1.5E+72 kg-m^2/s^2
   = 1.5E+72 kg-m^2/s^2 or 1.5E+72 joules

From the Heisenberg Uncertainty equation:

$$\Delta E \Delta T = h / (2\pi)$$

A Philosophy of Healing and Spirituality

The final primordial frequency that promoted all the physical energy of the universe is estimated as:

$\Delta T = h / (2\pi \Delta E)$

$= 6.626076E\text{-}34 / (2 \times 3.14 \times 1.5E72) = .7E\text{-}106$ (seconds/vibration)

In this model of "Nothing before Time," very fast primordial vibrations were fundamental in creating God and the universe approximately 13.75 billion years ago. I have used known equations and my best assumptions to develop a philosophical model of "Nothing before Time." All accepted physics and cosmology models have assumptions.

From relativity, the beginning very dense universe had, and black holes have, very different space and time characteristics. Light cannot escape black holes. God, Light, could not escape the beginning universe. God, Light does not escape but expands the universe.

After near death and spiritual experiences, it was important to think of and model "Nothing before Time". This creative model supports later spiritual models. All discoveries begin with dreams and assumptions.

Everybody's crazy if not believing there was uncertainty as to whether the universe was to exist. Assuming the Heisenberg Uncertainty principle existed before Creation of the universe allows creative models of God and His spiritual properties. I hope others will improve my models.

Neuroscience

—⚏—

NEUROSCIENTISTS STUDY NEURON FIRING POTENTIALS, frequencies, locations, spike shapes, neurotransmitters, neural networks, and their connectivity to understand and improve brain and thinking processes. They study global effects of electricity within the brain by analyzing *charge distributions on the scalp with electroencephalograms*. I include neuroscience with only enough details to stimulate feelings of subconscious and conscious healing. It takes the mind to understand and heal the brain and mind.

My neuroscience source is based upon 36 CD lectures, *Understanding the Brain*, by Professor Jeanette Norden, of Vanderbilt University School of Medicine, and The Teaching Company, 2007, and my physics background.

Neuron chemical activations accelerate electrons and, to a lesser extent, positive nuclei. Accelerated electrons, from one neuron activation, create electromagnetic radiation that adds energy to its membrane first and then other neuron membranes as it traverses throughout the brain. Synchronized neutron activations create integrated electromagnetic resonances throughout the brain or components of the brain. One neuron can stimulate other neurons to resonate with synchronized frequencies. Electromagnetic radiation, EMR, is integral in creating consciousness and cognition.

There is uncertainty in atom behaviors. Their activities are governed by probability laws. Similarly, there are probabilities and uncertainties in the timing of individual neuron activations. Integrated EMR, from synchronized neurons, can create "certain" conscious ideas. "I am eating an apple."

Subconscious processes are multi-level reflections of conscious thinking that make us who we are. Subconscious processes need conscious feedback for them to understand and heal themselves. Mental dysfunctions occur when the conscious mind denies reality and does not provide truthful feedback to subconscious processes. Psychiatrists and mental reconstruction provide feedback for promoting and understanding mental healing for reducing inner stresses.

Neurons consist of a cell body, one axon, and up to 7,000 dendrites. Axons send chemicals through synapses to dendrites of other neurons. Dendrites receive chemical signals mostly from axons of other neurons. Axons and dendrites are physically and chemically connected by synapses.

Firing pre-synaptic neurons affect post-synaptic neurons by transferring neurotransmitters through their axons to dendrites of other neurons. Neurotransmitters are chemicals that are transferred between neurons to influence one another. Neurotransmitters promote or suppress activations of post–synaptic neurons. Nuclei are groups of neurons forming networks for specific purposes. Neuron connections and communications are more complex than those of the internet.

Neuron and synapse activations and responses are affected by neurotransmitter concentrations. Plasticity is the property of neurons and synapses to change their internal parameters or functions over activation histories. Neural networks, neurons, and neural membranes must increase structure to store a lifetime of memories.

The brainstem is located at the top of the spinal cord, receives signals from nerves throughout the body, and transfers signals to various components within the brain. The brainstem is composed of several groupings of brain cells. The reticular formation extends along the length of the brainstem and is most active while sleeping. The aminergic cluster near the top of the brainstem is concentrated in the dorsal raphe nucleus and is most active during waking. These two areas of the brainstem compete to suppress each other's activity for sleeping or waking dominance.

The limbic system surrounds the brainstem. It is an older part of the brain and includes the brain's fast response system. If stimuli become too strong and fast, neural networks in the brainstem activate the hippocampus and the brain's fast response system. The limbic system produces our fast, emotional fight or flight responses. During normal activities, the limbic system passes information to the higher reasoning cerebral hemispheres.

The cerebral hemispheres surround the limbic system. The cerebrum is the newest developed part of the brain and processes higher reasoning functions.

Dark grayish matter is found a small distance below the surface of the cerebrum and is composed of mostly neuron cell bodies. It is associated with cognitive processing.

White matter is made up of millions of glial support cells and nerve fibers, or axons, below the cortex. It transmits signals between cerebral regions, to and from lower areas of the brain, modulates neuron action potentials, affects how the brain learns, and may affect learning dysfunctions.

At times, I try to feel which areas of my brain are active with different thoughts and emotions. I have worked to increase "brain" awareness, with limited success.

Nearly 24,000 genes comprise the blueprint of 100 trillion cells in our bodies. There are approximately 85 billion neurons and 600 trillion connections or synapses in the human brain. That's a lot to think with and about.

The brain is complex and takes a long time to heal. It is amazing that activities, within this complex brain structure, allow us to focus on one idea or see one object!

We can improve our offspring's genes by experiencing emotional limits at times and overcoming bold physical and mental challenges.

Introspective study, confident knowledge, and mental reconstruction make changes to, and develop, "confident, robust" genes for the next generation. It is important to relax after stressful events to give the brain and mind time to recover and integrate activities into memory and brain structure. The brain, like muscles, needs to relax to recover and grow abilities.

If nerve resonances last long enough and are strong enough, they activate neuron resonances to develop consciousness. A detailed model of consciousness is presented in my "Mind" essay.

Neurons connected with sight stimuli are thought to be the fastest firing neurons. Stimulated neurons normally activate or spike 20 to 30 times per second. Under the most stimulated conditions, neurons do not spike faster than 100 times per second. A typical neuron spike lasts about one thousandth of a second. Negative impulse potentials from pre-synaptic neurons slow spike rates of post-synaptic neurons.

Neurons fully discharge rapidly and recharge relatively slowly. It must be true that after firing, overstressed traumatized neurons again overcharge and remain overstressed and rigid. Recall therapy and mental reconstruction release neural energy at limits from traumatized networks to return them to more normal energy levels.

Neurotransmitter sharing between neurons is not nearly fast enough to produce or control an expected death flash of emotional memories, as presented in "The Flash" essay. These exceedingly fast experiences may provide insight between physical, mental, and spiritual time frames. Electromagnetic radiation, EMR, traveling at the speed of light, constructs memories in the brain and wisdom within the soul. The brain is physical. The mind is spiritual and not limited to physical restraints.

We can think of typing one moment and a childhood experience years ago in the next moment. Mental reality is beyond physical reality, and spiritual reality is beyond mental reality.

There are residual effects from neuron firings with their EMR expanding outward at the speed of light. Neuron activations have delayed influences along axons through synapses to numerous connected dendrites for influencing other neurons. Coordination of neural activations is fundamental to learning, memory, and other mental functions.

Each neuron has unique activation characteristics and spike shapes. EMR spike profiles from each neuron are different. Snowflakes are different.

A firing neuron affects its own membrane greater than other cell membranes. EMR from neuron firings dissipate and have less effect on more distant neuron membranes. EMR spikes do not completely overlap creating continuous EMR resonances within the brain. Repeated EMR transmissions, reflections, and absorptions culture mental hologram details on brain cell membranes throughout the brain. Eventually, EMR splits into "Strings" affecting individual atoms and molecules. While alive, EMR continually filters throughout the brain.

Multiple diffracted and reflected EMR in the brain have less energy but deposit more refined details on neuron membranes. Highly reflected EMR adds definition by overlaying refined harmonics on earlier neuron reference EMR imprints. Depending upon spike profiles, brain cell membranes may receive EMR from remote brain cell activations.

Neural networks produce a relatively slow transmission of chemicals throughout the brain, but transmit EMR at the speed of light. Signals from sense nerves must vary slow enough, and last long enough, for the brain to produce awareness and consciousness for engaging environments. We sense environments with our eyes, ears, taste, touch, and smell to develop a limited model of human reality.

Erratic high-energy, traumatized neuron activations disrupt normal synchronized charge contours on brain surfaces. Consciousness is created by symphonies of electromagnetic resonances on brain cell membranes, brain components, and on surfaces of the brain.

The brain's surface charge contours vary with perception and analytical activities. Each glance produces a symphony of changing neuron activations for a flowing human awareness. Brain surfaces are not perfect conductors of electricity. They resist electron flow to some extent allowing varying charge distributions on brain surfaces.

Dreams, we sometimes become aware of, are mental hologram scenarios constructed by resonating EMR within the brain. Dreams appear in three physical dimensions and include emotional and spiritual dimensions, such as love, caring, certainty, uncertainty, and so on.

At times I have worked to recall pleasant and spiritual dreams. Low energy creative ideas are as easy to evaporate from memory as are dreams. After reading the article below I have worked to recall dreams, sensed as exciting and useful.

"During REM, the hippocampus takes five to seven days to transfer select memories to long-term storage in the neo-cortex, according to a study led by Mark Blagrove, director of the Sleep Lab at Swansea University. 'Dream lag' is associated with more positive emotions about previous events—which scientists chalk up to the way we reprocess memories in our dreams. This means if we spot our former spouse today, next week's dream will put him in a softer, kinder light." This information was from an article in:

www.oprah.com/health/Facts-About-Dreams-Dream-Facts.

Our faces are contoured by persistent electromagnetic activities and thoughts within our brains. Continued frowning keeps the brain tense. Focusing on emotional negative thoughts causes the brain, forehead, and face to become narrow. We become narrow minded.

Human awareness consists of millions of electromagnetic frequencies within the brain. The brain has a capacity similar to the Internet. With one search phrase, the internet can find millions of matches in seconds. The brain makes similar numbers of subconscious activities

Neuroscience

in seconds. Brains and the internet used together wisely are powerful tools and may advance human knowledge exponentially.

There is a relationship between nerves and neurons. Each physical bruise and scar on the body causes a physical bruise and scar in a related area of the brain. Bruises heal quicker in the flesh than in the brain. Psychological and reasoning failures affect the brain more globally and heal more slowly. Emotional scars can be healed by mental reconstruction and recall therapy.

When trauma occurs, the brain does not have time to react normally. The reactive limbic system does not transmit emotional trauma data to the cerebrum. Cerebral processing shuts down creating a trauma moment of insanity. A trauma moment of insanity is when the brain cannot develop a response to a fast, overpowering trauma. Sense nerve activations overpower normal brain functions creating high energy trauma scars in the back of the upper neck, the throat, brainstem, and to a lesser extent in the upper brain. My "Psychiatric Exercises" and "Mental Reconstruction" essays support this conclusion.

Our subconscious response system reacts quickly but without detailed analysis. Thinking is mostly fight of flight. Face, neck, throat, and jaw muscles tense preparing the body to react. An arm jerks the steering wheel to the left. We are saved from an "expected death" near car accident.

Reducing energy usually helps the limbic system promote emotional memories to left brain resonances for detailed analyses. Without upper brain analyses, trauma memories sporadically activate, disrupting normal brain activities and causing inner tensions and uncertainties.

Why is the mental reconstruction process so long? When there is a rupture in emotional processing limits, the original limits cannot be mended and must be purged. A new, wider, and stronger emotional limit system must be constructed to process reactions to trauma with more reasonable, creative responses. Creative thinking expands with wider, more logical limits. After purging trauma scars, newly constructed and genetic mental limits allow more in depth, less emotional reasoning.

When overstressed neural networks exceed emotional limits long enough, loss of mental control and manic depression ensues. Fast, high-energy thinking, with its uncertainties, develops a chemical imbalance within the brain. Brain or mental restructuring and psychiatric or pharmaceutical therapy may lead to cures for bipolar and other mental disorders.

Brain activity consists of millions of EMR resonances vying for energy, dominance, and consciousness. Many normal energy resonances are integrated and promoted to form longer lasting conscious resonances. Longer resonances are reflected by brain and brain component surfaces. Mental hologram time stamps and precise energy levels and frequencies organize our memories. We remember what happened a minute ago and what happened last year.

The sharpest neuron EMR spike segments travel to more distant neurons before being absorbed. Two radios, at different distances from the radio station, tuned to the same station will receive the same music. Each neuron is a mental radio station and mental radio.

I am unaware of researchers studying neuron and glia membrane fabric to understand hologram development as foundations of subconscious processes and thinking. Brain cell membrane fabric has capabilities beyond photo film for humans to remember and recall so much data. Proof that the mind processes holograms is that we experience dream scenarios.

A major effort in mental reconstruction is to reduce the energy of traumatized neural networks to make the brain more efficient. Computers using less energy, with more refined electricity, are faster and more efficient. The brain has similar characteristics. High energy resonances construct less refined details for storing emotional memories on neural membranes.

This work is a new and different way of modeling and healing the brain and mind. Reducing inner tensions improves thinking, creativity, and quality of life.

Action potential and memory structures include the limbic, pre-frontal, hippocampus and other areas of the brain. The prefrontal cortex is important in learning, and in unlearning memories such as in "Desensitizing Therapy" to reduce effects of ingrained combat trauma memories.

Traumatic and emotional experiences construct mental limits for ease in controlling normal thinking. Reasonable decisions and behaviors depend upon an individual's history of social and physical successes and failures. Emotions also activate physiological responses. The pre-frontal cortex processes emotions and is active in moral decisions. Morals are products of heredity, learning, reason, and survival.

In language, meaning is mapped to sound. Language and music are more easily learned early in life. Adults become accustomed to meaning in the sounds of their language. Sounds of other languages have little meaning, and their words become less conscious.

Certain drugs ruin lives. Cocaine and heroin activate the brain's pleasure reward system creating an internal subjective sense of joy. Joy for doing nothing creates a false mind. Anticipating uncertainty and the excitement of expected success develops a feeling of joy.

In my earlier books, glial cells, also called astrocytes, were presented as support cells in the brain. Neuroscience now understands glial cells to have an important role in axon pathway growth and direction. Glial cells guide axons to connect within specific neuron areas. Brain growth is preplanned. In a healthy baby, there is little randomness in the trillions of neuron connections.

There are 150 types of neurons in the human brain. A healthy brain is guided by heredity, physics, and biochemical processes as it grows. A brain with 85 billion neurons functioning together is a miracle of life. There must be spiritual guidance.

We have completed a brief introduction to neuroscience to develop a feeling of how the brain works, including some of my insights. The goal is to heal and improve brain and mind activities.

The more neuroscientists learn about brain component activities and communications, the better the chance of healing the brain, improving reasoning, and managing pain. We do not need detailed models of the brain to stimulate healing and creativity. We only need to study the brain enough to help heal and expand mental abilities, and reactivate our innate baby spiritual communication skills.

Everybody's crazy if we don't believe studying brain processes can heal the mind, and enhance inner awareness and cognition. It takes the brain and mind to study neuroscience.

Physics of the Brain

This essay emphasizes electromagnetic radiation, EMR, activities and control within the brain. Less effort is directed toward chemistry. Studying intermediate characteristics of the brain may stimulate inner healing and creativity.

We choose freedom of thought, action, and belief or allow others to dictate our thoughts, actions, and beliefs. We can be true to ourselves by purging emotional and trauma energy, others and various injuries have ingrained within our brains.

Each neuron EMR spike imprints detailed mental hologram information on numerous brain cell membranes for developing thinking and memory. Neuron activated EMR passing through its own cell membrane splits it into "reference beams" creating "coherent" EMR that constructs small components of many integrated mental holograms as it passes through membranes of many neurons and glia.

If photographic film absorbs light energy to create and store three-dimensional images, then certainly DNA within brain cell membranes absorb EMR and store mental hologram imprints. Human three-dimensional neural membrane "photo film" creates higher dimensional hologram imprints that are always present and ready to "view" quicker than family photos.

Memory holograms are much more complex than laser holograms. EMR with distinct frequencies filtering through the brain may construct holograms in one nucleus, one component, or throughout the entire brain. A nucleus in the brain is a grouping of neurons with a specific function.

Our minds imagine and construct three-dimensional visions when viewing a two-dimensional photograph or television screen. EMR resonances ingrain four, and higher, dimensional mental holograms by "writing to" and "reading from" a complex array of three-dimensional neuron membranes.

From an engineering perspective, mental holograms must have many dimensions. Neuron membrane segments are located within three spatial dimensions at many angles. To model activities in the brain, we must include membrane segment location, orientation, thickness, and chemical variations.

Mental holograms consist of three dimensional scenarios and backgrounds, emotional dimensions related to self, speeds of detail changes, and shades of colors, on three dimensional, complex arrays of neuron membranes. Mental holograms and their changing content are the working tools of cognition and memory.

Physical and chemical processes develop activation potentials. Light or EMR from neuron activations continually read from and write to brain cell membranes – similar to reading from and writing to computer CDs. Light is a small part of brain EMR.

EMR absorbed by less fixed neuron and glia body fluids have less influence on hologram construction, memory, and thinking than that absorbed by more fixed cell membranes. Neuron activation frequencies are influenced by its chemical buildup and neurotransmitters from other neurons.

The fabric of brain cells must have amazing imaging properties. EMR and brain cell membranes have recursive relationships. EMR constructs thinking through "reading" and "writing" information from and to neural membranes.

Coherent light, absorbed by brain cell membrane segments, has the same frequencies and the same phase angles. Coherent light has wave highs and lows in the same phase. Millions and millions of slightly different EMR frequencies and wave shapes activate unique responses from each neuron.

Dreams are our inner hologram language, which briefly rise to consciousness. Verbal languages are tools for communicating information between human beings. Integrated semiconscious ideas produce feelings and emotions that influence our thoughts and activities. Pondering specific thoughts over long periods of time develop stronger, specialized neural networks for creative ideas in areas of concentration.

Repeated thoughts make related mental holograms brighter and clearer. Similar visions and experiences construct similar mental resonances and holograms. There is so much EMR traveling within the brain that some coherent EMR must be absorbed in brain cell membranes. Resonating coherent EMR striking cell membranes at several different angles has more influence than non-coherent light waves in constructing mental holograms.

Neurons and nuclei have specific resonances similar to radios having specific resonances to receive specific radio signals. Radios at different distances from radio stations are sensitive to the same EMR radio waves. EMR frequencies from one firing neuron are absorbed more by neuron membranes with resonances for those frequencies at different distances from the firing neuron, to form a mental hologram distributed throughout the brain with specific characteristics.

Neural membranes have specific EMR resonances. An EMR frequency may be transmitted through many brain components but absorbed mostly by neural membranes with resonances for that distinct frequency. Electromagnetic spikes from each neuron have unique energy characteristics and profiles. Neurotransmitters sent along neuron axons to dendrites of other neurons also have distinct characteristics. A unique neuron "footprint" is recognized by billions of brain cell membranes

Let's consider paths that EMR, from one neuron activation, takes. This is my "Brain String Theory." An electromagnetic spike, from one neuron, explodes in all directions. This light is:

1) Reflected by its inner membrane surface;
2) Transmitted through its inner membrane surface;
3) Absorbed in the fabric of its own membrane;
4) Reflected by its outer membrane surface;
5) Repeatedly reflected between inner and outer membrane surfaces imprinting energy and information within its own membrane; (EMR is absorbed by cell membrane resonances.)
6) Transmitted through its outer membrane surface;
7) Absorbed by non-cell matter in the brain, or transmitted to the surface of another neuron or glia cell;
8) Reflected by another cell's outer membrane surface;
9) Transmitted through another cell's outer membrane surface;
10) Absorbed by another cell's membrane;
11) Reflected by another membrane's inner surface;
12) Absorbed within another cell;
13) Similar activities continue throughout millions of brain cells.

Resonating electromagnetic waves die out as their energy is absorbed or escapes the brain. Awareness of one moment dies out as energy dissipates and is reborn by resonating EMR from the next overlapping generation of neuron activations. Neurons are affected more by EMR from near than distant neurons. Neuron information is passed along throughout the brain by EMR and slow axons and dendrites.

From incoming EMR, brain cell membranes either reflect or refract light. Light absorbed within and passing through multiple membranes refracts into widening angles. Successive membrane absorptions create an increasingly spread out and detailed holographic imprint. EMR waves continue through membranes until strings or quanta of light energy are deposited within one atom or molecule – thus: my "Brain String Theory."

Traumatized neural networks, and their high-energy EMR, negatively influence the culturing of normal and emotional thoughts. We need to purge excess energy from traumatized neural networks to reduce its emotional, sporadic, and disruptive influence.

An individual who thinks of, and reacts to, many different activities and challenges will have more diverse mental hologram building blocks. Our minds compare all things we do to the content within our fundamental mental holograms to construct ideas and reason.

At any time, the brain produces millions of subconscious resonances vying to gain energy to influence consciousness. Subconscious EMR resonances integrate to increase energy for developing conscious resonances. Longer resonances are reflected between brain component surfaces. Mental holograms include time stamps for organizing and sequencing memories.

Complex subconscious processes integrate to form simpler conscious processes. Subconscious and conscious processes are more diverse for individuals who speak different languages, and experience different challenges and environments. Two individuals sharing the same idea have very different subconscious processes for developing that idea. Subconscious processes are cultured by genetics and histories. Thinking processes appear as analog or continuous mental hologram scenarios created by overlapping EMR from neuron activations.

Humans have cultivated and defined discrete words to communicate with one another. Some of us receive spiritual feelings and ideas and communicate them to others. We must be aware of higher dimensions within our souls to translate analog spiritual wave messages received into discrete spiritual words for sharing with others.

Truthful EMR, spiritual resonances, are absorbed within our souls. We have a guiding light to live by. Our thoughts are absorbed and reflected by spiritual wisdom within our souls. Our souls have perfect communication with God.

Our souls in higher spiritual dimensions are sensitive to very long, low-energy wavelengths. They extend beyond our physical bodies. Spiritual wave lengths may extend over galaxies. God's fundamental Big Bang wavelength continues to expand at the speed of light creating the edges, or limits, of the universe.

There is little reason to believe that "virgin light originally from Nothing" and still expanding the boundaries of the universe, is anything like light we are familiar with. Virgin light is directly created by the Big Bang and not emitted from atom excitations.

Our eyes are only sensitive, and react, to light, a small part of the electromagnetic spectra. We should not limit God to man's limited sensitivities. God is sensitive to, and learns from, all electromagnetic and spiritual frequencies.

Unfortunately, trauma scars eclipse spiritual communication between minds and souls. Information absorbed by our souls is integrated as wisdom independent of time and space. God is omnipresent and everywhere the same. Spiritual waves are independent of space, physical time, and matter. Spiritual waves only interact with light or EMR, and not with atoms and matter. Interactions with matter would is too slow for the extreme speed of spiritual waves.

Truthful thinking and surrendering free will enhances spiritual communication and blessings. We must clear our brains and minds of trauma effects to reclaim our baby spiritual abilities.

There is no awareness without conflict. Conflicts within trauma memories affect our thinking security causing unwarranted guilt. "Why did this happen to me?" "Why was I in the wrong place?" We must learn from, avoid, adjust to, and control, conflict. Conflict means different things to different people. It may mean avoid or stop to most people but a challenge and go to the bold.

We can break the mental chains of childhood traumas and indoctrination by becoming aware of the effects conflicts have on our minds and behaviors. Expanding mental limits helps us understand ourselves, others, the universe, and God. Relaxed minds are healthier, confident, creative, and promote longer lives.

Scientists and doctors should expect out of control actions and reactions when brain limits are exceeded. Doctors should question patients to understand their mental limit breaches and help restore more stable emotional limits.

When adjusting inner processes, minds may become preoccupied. If practicing mind expansion, individuals should expect temporary slowing or racing thoughts followed by creative, reflective thinking and possibly spiritual awareness. Control originally lessens during mental expansion but becomes greater later on.

I hope my mind models and "brain string" theory are realistic enough to help readers release trauma energy and heal their afflictions. Mental afflictions are difficult to recognize since most of them have been ingrained since childhood. Research should focus on studying brain cell membrane properties and the development and processing of mental holograms.

I am grateful for having, and been cured of, bipolar disorder, and having received spiritual blessings and wisdom. I have presented ideas as truthfully as I understand them and will continue improving healing processes. *A Philosophy* of *Healing and Spirituality* is meant to help readers develop their own healing and spiritual processes.

Everybody's crazy if not believing that studying electromagnetic and spiritual properties within the brain are as important as studying the chemistry of the brain. The brain is physical and the mind is spiritual

Spiritual Physics

—⚏—

SPIRITUAL PHYSICS DEVELOPS MODELS THAT cross boundaries between physical and spiritual existence. There were only two differences in existence before time began. There was a point existence and infinite homogeneous existence, without boundaries. The Big Bang created physical properties, space, and time for differences to exist and evolve within space. A goal is to inspire the science community to consider philosophical models of creation, the brain, mind, and God.

Mind and spiritual models use science, the Bible, and my spiritual awareness to integrate science and spirituality. In curing my bipolar disorder, inner awareness added understanding of the mind and gave insight into God's dimensions. Physics and engineering principles are used to understand and heal the mind, and develop spiritual reasoning.

If we completely understand our minds and elementary particle physics, we will understand God. In spiritual dimensions, God is within us and surrounding every atom in the universe. He is omnipresent and omniscient.

Without conflict, uncertainty, and energy transfer, the mind and universe cannot exist. God integrates universal histories including physical uncertainties to construct spiritual certainty and completeness each quantum of time. God integrates atom and galaxy uncertainties into complete spiritual certainty.

Without certainties and uncertainties, human life cannot exist. Genetics brings some level of certainty to human development and life. However, we are never absolutely certain what our next thought or action will be.

Reasoning through and integrating physical uncertainties increases mental certainty and builds confident, spiritual minds. Thoughts are never complete without reflection to and from an omnipresent, omniscient God. We study physics and other sciences to understand God's reasoning for creating the universe, and man. Humans need uncertainties, challenges, and completeness for spiritual lives.

Humans search for certainty in life through religion. Some religions proclaim that their spiritual books are, and spiritual leaders were, perfect. Perfect includes being certain and complete. It was dangerous to question perfect religions a few hundred years ago. Questioning could lead to execution by "perfect" religious followers defending their "perfect" religions.

Early scientists were jailed if they disproved accepted Christian beliefs. Early Christian leaders were the self-proclaimed protectors of all important knowledge. For this reason, philosophers did not question religions. Religions controlled governments with authoritarian rule. Disagreeing was risky. Some religions proclaimed having the only certain path of being accepted by God

Humans need uncertainty to understand certainty. A basketball game between an NBA team and a six-year-old team has little uncertainty or excitement. Humans love excitement of overcoming difficult uncertainties to develop certainty and completeness.

From my models, God was created from a very fast primordial wave in one 10^{-106} second vibration - a very, very small fraction of a second. In my models, a 10^{-106} second vibration defines the smallest quantum of spiritual time. This very fast vibration and speed allows God to be aware of and manage activities in a very big universe.

Scientists believe that the shortest physical time is 10^{-43} seconds for light to travel the shortest length, 10^{-35} meters. These two values are theoretically defined using fundamental physics constants and are so small they can never be measured.

God is aware of and records our thoughts, life events, and all activities in the universe. He builds awareness of universal completeness every 10^{-106} seconds. Man's purpose in an evolving universe is to reflect good relationships and lives to God. God is aware of, and controls physical activities and relationships in the universe with His physical laws. He gives humans and living things limited free wills to control limited awareness, minds, and physical environments.

We sometimes understand near-term earthly purposes but have little understanding of our universal and spiritual purposes. Through God's spiritual dimensions, our lives affect the entire universe to some very small extent. We may choose to have or not have a relationship with God. Some individuals sense God strongly and some choose to ignore Him. It depends upon one's experience and attitude toward spiritual surrender. Some people feel too powerful or important to surrender to God.

Anything traveling near the speed of light "observes" time as slowed down and space compressed in the direction of travel in a relative reference frame. God is Light and has very different abilities and properties than humans.

Light does not lose energy in space but normally spreads out or is absorbed within matter. Light, God, has very fast spiritual information waves that are independent of matter and physical time.

God is always traveling at the speed of light relative to humans and matter. From relativity, God views humans as constant and independent of time and space. Humans view God as always traveling at the speed of light, constant, and independent of time. God has "complete spiritual awareness" of all events in the universe, which have occurred up to the current time.

Scientists learn about God and His universe through structured, repeatable experiments for proving theories. A successful scientist does not declare he is the only true scientist after discovering some important principle of the universe.

Some spiritual leaders who have received messages from God claim they and their ways are the only true paths to learn about, and receive messages from, God. Power has corrupted many short time spiritual leaders. Spiritual leaders must be humble after receiving spiritual messages to communicate them truthfully. Patience with self, others, and God is a virtue.

DNA is the architecture of human life. Think of the impossible, difficult task, a human architect would have designing a human. DNA is God's miracle of human life. We are molded by our parents, ancestors, and the universe through God.

We are limited in sensing and reasoning about, our lives and our speck in the universe. Scientists search for knowledge to increase human comforts and longevity. It takes imagination to integrate new ideas with related memories to develop knowledge. God senses and records all activities and relationships, in the universe, independent of time and space.

Memories with similar characteristics are encoded with similar resonances and "strong" time stamps for organized recall. Subconscious processes do not need to search through all memories to recall similar events. Activated senses promote the recall of similar events with similar resonances most readily.

Memories have time stamps relative to all other memories. We can usually recall the order of events over the last day or two. With healthy minds, we do not confuse childhood or high school memories with recent memories.

Nothing physical is ever final, complete, or holy. Time continues. Anything humans build deteriorates over time. Spiritual thoughts are independent of time and evenly integrated throughout the universe; they will last forever in heaven.

The brain and mind increase in complexity to make physical efforts less strenuous and promote longer life. Science instruments allow us to expand "sensing of and reasoning about" the universe. Different laws, forces, and influences apply for atomic, human, earth, sun, galaxy, and universe sized entities. Light, space, time, matter, and their interactions are different for different sizes of existence.

With increasingly complex, precise language, minds become more organized, integrated, and specialized allowing greater accomplishments, hopefully, for God's benefit. Man's spiritual wisdom can be beneficial to God. We hope to be some benefit to our children, mothers, fathers, and God. God needs prayers at human levels to become more holy or complete each quantum of spiritual time.

We sometimes may feel we do things perfectly. We make mistakes. Spiritually, we must be truthful about our communications, thoughts and accomplishments. I have good and bad thoughts. I try to understand bad thoughts and make them more positive and spiritual, and only act upon good thoughts. Unfortunately, bad things happen to good people.

After death, the brain and body deteriorate. There is no longer EMR resonating throughout the brain from neuron activities. However, there is faint outside radiation from various sources. Very low energy filtering throughout decaying neural membranes may develop a small low-energy spiritual awareness. Low electromagnetic energy in the brain, (and in computers,) is easier to control and promotes creative, spiritual thought. Our remains may be able to give spiritually after physical deaths.

Spiritual leaders should teach followers to distinguish between parables, beliefs, and facts. If they do not do this, science truths will make traditional religions obsolete. Religions with good spiritual principles will be able to incorporate science truths to better serve God and His people. Human speaking and writing is never perfect. With time and effort writing can always be improved. Words also change meaning over time.

I write from experiences and with words I understand. Biblical writers could only do the same. With some understanding of traditional spiritual books, science, technology, and spiritual experiences, we have some small chance of advancing understanding of the mind and God.

Scientists look at the world differently than religious leaders. Empty space is spiritual existence, the same everywhere, and independent of location within the universe. We pray and God becomes aware of our prayers even if we were in empty space.

Scientists understand some of God's non-changing physical laws. Repeated experiments verify discoveries as facts. Scientific discoveries and facts make life easier and more exciting.

Atoms absorb and emit light energy. God constructed the universe such that little things have the probability of making big things with greater stability and certainty.

Mathematics and science provide rather precise models of electromagnetic radiation. EMR is a link to higher spiritual dimensions. Light is spiritual. Imaginary numbers are needed to describe its properties.

Scientists have proven that laws governing galaxies and the universe have amazing consistency. Higher dimensions and laws must influence such consistency over very large distances. With His constant physical and spiritual laws, God organizes and guides every aspect of an expanding universe.

God gave human minds abilities to build upon earlier thought foundations. With free will, humans have extended thinking structures to build advanced environments and devices.

I am not sure why Man is limited to such a small awareness within his mind, body, and environment. However, scientists have developed huge imaginations and devises for discovering and understanding the universe. God guides physical, mental, and spiritual advances.

At conception, we received God's complete wisdom. Human awareness of spiritual wisdom becomes repressed as we grow mentally and physically and learn to navigate our environments. Humans have ability to regain spiritual wisdom through humility, meditation, and mental reconstruction. Humans must be spiritually reborn to attain everlasting life

Developing strict scientific criteria for determining facts has allowed an explosion of useful machines and technical devices that have enhanced our knowledge and lives. No recent religious awakenings have occurred that have radically advanced spiritual communication skills and lives. We must distinguish between beliefs and facts:

Belief – a mental acceptance of something as real or true. Belief may or may not imply certitude in the believer. Faith always implies trust and confidence even when there is no evidence or proof. Beliefs imply intellectual acceptance but offer no proof.

Fact - something that exists, interacts, or happens and has objective reality as understood by a perceptive, reasoning mind, or as repetitively and consistently proven through scientific tests.

Small atomic size energy changes occur in well-defined discrete up or down steps. God's wisdom includes knowledge of quantum activities:

- Spiritual knowledge of physical events becomes independent of time and space, and is the same throughout space and time.
- Spiritual knowledge of physical and spiritual events is "instantly" transmitted throughout the universe.
- "Spiritual dimensions" multiply rather than add for integrating spiritual history and wisdom.
- God predicts, influences, and organizes spiritual events throughout the universe in spiritual dimensions.

There are many kinds of evil and suffering in the world, yet, most religions conclude God is perfect. Humans with their uncertainties need a solid standard to look up to. Field forces (such as gravity) and light always act and react consistently throughout space and time. They give the universe consistent structure that provides man a place to live. God has created consistent laws guiding evolution of the universe. Man is never consistent very long.

We refer to the universe as being physical; however, God is intertwined and integrated throughout the universe in higher dimensions. God controls constant physical forces and nurtures spiritual relationships while allowing free will. We must obey God's physical laws, but have free will to obey or disobey God's spiritual laws.

Gravity and other physical laws govern physical relationships. Every atom in our bodies is attracted to every atom in and on the earth. To a lesser extent, atoms in our bodies are affected by every atom in the universe. However, it takes time for a very weak gravity to reach us from distant stars.

Spiritually inspired believers work to discover truths to improve lives on earth and cultivate a path for eternal life. Traditional religions look to the past and restrict future thinking and actions. Even though churches may provide spiritual guidance, followers must be responsible for their own spiritual endeavors for everlasting life.

We must reason about events in the past to understand and develop a structured, creative future. Lives today are very different from lives one hundred years ago. Technology gives us more opportunity to learn about and love one another and God. Unfortunately, technology also gives us more opportunity to be self-centered, and do evil.

Should we live spiritually and worship the same as ancestors lived and worshiped two and six thousand years ago? Conservative Christians believe mankind can never be more spiritual than Jesus was two thousand years ago. Can we not learn from Jesus and improve our spiritual lives with the advantages of technology? Conservative Christians say no.

We can become better Christians by following Jesus' teachings for praising God and by studying science for understanding His universe, and God. The better we understand God, the better we can please and serve Him. We need to be intelligent in our beliefs. Israeli scientist Dan Shechtman was not believed in the 1980s for his discovery of crystal pentagonal symmetry or quasi-crystals. He faced skepticism and mockery that prompted expulsion from his U.S. research team before his research won widespread acceptance as a fundamental breakthrough. His work violated accepted principles of chemistry. He continued when no one believed in him.

Shechtman was awarded the Nobel Prize for chemistry in 2011 for his discovery. The primary use for his work is converting low-level heat energy into electrical energy. His discovery has changed chemistry forever.

Spiritual technology for communicating with God may be discovered and refined. We must be intelligent in accepting and rejecting beliefs. So many believers are caught up in cults that are primarily for the benefit of cult leaders.

I work to expand understanding of the brain, mind, and spiritual communication skills. Anyone attempting to go beyond current science principles or traditional religious practices will endure skepticism until breakthroughs are understood and accepted. It is short sighted to believe fundamental science and spiritual communications cannot be technically expanded and improved. To develop science and spiritual technologies, we must have patience and persistence in exploring beyond the accepted.

I have developed brain and mind healing, and spiritual communication innovations. New discoveries must be testable with overwhelmingly successful results to be accepted. Testing and acceptance is difficult to accomplish with mental and spiritual advancements. If we have been brainwashed by current science and traditional religious practices, creative reasoning is blocked for discovering physical and spiritual truths. Jesus' healing miracles were important in Jesus being widely accepted.

Entropy or disorganization increases in the universe over time. Organization increases and entropy decreases in spiritual dimensions.

Heaven becomes more organized over time to record activities of an increasingly complex universe. Cosmologists will discover more about spiritual dimensions through analysis and integration of physical histories and spiritual relationships. Scientists must integrate physical and spiritual histories to think holistically for understanding God.

Everyone is crazy if thinking we cannot integrate physical uncertainties into spiritual certainties. Boundaries defined centuries ago have separated spiritual and physical studies. Advances in science will integrate the two disciplines. Both will be enriched.

Philosophy of Perfect

God communicates to human minds and souls through His perfect waves and resonances. His perfect spiritual wisdom when received can only be translated into imperfect human words and language. Writers and translators of spiritual books, including the Bible, are never perfect. Humans live with physical and mental uncertainties but some strive for spiritual certainty.

Spiritual translations may be truthful, or biased for the benefit of the receiver and his people. Different human experiences, words, and languages produce different shades of meaning in conversations and writings.

There is no perfect "Word of God." Perfect spiritual waves have perfect spiritual wisdom. If God is perfect, He cannot speak in imperfect words. He chooses leaders to truthfully translate His spiritual wisdom. Spiritual books may contain truthful word translations of God's perfect spiritual waves. "The Word of God" is a good traditional shortcut relating to spiritual truth.

"Perfect" is often a word used to intimidate and control. Fundamental Christian preachers refer to a perfect Bible and God's Perfect Word. Spiritual leaders emphasize that perfect spiritual books cannot be questioned, added to, or subtracted from. Humans, with their weaknesses, uncertainties, and fears of mortality are attracted to the word "perfect," and an "all knowing, all powerful, perfect God."

As a scientist aware of God's unchanging "perfect" physical laws, I believe God was perfect in creating, and is perfect in controlling and evolving, the physical universe. With limited abilities, humans are not able to understand spiritual perfection.

As a Christian I believe Jesus set the standard of living a spiritual life. However, He did not teach science to improve followers' lives. Jesus' miracles must have included physical and spiritual technologies. Did Jesus understand the technologies of His healing miracles? Would Jesus have been "more" perfect if He shared His healing technologies with others? There would be less suffering today. Today, researchers and physicians share their healing technologies. We know so little about "perfect."

If someone is perfect one day, can he become more perfect later? Perfect cannot change and must be constant for all times. Christians believe Jesus' life, miracles and crucifixion defined perfection and His spirit will continue to save believers' souls for a billion years and then forever.

Miracles happen beyond my ability to understand them. Creation of the universe and human life are miracles. I may understand some things that others would consider miracles. Others may understand things that I would consider miracles.

I am inquisitive about Jesus' early years. His early years must have been difficult knowing what was expected of Him. He needed thirty years of preparation. I suspect persistent stress of expectations caused Jesus to become bipolar. Jesus abilities extended beyond normal limits. Bipolar disorder heightens spiritual communications and skills.

Human spiritual abilities are limited by life's traumas and selfish pride. To be truly spiritual and know God, we must reconstruct our brains and minds to be clear of trauma effects and achieve a "Clear Mind." With clear minds, we can better learn spiritual principles from God.

Was Jesus spiritually perfect His entire life? Can we not question all things to deepen beliefs? Could God have been more perfect for

Philosophy of Perfect

humans over their history? Many of us believe God is perfect in spiritual dimensions beyond human understanding. Many of us feel inferior to anyone described as "perfect." The word "perfect" is difficult to deal with.

I use the word, "perfect," only when someone has done something better than imagined. Perfect inspires an atmosphere of awe. Can someone be perfect and more perfect later? Calling a young child a genius ruins their lives. The word, "genius," is closely related perfect. The poor child has to continuously "act" like a genius.

There must be reasons for suffering. Humans can only interpret God's Holy purpose. Everybody's crazy believing human words are perfect. However, God's ever present spiritual waves are perfectly truthful in defining God and His universe. Everybody's crazy calling a child a genius. High expectations often become over stressful causing disorders and distortions. Misguided geniuses treat others as inferior to maintain a superior status.

BRAIN SECTION

Brain

"I wish I had a brain!"

— Strawman, Wizard of OZ

WITHOUT A BRAIN, WE ARE "straw people." I develop models of the brain, using physics and neuroscience, for thinking about, studying, and healing the brain. My models are intuitive and creative. I heal my brain and mind mostly with physics.

In this and later chapters, we strive to understand emotions to release repressed trauma energy from the brain. The overstressed usually talk fast and emphatic, seem nervous, and overreact to seemingly minor things. Lowering the emotional energy of the brain promotes calm, less pressured, creative thinking

A goal is to heal the brain and prevent mental disorders and injuries. Models of brain structures and functions add understanding and promote change. The brain and mind are an integrated entity for analyzing sense information from nerves and developing conscious control. Normal conscious processes do little toward understanding and improving subconscious efficiencies. Subconscious processes were developed mostly genetically and early in life. It takes conscious effort to heal and improve subconscious protocols. The mind consists of spiritual dimensions beyond three spatial and one time dimensions. Spiritual thoughts roam heaven forever within God's omnipresent and omniscient dimensions. Spiritual thoughts extend beyond the physical brain to become integrated within souls as unchanging spirits, independent of space.

Physical and spiritual histories of the universe are integrated into one complete, holy spiritual system, God. This spiritual integration is similar to billions of neuron activities integrating to develop a single human thought. Think of the coordination needed for billions of activating neurons to develop one idea. The mind "must" have a spiritual component. Integration is a strong concept in my theories on the universe and God.

Early in life, we need parents to nurture and give us confidence to think, communicate, and explore. To communicate, we need someone to communicate with and listen to us. How well we think and communicate depends upon the encouragement and confidence others have given us when we were young, and the confidence we have fought for during our lives. The brain is physical and grows with experiences, or atrophies from disuse.

The brain and mind develop a recursive system. We must use our minds to stimulate our brains to release engrained trauma tensions, and to understand and heal emotional inner processes.

The next generation clings to ideas and principles from earlier generations, often without questioning. This is especially true about the brain, mind, health, and religion. Several ideas that were slow to change are: "The earth is flat." "The heart is the center of the mind." "There are many jealous gods." "Bloodletting heals." Today, we continue activities that promote good and poor health.

Ponce de Leon traveled to Florida in search of the Fountain of Youth when he only needed to stimulate his longevity genes. Researchers have discovered longevity genes in lower life forms such as yeast. They are searching for master regulator genes related to natural defense mechanisms against stress and aging in humans as part of the Longevity Genes Project at Albert Einstein College of Medicine, Dr. Nir Barzilai, director.

Emotional and trauma limits developed in youth, build defenses against early stresses. One exercise was to briefly stress my mind to limits and then quickly calm down. With less persistent inner stress, we live longer. Our inner stresses have existed for so long we do not recognize them as being present. Similarly, we are unaware of high blood pressure. A further goal is to help readers reduce their overall stress and slow aging.

Today, many look to the Fountain of Youth in plastic surgery, Botox, and a host of vitamins. In reality, the Fountain of Youth is a relaxed and frequently stimulated mind, exercise for stimulating longevity genes, healthy eating habits, and a little sunshine.

In the future, brain scans will correlate brain fabric, mental hologram characteristics, and thought construction for improving mental technology. We cannot imagine mental healing technologies in the next one hundred years. Humans have just begun to think.

From genetics and experiences, some people handle stress better than others. If persistently beyond limits, humans lose control. By resolving conflict and reducing inner stresses, the brain re-grows. Mental limits expand and we get smarter.

The brain is not so different from the body's immune system. Stress can overwhelm the brain and affect the body's immune system. Similar to immunization, controlled conflicting stress can prepare the brain for higher levels of persistent or unexpected stresses.

The brain's immunity to stress can be developed just as the body's immune system can adapt to combat infectious diseases. Forcing the mind to limits is much like working out with weights. Afterward, normal activities are easier.

Millions of electromagnetic frequencies and resonances iterate and integrate to form subconscious sub-thoughts each fraction of a second. Thousands of subconscious sub-thoughts integrate to form conscious thoughts.

The subconscious mind is aware of every nerve and muscle cell in the body and every neuron and glia cell in the brain. The conscious mind only needs to send a holistic signal to move a leg. The subconscious mind activates the correct subset of leg nerve and muscle cells to move that leg.

Writing develops mental organization and precision, refines understanding, and reduces anxieties and insecurities. Writing is part of mental healing.

Thinking does not need to be in words. Picture thinking can be easier and more efficient at times. We construct visions of the road ahead as we navigate toward destinations in our cars.

Long term thoughts and moods are reflected on our faces. Contours of our faces are related to contours within and on our brains.

We can recognize long term mental characteristics by analyzing older faces. We can tell who has:

- had a hard or easy life;
- loved or hated;
- developed little or greater understanding and confidence in life;
- been abused or victimized;
- had faith or uncertainty;
- or has been deceitful or nurturing.

Normal memories are spread throughout the brain to become part of the mind's recall system. The brain and body accept and store energy and then use that energy for recall and activities when stimulated. Decisions and behaviors depend upon earlier success and failure histories. Morals are products of heredity, histories of emotional reactions, and consistent reasoning. Having human genetics, we do not look or act like cats.

Clinical or Unipolar depression becomes a neurological disorder with a neurotransmitter imbalance. From inner sensations when and after performing conflicting neck exercises, overstressed neural networks release energy mostly in the brainstem, upper neck, and upper throat. Antidepressants can increase monoamines including dopamine, norepinephrine, and serotonin to restore chemical balances for maintaining more normal thinking.

The hippocampus is active during prolonged stress. Losses and stress cause depression and too often lead to bipolar disorder.

Cocaine and heroin activate the brain's pleasure reward system, creating an internal subjective sense of joy. Uncertainties that end successfully develop pleasurable experiences. Love can bring Joy. Joy, without reason or accomplishment, corrupts reasoning.

Bipolar disorder includes neurotransmitter imbalances. Moods often become elevated. At first, there is some benefit. Thinking becomes faster and moods become pleasant. Confidence builds and in mania, one may think he can reason through anything.

As moods elevate, emotional limits are broken, and reasoning collapses. The bipolar mind goes wildly out of control searching for lost sanity. Normal thinking and reasoning degrade, but spiritual insight may become more acute.

Subconscious resonance energies from rods and cones within the eyes integrate for constructing vision and conscious. We are not aware of individual rod and cone activities. The mind integrates awareness for sight. Sensitivity integration is spiritual. Similarly, we only see integrations of atom when viewing our skin.

Minds are constructed from integrated neural resonances. Reactions to various stimuli activate related neural networks, nuclei, and components within the brain. With psychiatric exploration and patience, we can explore a wide range of mental integrations for creative healing paths.

Neuroscientists work to relate learning to physical changes within the brain. Spines, stubby mushroom-like growths on dendrites, change shape over activation histories. Exercise and learning can cause dendrites to sprout new spines and synapses. Continued analysis might relate spine growth to various learning experiences. Spine protrusions on dendrites store synaptic energy and help transmit signals to its neuron body.

Studying stress effects on spine grow may help overstressed victims reduce or unlearn trauma effects. Traumatized neural networks produce erratic high-energy, EMR, activations that degrade normal charge contours on the surfaces of the brain. Smooth EMR contours on the surfaces of the brain reflect more confident, holistic, and complete thinking.

Normal brain functions must increase energy to override, or work around, disruptive activities of traumatized neurons to overcome adverse effects. After purging excess trauma energy, the brain no longer needs to avoid trauma effects and develops more efficient, thinking, emotions, and responses.

Consciousness is constructed by synchronized neuron chemical activations that produce charge and voltage variations within and on brain components and surfaces. Consciousness is a resonating symphony of "flowing" electromagnetic activities. Resonances must vary slow enough and last long enough to produce consciousness for humans to engage in environments. Brain surfaces resist electron flow forming charge profiles on brain surfaces for awareness and cognition.

The limbic system contains complex interconnected nuclei (neurons connected for dedicated purposes) involved in learning, memory, emotions, and executive functions for organizing sensing, memory, and other inner processes. Memory structure includes limbic, prefrontal cortex, and hippocampus areas of the brain for positive learning. The prefrontal cortex is important in learning and unlearning memories. Desensitizing Therapy is important to reduce the fears and effects of military experienced Post Traumatic Syndrome.

Normally, males and females are easily recognized. Brain sex may not be so obvious. In her CD lectures, professor Norden discusses sexual orientation. A boy fetus' testicles must produce testosterone to his growing brain, at a critical time of development, for him to form a boy's brain. If not enough testosterone is produced at this critical time of brain development, a physical male develops a female oriented brain and mind.

If a mother has high levels of testosterone or is taking certain drugs at a critical developmental time, a physical female baby will have a male's sexually oriented brain and mind. This discovery may help expecting parents connect the right mind with the right body. However, the important thing is to have a healthy, happy baby, child, and adult. From observations, if a woman is aggressive most of her life, she may develop male sexual orientation.

Human sexual orientation is not their child's fault. With today's technologies, parents will have more options in the sex orientation of their beautiful babies.

After reading Dr. Norden's theory on sexual orientation, I am also aware of theories that genetics affect sexual orientation of children. Sexual orientation will be an interesting topic in the future.

Humans have greater ability to configure their brains than originally thought. Our brains are rigid when we are tense and stressed. After stressful interactions, our brains and faces remain tense unless we relax them. A relaxed, supple brain creates a versatile, creative mind. For many of us, our brains have remained tense for so long we do not recognize the inner tensions. Frowning restricts blood flow to the brain, and the brain remains tense. Practice smiling or laughing to relax the face and brain.

We revert to our childhood minds briefly, at times. In need, children surrender to parents with broadened, questioning faces and open minds. Surrendering cares to God relaxes the mind. The holistic right-brain becomes dominant and open to expected good and spiritual ideas. With eyes focused long distant and the mind focused on the future, the mind becomes right-brained, more relaxed, and moldable.

Relaxing the brain and body is good for health and creativity. Many of us remain tense night and day. Broadening the face and brain becomes easier with practice. Increased blood flow to the brain may cause the face and scalp to feel flush. Heart beat awareness within the brain often occurs. These sensations became apparent after years of mental reconstruction. A less tense body and brain lowers blood pressure and reduces heart attacks.

When a person is stressed, he is mostly concerned about his own wellbeing, and not open to nurturing others. The brain is meant to be a holistic organ. If the brain is stressed, brain cells are stressed and more concerned about their own functions and wellbeing. They do not share information as freely and are not as open to integration functions and healing. Relaxing the body and mind allows brain cells to work together as an integrated, spiritual whole.

If all nations were governed by relaxed, creative minds there would be more creative reasoning in solving national and world problems. People would think less emotionally and selfishly about their activities and religions. Leaders would think more about the good of the entire world.

It is sinful when religions brainwash followers to feel and act superior because of their "limiting, perfect" beliefs. Religions should never encourage followers to act superior to anyone. Good parents and teachers do not feel or act superior to their children or students.

No thought or physical interaction occurs in the universe without emitting light, or electromagnetic radiation. A brain, healed of trauma effects, will have lower energy levels with longer wavelengths. God responds to longer, "spiritual" wavelengths.

God integrates light, EMR, from all activities throughout the universe to construct His perfect, complete truth. Many of us feel we can pray anywhere and God is there, with consistently perfect information, awareness, and wisdom to nurture us. Being listened to by God, or important others, is healing, comforting, and confidence building.

Spiritual information, even that which is created by human minds, travels "instantly" throughout the universe by God's higher spiritual integration dimensions. Humans should not be so arrogant to limit God to human sensed dimensions, awareness, and abilities.

Psychiatry and psychology have done little in analyzing how mania inspires spiritual receptiveness. Psychiatrists do not accept or reason about unusual spiritual sensitivities. From a few manic-depressives I have talked with, spiritual themes are similar. However, words are different depending upon language, experiences and vocabularies. Researching manic episodes, we may discover the nature of the inner mind, prove God exists, and discover more about His nature.

The brain and body are temporary houses of the mind and soul. The soul consists of mental holograms that have been infinitely multiplied into unchanging spiritual holograms within spiritual dimensions, independent of physical space. Upon death the soul escapes the brain and mind into spiritual dimensions.

Everybody's crazy if only studying chemistry and anatomy and not physics of the brain. Light and EMR create our spiritual minds. Studying the brain expands the mind and soul.

Healing the Body

—⋙—

ACTIVITIES OF THE BRAIN MIND, and body, including expressions of the face, are intricately connected. As the brain, body, and mind heal and become healthier, the face heals and becomes more relaxed and healthier. Appearance improves to express a new, creative mind and self. Healing the face lags healing the brain and mind to some extent. Wrinkles take time to heal. A healed, or renewed, mind and face have more ability to heal the body.

Healing the body is similar to healing the mind. Envision billions and billions of stars in the sky. The universe and God are alive. The stars twinkle through the earth's atmosphere. Imagine billions of neurons firing, or twinkling, in the brain. The brain and mind are alive. Nerves are connected to the brain and muscles. Stressed nerves stress the brain, body, and muscles. Awakening and healing nerves heals the brain and body. Chiropractors can help do this.

Let's look at a specific healing example. I had realized for some time that my more athletic left hand and arm were weaker that my less used right hand and arm. I began thinking of ways to express this loss of strength, quickness, and ability to my chiropractor. I rotated my right hand and wrist back and forth as fast as I could. To my surprise, my left wrist and hand was not able to rotate back and forth nearly as fast.

My chiropractor said I have a nerve problem. With a diagram, she showed me that nerves in my left arm and wrist were connected to nerves near the middle of my back and just on the right side of the spinal column. With a vibrating devise, she activated nerves to the right of my spinal column. In the most related location on my back, the pain of the vibrating machine was excruciating. My chiropractor refers to this procedure as opening the nerves.

To my amazement, immediately after this procedure, I could rotate my left hand back and forth almost as quickly as I could my right hand. Additional sessions were needed to increase and maintain abilities of my left hand. With more strength in my left hand, maybe my tennis game will improve. After three months, my left hand and wrist have remained as active.

This energy release process from the back is similar to my psychiatric exercise and mental reconstruction energy release, healing processes. The mind, brain, and nerves, when forced to limits, release excess trauma energy, heal, and function as they should.

Stressful activities of the left arm had made nerves to the right of the spine rigid. Overstressed nerves and neural networks store excess trauma energy. Vibrations briefly stress nerves and connected neural networks to limits releasing their repressed, pent-up energy for them to become more resilient. Releasing repressed energy restores nerve and brain functions. With less disruptive energy, overstressed nerves heal and function more normally.

With excess energy, machines, nerves, and brains overact, and may self-destruct. Neurons and nerves, with excess energy, are painful when stimulated. With excess energy, nerves are stressed similarly to tiny string balloons being overly inflated. Chiropractic vibrations pop the "mini-balloon nerves" and release their energy. Nerves and neurons become more normal.

My right back sensitivity and pain was hidden until strong vibrations activated overstressed nerves. This alternative healing process required chiropractic care.

Once when stretching while playing tennis, my back began to hurt significantly. The next day my back seemed to be healed. I had had a slight joint displacement. Stretching beyond my normal limits caused a vertebra to slip back into its less energetic, normal position.

If we always do the same activities, abilities remain the same or degrade with age. Readers who receive chiropractic care and practice mental reconstruction will stay healthier and live longer. Healthy minds and bodies have more effective defenses against diseases, stress, and disorders. We should not under estimate the power of the positive, spiritual mind.

Everybody's crazy if not using our minds to help heal our brains and bodies. We have over eighty-five billion neurons for cultivating awareness and thinking, and for healing our brains and bodies.

Subconscious Processes

SIGMUND FREUD IS CREDITED WITH modeling the mind as consisting of two parts - subconscious and conscious. Subconscious processes include integrating sense data with related memories and iterating until processes last long enough with enough energy to converge to consciousness. Eighty-five billion neurons and billions of nerves construct the nervous system for developing subconscious and conscious processes. For each conscious idea we are aware of, there are millions of subconscious sub-ideas.

The brain is as active while sleeping as during waking. Subconscious and conscious activities are separated by electromagnetic frequency and energy levels. Electromagnetic resonances in the brain that break through energy and time barriers, construct consciousness. Many subconscious processes may have enough energy to create conscious but do not last long enough.

During sleep, the brain organizes, prioritizes, integrates, and tests short and long term recall. Sodium, potassium, and other chemicals, filtering through membranes, create neuron action potentials and activations. During waking, active neurons create waste or toxins. A vital subconscious function during sleep is clearing neurons of their toxins.

EMR resonances are fundamental tools that construct subconscious and conscious processes. Consciousness includes mental hologram scenarios, words, feelings, and emotions that last beyond energy and time thresholds. EMR resonances in all directions within the brain, interact with each other constructing higher dimensional mental holograms imprinting memory information on neural membranes.

Millions of subconscious resonances compete and integrate to develop long lasting, high-energy conscious resonances. Resonance energy levels from senses, memories, emotions, and pains determine which subconscious activities develop consciousness.

Years ago when highly manic, I briefly gained awareness of normally subconscious processes competing to become conscious. Unusual sensations, awareness, and thoughts occur when a manic mind is extended beyond limits and expecting death.

As energy diminishes from current memory and sense activations, and the next iteration of activations converges to create the next moment of consciousness. Thoughts are stimulated in many ways. All memories are subconscious unless currently conscious. Recollection of various memories may be easy, difficult, or impossible. Feelings and emotions are integrations of semi-conscious memories. An old friend may stimulate recollection of "impossible" memories.

We may follow every word on a radio. Radio content becomes semi-conscious if we concentrate on something else. Certain words, or an increase in volume, may again attract consciousness.

Subconscious processes occur faster than waking thoughts but may become conscious as dreams if abruptly awakened. Dream processes organize and integrate the previous day's experiences with related historical memories to form new memories. Memories are imprinted as higher dimensional holograms (created by complex EMR resonances) on neural membranes with synchronized resonances. New memories are organized and stored with related historical memories. Specific energy levels, frequency variations, and time stamps are compared.

Reconstructing the brain makes dreaming and other subconscious processes more realistic and energy efficient, with less distortion, when phasing out of sleep. Sporadic baby and childhood attentions and perceptions make early subconscious protocols inefficient. Brain activities and memories should become more organized with refined adult energy levels and frequencies.

Thought and memory are developed non-linear, iterative subconscious processes. We are vaguely aware of the numerous assumptions and decisions made by subconscious processes for constructing consciousness. Becoming more aware of inner assumptions and decisions improves mental abilities, and gives confidence in one's thinking.

Healthy subconscious processes promote strong, long-lasting resonances for developing confident conscious thoughts. Recursively, the conscious mind influences subconscious processes. Together, the brain and mind are an iterative feedback system. The subconscious mind is the foundation of conscious thoughts and abilities, but has difficulties understanding its own processes. We must stimulate subconscious processes to limits at times to help them understand and improve integrations for consciousness.

Let's make a model to distinguish between subconscious and consciousness processes. Subconscious processes occur faster than dreams and use less energy.

Suppose a potential conscious thought consists of ten related EMR hologram resonances or sub-ideas: "abcdefghij-KL." K is conscious evaluation parameter. K is an on-off switch. It has a zero beginning value and switches to "on" when consciousness is achieved. L places a time stamp when conscious thoughts are created, related to, and ordered with historical memories. Constructing consciousness is no simple process.

As subconscious resonances form and iterate, adding to and replacing earlier sub-ideas; some hologram sub-ideas become excited above subconscious energy limits: "abCdeFghiJ-KL." C, F, and J now have energy beyond sub-idea thresholds. However, the average energy of this subconscious model is not strong enough for an idea to become fully conscious. Conscious ideas must have a majority of sub-idea components above conscious sub-idea thresholds. Capital letters represent sub-ideas above threshold energies.

Upon further subconscious excitement and iterations, more sub-ideas exceed the sub-idea energy limit. If the majority of sub-idea hologram resonances are elevated above sub-idea thresholds, a subconscious process develops a conscious idea: "AbCDeFGhiJ-KL." If half of synchronized sub-ideas are below and half are above subconscious limits, we have feelings of almost having a conscious idea. Studying or emotional thinking in an area may escalate old memories into conscious ideas. A highly emotional "Flash" or my spiritual message, "Don't leave God out," may have constructed: an "ABCDEFGHIJ-KL" "Perfect" high-energy conscious spiritual idea.

Thousands, maybe millions, of stimulated sub-ideas may be needed to construct one conscious idea. The brain is complex. Simple models of constructing consciousness may help us recall better and think more precisely.

Processes that were once conscious fade into subconscious processes as their energy dissipates. New sense and related memory activities promote the next conscious awareness and idea. As an example, the mind concentrates on words to be typed. Finger and typing processes have become mostly subconscious. Our fingers know what to do. This is similar to not remembering steps when running, but remembering checkpoints along the path and the destination.

With learning and practice, routine activities are mostly performed subconsciously. With practice, we can become aware of and control more subconscious activities. Study and concentration make sub-ideas conscious and uncertain things certain. We improve memories.

Einstein must have had many uncertain sub-thoughts and thoughts while working to construct his famous relativity models that have given scientists a better understanding of the universe. To be creative, we need to accept uncertainties and relax to make them more certain. Study in fields of interest at your pace to become a more certain, creative person. Creative people are guided by imagination and not limited by past memories. Nurture your mind with patience creative ideas will evolve.

During twenty years of experimenting and writing, healing feelings have been pleasant and positive. I am still as excited as ever in practicing, and writing about, mental reconstruction. The integrated brain-mind is complex and requires stimulation and time to mentally reconstruct. Mental and spiritual rewards have been fascinating and wonderful.

Everybody's crazy if not believing that simple subconscious models can improve awareness, memory, consciousness, and control.

Dreams

"Here we are, all, by day; by night we're hurled by dreams, each by one, into a several world."

— WILLIAM BROWNE

"Some men see things as they are and say why. I dream of things that never were, and say why not."

— ROBERT KENNEDY

DREAM REASONING IS DIFFERENT AND less limited than in waking. We dream impossible dreams and accomplishments. Dreaming includes imagination to do things beyond the normal. In mania, we lose normal waking reasoning and believe we can do impossible dreams.

We are sometimes aware of three-dimensional holographic characters in dream scenarios. We see ourselves in dreams, as we believe others would observe us, or in ways, we wish to, or wish not to, be observed.

From my computer programming days, I believe dreaming must be an involved process with complex comparison criteria. Developing computer instructions for comparisons can be complex with various levels of precision. Dream holograms are processing tools for the subconscious mind. Dreaming is, and should be, a selfish inner process. Dreams organize recent memories with similar historical memories to prepare for future recall.

Dreams are often forgotten. Highly emotional dreams are more easily remembered primarily because we are often awakened by them. The energy of most dreams is too weak to be remembered. High-energy dream scenario resonances have energy levels near that of waking resonances and are more easily remembered.

Waking awareness is based upon reactions and expected reactions to environments for satisfying physical and mental needs that have built-up over short or longer periods of time. Sight allows us to see fast moving things, other physical reactions are slower.

Dreams progress exceedingly fast since they are free of waking physical restraints such as waiting for slow moving limbs. Neurons fire from one tenth to nearly one hundredth of a second. Billions of neurons in the brain fire within tenths of a second. Each firing neuron produces an electromagnetic spike profile that lasts around one thousandth of a second. Overlapping spikes from active neurons integrate to form continuous electromagnetic resonances, or mental hologram scenarios. Mental hologram or dream "awareness" may occur faster than one hundredth of a second in expected death flashes. The subconscious mind processes like lightening.

Dreams exaggerate images, emotions, and actions to enhance integration with related historical memories. Distortions are caused by comparisons of new activities and sensations with limiting memories. Comparisons include other actions and reactions we wished we had done.

The subconscious mind constantly compares current observations and activities to emotional and trauma limits for security alertness. Comparisons are performed quickly with low energy, unless threats are sensed at or near emotional or trauma limits, then waking energy rises quickly.

The dreaming brain includes greater freedoms and wider limits than when awake. We can fly in dreams mostly because we floated or "flew" in the womb. We do not need to be limited to normal perspectives in dreams, but we observe ourselves as a character in a play. We may even feel we experience God viewing ourselves in dreams. Hopefully, this is not true in nightmares.

Sigmund Freud developed psychoanalysis, for discovering meaning in dreams. In his view, most dreams relate to the previous day's activities. Dream images and backgrounds dramatize daily occurrences. Emotional events during the day are more prevalent in dreams.

Dream exaggerations may be due to integrating emotions and reactions with erratic emotional and trauma limits. Subconscious processes integrate, interpolate, and extrapolate to relate new memories to historical memories.

Freud claims we can always determine the meaning of dreams. He translated dream scenarios into meaningful thoughts.

Dr. Freud emphasized that recalling traumatic, repressed memories frees a person from adverse, ingrained effects. He refers to remembered dream scenarios as "manifest dreams." Manifest dreams consist of the visual images we become aware of. A part of Dr. Freud's dream analysis is discovering the origin of dream distortions. Dream-content or meaning is revealed through analog or flowing processes.

Let's be more precise in understanding dream distortions. The brain operates through electrical and electromagnetic properties. Sound, sight, and words must be converted to electromagnetic and chemical properties for creating cognition and long term memory. Dream image and scenario distortions are due to difficulties in integrating and encoding emotional sounds, feelings, smells, sight, reactions, and so on, into EMR mental holograms.

Dream encoding depends on genetic and learned inner technologies. The subconscious mind stores meaningful memory information with its coding technology. Recall activates encoded mental hologram memories from neural network membranes back into meaningful conscious resonances. Dream encoding is more complex than that of secret military encoding.

Sometimes we seem to struggle with difficult tasks in dreams for hours. We often awaken to find the task was unnecessary or nonsense. Our subconscious processes seemed to waste energy and emotion. However, there must be a future purpose. Scenario repetition in dreams may add importance to activities and make them easier to recall.

For possible experiments, neuroscientists may expose patients to various emotional videos, then abruptly wake them up after little sleep, to discuss dream distortions. This work may help scientists understand subconscious encoding.

I have experimented to develop awareness and control of dreams. This experiment is called, "Dreaming While Awake."

By lowering the energy of the brain, with eyes closed, I have been able to develop an image of a scary ole dream dragon. I void my mind of words, concentrate on the darkness, and wait. Eventually, I am aware of a big ornery ole dragon coming toward me. He is scary! He gets closer and closer; the dream disappears. I did not remain calm enough, and the dragon dream was gone in a poof. I did not give up. After much practice, I stayed calm so the dragon did not "poof" away so quickly. I finally mastered this task. What do you think happened?

One of two scenarios happens when the big, mean, ornery dragon comes to get me. He gets closer; I feel the closeness! I wince a little; he gets me! I experience a brief emotional black out. I am a goner for sure! But wait! The next thing I am aware of is sliding down the dragon's throat and laughing as the dream ends.

Why do I laugh? The reason is genetic. Throughout childhood, we were taught to avoid sharp teeth. Staying calm during the dream attack, tricked the subconscious mind and forced it to continue the scenario.

My dreaming mind placed me in the dragon's throat. I was no longer afraid because from childhood on I only feared sharp teeth and not of being swallowed. It was funny also because, as the dream image dissipated, I became aware, that a dream dragon cannot really eat me. Rapid releasing tensions added to the humor. This was one emotional dream option.

That brief dream blackout created an "unconscious trauma moment" and a trauma scar during this emotional dream. The subconscious mind momentarily did not know what to do. After composing, it had me sliding down the dragon's throat.

Oh, about the second scenario! This scenario is simpler. The big mean, ornery dragon comes to get me. He gets closer; I feel the closeness! I remain calm. The dragon suddenly looks sheepish, and gets smaller as he quickly turns and runs away. I have a small feeling of victory with this option.

I was unable to predict which scenario the dragon will choose. Slight differences in facial expression may affect my dragon scenarios. I have used patience, calmness and imagination to explore subconscious limits and make dreams conscious and somewhat controlled. Persistence and patience were needed to practice the dragon dreams.

The next dream experiment is "Asleepened:" Upon closing my eyes and becoming calm, I eventually produce a flowing kaleidoscope of colors in a similar manner to "Dreaming While Awake." Without thinking in words, I slowly increase the flow of the kaleidoscope colors. I calmly move my eyes from side to side with a slight flutter of my eyelids to imitate Rapid Eye Movement, REM. The right-brain becomes dominant. What do you think happens?

The whole body begins to twitch. I have tricked my subconscious mind, again, and am on a dreaming-waking boundary. Here's what happened. My eye movement, fluttering eyelids, and the flowing kaleidoscope of colors, simulated REM dreaming characteristics. I did the reverse of being abruptly awakened from sleep. I was abruptly "asleepened."

This reversal shows how words were developed for waking and sleeping states. While awake and stimulated for sleeping, I quickly fell asleep. Nods caused by muscles briefly relaxing awakened me, as I quickly fell asleep again. The quick repeated changes in state caused the twitches. I have experimented to discover limits between waking and dreaming. Dream scenarios become more like waking activities after mental restructuring.

From a neurological standpoint what happened? I'm awake and aminergic neurons within the brainstem are firing as they should. I create activities stimulating REM dreaming. Reticular formation neurons become excited and begin firing for dominance. Stimulated dream like activities briefly suppressed aminergic activities and the waking state. In brief sleep, muscles relax and nodding reactivates aminergic neurons for waking. There are emotional and energy limits between dreaming and waking.

Without an organized, complete set of emotional/trauma limits, thinking becomes faster and less controlled. Subconscious iterations lose resonances without converging to complete thoughts and reasonable decisions. When manic, with lost subconscious convergence, one believes any "dream." Thoughts are no longer compared to, and resolved with, historical memories to maintain consistency and sanity.

In my 1988 manic episode, in Phoenix, Arizona while consumed with inner thinking, I entered a place where people were dancing. To my amazement, I saw images of dancer's previous feet and leg images trailing their most recent feet and leg images as they fast-danced. The trailing, or "slowly" disappearing, images looked like images of fast moving cartoon characters.

I only worried briefly, and theorized that this strange sight was caused by my mental reconstruction. I did not think physical reality had changed. In this unusual experience, previous images lingered longer in my eyes and brain than usual. This unusual vision occurred only once. Vision inner timing and memory processes were reconstructing.

Normally vision images dissipate quickly as we become aware of the next images. However, watching a fast rotating wheel, we become aware of an "integrated blur" of the rotating wheel. We are aware that our eyes and mind of not able to see or understand reality.

Sleeping and dreaming processes are faster but less energetic than waking processes. Sleeping and dreaming organize memories with senses of timing, while rejuvenating body, mind, and soul.

Before sleeping, relax and broaden the forehead and face. Rub horizontally between the eyebrows. Forget the stresses of the day. Pleasant dreams may solve yesterday's problems. Tomorrow will be a successful day. A relaxed mind nourishes body, mind, and soul.

Trauma related activities stimulate bizarre disconnected dreams. Exaggerated movements and activities in dreams, and in plays, make activities more memorable.

When trauma energy is released, dreams become more connected and helpful to waking activities. In psychotherapy, one recalls trauma events to release excess neural energy and dissolve inner conflict and stress. Releasing neural emotional energy promotes mental healing. With psychiatric exercises and processes, trauma memories are not recalled when releasing emotional energy for promoting mental healing.

Waking mental processes continually prepare muscles to act and react. Activating muscles uses more energy than dreaming processes. Normally higher waking energy makes recalling lower energy dreams difficult. This is good. Otherwise, it would be difficult to distinguish between waking and dreaming activities.

Brain activities are electromagnetic and chemical and can act and react very quickly. Slower waking processes are needed for controlling slow moving bodies and limbs. Dreams need little control of muscles and the body so dream processing is much faster. Energy of most dreams is too weak to be remembered very long.

During manic episodes, mental energy is high and the mind is not as constrained by normal waking limits and is more creative. Creativeness is developed by subconscious dream processes that become conscious at times. However, discoveries are completed by methodical, conscious step by step processes and reasoning.

Dreaming characteristics become more active by high, manic energy. In mania, it is difficult at times to distinguish between waking and dreaming processes. Normal thinking occurs within certain mental energy levels. Our thinking limits are different depending upon emotional successes and failures; attitudes, feelings, truthfulness, and trauma memories. Insanity is often referred to as dreaming while awake. The brain manages thinking energy.

If we are able to lower the energy of the brain enough, minds feel free of body sensations and responsibilities. Awareness may briefly extend to experience a glimpse of God. After spiritual experiences, earthly activities seem less important

Dream scenarios have become more like waking experiences. If I dream of throwing a ball, my arm begins to move. The beginning of the arm movement awakens me without completing the motion. My mind has been my laboratory.

Analyzing dream content improves reasoning ability. Understanding our brains and minds is essential for staying healthy. We can improve our minds. The best perspective is to be comfortable with who and what we are. With patience and determination, we can become who we should be.

Continuous processes, such as thinking, must iterate and converge to meaningful, flowing conclusions. Subconscious, dream resonances must be reflected by some energy or emotional boundary or reasonable conclusions are not developed.

I consider a dream distortion model. Baby, and early trauma, memories were stored erratically and unorganized, but have formed thinking limits. Dreams include distorted images, misplaced characters, and unrealistic actions. In dreams, new memories are compared to earlier limiting high-energy trauma memories for constructing long-term memories. Current activity comparisons to early trauma memory limits cause dream distortions. Converging memory comparisons improve reasoning.

Threatening experiences and unresolved memories of conflicting experiences may extend the brain beyond mental limits and out of control. When we talk confidently we also have awareness of follow-up ideas related to current ideas being spoken. Without those semi-conscious related ideas we do not have confidence to continue speaking. The dreaming, subconscious mind builds those supporting relationships for us.

We have social communication limits that we cannot go beyond without offending others or getting in trouble. We normally know what and when to say things. Social communication limits are normally subconscious but current thoughts and related histories make communication limits become conscious. Even if we thought someone was fat, we would not say so.

The better we understand our dreams and subconscious processes the more we can improve thinking and speaking. When making subconscious processes conscious, we have more control over our minds.

I would be remiss if I did not mention that dreams had an important role in biblical stories. A well-known dream was pharaoh's dream about an oncoming famine that Joseph interpreted and helped Egypt prepare for. In biblical times, dreams were often demanding messages from God. Noah received a dream warning of a great flood and for him to build an Ark. These stories present spiritual communication miracles that changed history.

I have received messages from God differently. My inner message, "Don't Leave God Out," was surprising, demanding, and dramatic while awake and thinking of finishing a healing manuscript. Believing this message, I have written spiritually for twenty years.

Sometimes, when calm with daily thoughts, creative, spiritual ideas arise into consciousness as an unexpected shift of attention. There is an immediate sense that these creative ideas are better than I could have had on my own. These creative ideas are harmonics of my demanding message, "Don't Leave God Out."

Everybody's crazy believing we cannot do inner research to understand our dreams, and inner messages. Dreams have subconscious reasoning that is not limited by waking reason. Dream distortions encode emotional relevance between new and historical memories. Upon awakening or near awakening, mental energy may become strong enough and last long enough for subconscious dream processes to develop consciousness.

The Flash

—⌇—

*"Death be not proud, though some have called thee
Mighty and dreadful, for thou art not so . . ."*

— John Donne

It was the night before registration for spring quarter at Virginia Tech, in 1967, and there was a party in Lynchburg, Virginia. I attended this party and returned to my parents' home after midnight.

I needed to wake up at 5:00 A.M. and travel one hundred and twenty miles to Virginia Tech to register for classes. The alarm awakened me. I had never felt so tired but left for Blacksburg at 6:00 A.M.

After about an hour, I began nodding while driving. A dangerous thought occurred that I could rest while driving. Several times a nod would awaken me. My tiredness continued.

It happened! I fell asleep. My head nodded down and awakened me. As it recovered, immediate awareness swept throughout my being. My foot had relaxed on the accelerator. The speedometer was reading 80 mph and a tractor trailer was a few yards in front of me going 25 mph.

I started for the brake, but immediately knew it was useless. Reason lost all hope of life continuing. In absolute fear, my emotional life "flashed" before my eyes as I prepared to die. A thought flashed to use the center lane to pass and avoid the truck. My arm jerked the steering wheel to the left. Tires screeched. Someone else seemed to be driving. I was a concerned and displaced bystander in a tragic play. There were two lanes up and one lane down this mountain.

As my car entered the center lane, another semi-tractor was coming down in the opposite direction toward me. My hand jerked the steering wheel to the right. Tires screeched again. With God's help, I went between those two tractor-trailers going 80 miles per hour. The ordeal was over in a flash. In less than a second, I was trembling like a leaf. Time slowed back to normal. I survived.

Feelings linger to this day that no racecar driver could have avoided those trucks without God's help. I had no difficulty staying alert the rest of the trip. This story never ended. I continued to wonder about the high energy, lightning "Flash" of emotional memories that occurred when I had lost hope of life continuing.

Later during high manic excitement in 1977, I worked to relive and understand that high energy "Flash" and its detailed realistic visions. Highly emotional manic episodes approached mental energy levels of the "Flash" adding ability to recall the highly emotional "flash" visions. I recalled emotional visions that began with fear or elation. Amazingly, all emotional visions had successful endings. So many "Flash" visions were recalled so hurriedly and profoundly in such a short time.

The "Flash" was a spiritual miracle. I survived the impossible.

"The Flash" is an important concept for my dreaming and mind development theories. The speed of the visions was amazing. I estimate that in less than one tenth of a second, one hundred vivid memories of "significant emotional events" flashed through consciousness. "The flash" occurred between the time I was aware of the truck and before my hand jerked the steering wheel to the left.

I have roughly estimated the "apparent time span" of all visions. Each vision seemed to last for a virtual time of ten minutes or more. Some visions appeared to last for extremely long times. In one vision, I was a young child peering out the window waiting and waiting for dad to come home. I was elated when I saw his car turn into the driveway.

Assumptions are conservative. Let's perform a calculation for the "Apparent Time Span of all Visions" (ATSVs):

ATSVs = 10 minutes x 100 visions x 60 seconds/minute

ATSVs = 60,000 seconds, apparent time span of all flash visions

Let's look at the ratio of the apparent time span of all visions and the actual time:

Actual Time (AT = .1 seconds):

Ratio = ATSVs/AT = 60,000/0.1 = 600,000

This rough calculation estimates that during "the Flash" my mind processed close to one million times faster than normal. Thank God, we have capacity to think very fast in "expected" death situations. Subconscious processes momentarily became conscious.

"The Flash" was an amazingly fast awareness of subconscious processes activating emotional memories to construct an emotional life saving decision. Can we learn to become aware of very fast subconscious processes at other times for our benefit?

If God gave me "the Flash," I have little capacity to understand it. If the brain has the capacity to process so quickly, I may be able to develop some understanding for future benefit.

During "The Flash," visions appeared as the perfect recall of emotional events. There were no distortions. No judgments were made during the "Flash." Judgments take time. I was simply an observer. Emotional scenarios occurred so fast without me feeling emotions or needing to rush.

My body was frozen while my mind was an unbiased, nonjudgmental observer to a number of plays meant to provide a decision to avoid a certain death car tragedy. My subconscious mind selected the correct emotional memory scenarios that empowered my hand to avoid an "expected death" car crash. I only observed my hand jerking the steering wheel to the left. My guardian angels in heaven and God controlled my hand that saved my life that morning.

Here is one "Flash" scenario. At nine or ten years old some older boys and I were building a bridge over a gully in a cow pasture out of old boards and pine logs we had cut. I slipped and had the breath knocked out of me. I ran crying through the pasture and up the hill to see my mother.

As I was running up the hill and observing the grass in the "Flash," I was amazed at remembering detailed images. My normal view of grass might be as from an older TV. In the "Flash" I viewed the grass in High Definition. I met mother at the front door. She gave me a hug and I returned to building our important bridge. The mind awakens when highly emotional.

It seemed strange that the highly emotional visions did not directly relate to the immediate task of avoiding a devastating car crash. None of them had anything to do with driving a car. The connection only seemed to be that all visions were highly emotional that caused my immediate life-saving reaction.

Mindfulness is to live briefly in the flow of each idea and moment without judgment or feeling threatened. Similarly, in the "Flash," so many emotional scenarios flashed through my mind without sensing any judgments. I gained insight into emotional, subconscious decisions.

From the flash, it is apparent that timing within remembered scenarios is "encoded" within memory. Memories can be recalled in either "flash" or normal conscious rates.

Can humans learn to recall at fast speeds for benefit during normal times? "Subconsciously jerking the steering wheel to the left" occurred immediately at the end of "Flash" scenarios. I was saved by fear, panic, my Guardian Angels' and God's intervention. "The Flash" was my proof that God is always present.

Everybody's crazy not believing subconscious processes can become conscious at nearly one million times normal conscious speeds during expected death situations.

Miracles

MY INITIAL MIRACLE OCCURRED WHEN I first took communion at Ivy Hill United Methodist Church, in Amherst, Virginia. I was about twelve or thirteen years old and felt emotionally high for two weeks. I asked my mother several times if Ivy Hill communions used real wine. She always said no. I have wondered about this amazing feeling over the years.

My second miracle was being saved from the "expected death" car near accident by a flash of emotional memories. See "The Flash" essay.

In 1977, I experienced another miracle when deeply depressed, suicidal, and standing in my carport. I felt more like being dead than alive and smelled of death. The air was becoming murky and closing in. Scenery was becoming shadows and drifting into shadowy dimensions. Soon, I would not be able to breathe. My vision was only in black and white.

As the shadows darkened and came towards me, I was in a hopeless dimension. I experienced shadowy surroundings with feelings of not being present. I existed within nothingness. Unexpectedly, the murky darkness receded and I slowly recovered a frail body and mind. I survived and slowly regained fear of continuing a hopeless life.

During this time, I could not recall a single word or speak. I had surrendered life needing death. As in "The Flash," I had no idea why I was saved. My Guardian Angels or Jesus in heaven may have asked God to save my life for writing this book.

A few months later a psychiatrist prescribed Haldol. After a week or so, all muscles in my body began cramping. While lying on a gurney in Lynchburg General Hospital, feeling uncertain of life, I again sensed the world around me continuing without my physical presence. Spiritual reality became more important than physical reality.

I "envisioned" my beloved parents, aunts, and uncles, looking down upon me with great concern. Some were living and some had passed on. They came together, spiritually, to save my life. My saints "observed" my body, as my feeble mind, and soul, began to evaporate into spiritual dimensions. My Uncle Hugh, a neurosurgeon, guided my spiritual direction. My parents, aunts, and other uncles supported my Uncle Hugh by placing their hands on his shoulders.

They were aware my soul was leaving my body and were praying for my soul's return to my mind and body. My Guardian Angels' faith was strong. With my angels' faith and Jesus' love, God returned my soul for me to live another day. A "dream miracle" saved my life.

When working on a book in 2008 and in good mental health, I attended services at Timberlake United Methodist Church near Lynchburg, Virginia. I was listening to an interesting sermon and the most beautiful spiritual understanding exploded into my mind. My mouth dropped open. Instantly, I knew my spiritual purpose and my relationship with God.

I looked back toward the minister. My beautiful spiritual wisdom vanished in a flash. I had had a brief glimpse of "Heaven." I have worked to recall this wonderful wisdom without success. I believe we all have spiritual miracles to look forward to.

I have had so many unexpected creative ideas during writing of my books. Creative ideas seem new at first, but after a while seem to have been known for a long while. So many ideas were more creative than I could have dreamed of, without God's assistance. I thank God for creative ideas and miracles that have come to my mind like spiritual seeds or diamonds in the rough. I must refine them with wordless thinking into sparkling diamonds, and then assign words to them for communication. I can only translate God's perfect waves into fragile words.

Often there are no words to express new spiritual and inventive ideas. However, vague words must be selected or we must define new words as new circumstances occur and societies develop a need, for example – "Selfie." I define "SCAP" to describe the inner healing sensations I have experienced for twenty years during mental reconstruction.

Everybody's crazy not believing in miracles. Miracles give hope for a better tomorrow and bliss in afterlife. Miracles occur unexpectedly beyond understanding. Answered prayers are miracles. After "expecting death," living each day is a miracle to cherish. Anything that occurs beyond understanding is a miracle to me.

Operating the Brain

—⋙—

ENGINEERS DESIGN, BUILD, AND OPERATE complex machines. I have experience designing and operating nuclear reactors. This experience has given me awareness of the need to understand and control complex parameters. Before getting into the nuts and bolts of operating our brains and minds, let's begin with simpler models.

Before we flip a light switch on, we anticipate a light coming on and being able to see things in a previously dark room. We associate the light switch with the light. We seldom think of what went into making the light switch, the associated wires, designing and manufacturing the bulb, and generating the electricity. Similarly, we become aware of thoughts but seldom think about how they came about.

Most of us can ride or operate a bicycle. With the left foot on the ground, we place the right leg over the bike and the right foot on the raised right pedal. We push forward on the handlebars and push the right pedal forward and down. We then sit on the seat and place our left foot on the left pedal. We rotate the pedals forward with our legs, adjust the angle of the handlebars and front wheel, continue balancing our weight on the bike, and continuing to rotate the pedals forcing the bike forward.

With experience, operating a bicycle becomes easy and seems natural without requiring much of the above thought. When riding a bicycle, we are operating our legs, feet, arms, hands, eyes, backs, bodies, brains, and minds. Much of this becomes subconscious, or semiconscious.

When performing normal and routine activities, thinking is easy, requiring little conscious attention to detail. Our subconscious minds take over managing well-known, repetitive tasks not needing full conscious control over decisions. Difficult tasks become easier after we have learned and practiced solution steps. A concert pianist is able to play mostly semi-consciously.

Operating the brain includes the following tasks:
1. Vision is a complex process between environments, light sources, relative locations, eyes, nerves, brain, posture, and minds. Eyes and brains react to brightness, color, movement, lines, speed of changes, and various details. Different portions of vision are processed by different neural paths from the eyes to areas within the brain. The brain must synchronize and integrate light from different eye and neural paths to synchronize visual content for consciousness and reactions. Sound content must also be coordinated with visual content. The brain is not a simple machine, however, all we have to do is open their eyes and see, if there is a light source.
2. The brain monitors and controls "autonomous" organs including heart, lungs, "digestive track," and other internal organs. Breathing is semi-autonomous. To some extent, we can control breathing. Some can affect their heart rate.
3. The mind has semiconscious awareness of skin and posture. A touch makes an area of the skin become conscious. Severe pain within the body or brain dominates awareness. Other awareness lessens. Pain and threats activate conscious operating procedures to avoid or attack.
4. Humans must eat, breathe, avoid danger, and maintain secure environments most of the time to live and control their lives. Humans seek security, pleasure, love, sex, entertainment,

friends, and competition. Normal brains and minds develop versatile abilities to perform survival and pleasurable tasks.

5. Our subconscious operating protocol mechanism must analyze importance of sensed activities, retrieve, and compare related memories to choose reactions or actions. Senses and subconscious processes activate necessary memories. Integration of current sensed data and related memories forms consciousness for solving problems, and constructing and storing new memories.

6. With vision we become aware of familiar and unfamiliar shapes and images. The subconscious mind is always analyzing vision for familiar and unfamiliar friendly or threatening images. Memory is always a part of vision awareness and consciousness.

7. Views of mountains may seem both powerful and peaceful. We are aware of the energy needed to climb or descend mountains, and we semiconsciously feel the power. A holistic vision of mountains in the distance activates the more relaxing right-brain. In distant visions no quick action is usually required.

8. Our souls are our pathways to God. During difficult and near death occurrences, and during extremely low mental energy levels, the mind becomes more aware of the soul and spiritual communication paths. Many people and I have received unexpected messages from God and felt compelled to surrender to His suggestions or demands. God influences the operation of our brains and minds.

I have listed several tasks that our senses, brains, and minds perform subconsciously and consciously, which allow us to live our lives and prepare for spiritual existence after physical death. Our brains and minds have developed operating protocols for prioritizing various subconscious and conscious actions and reactions.

Brain priorities are based on energy levels. High energy threats require fast forceful actions. A gentle touch can activate feelings of love and closeness.

Emotions are semi-conscious integrated memory activations producing a general level of consciousness. Reactions to images or events causing sufficient energy resonances promote recall of memories with similar resonances. Similar awareness recalls similar memories. Association is a fundamental function of the brain and mind.

Protocols for vision are initiated by light activating electromagnetic resonances in the rods and cones of the eyes. Each rod and cone promotes a resonance within the brain. There are millions of resonances in the brain at any one time. Synchronized resonances lasting a sufficient period of time develop consciousness. As views change, resonances, vision, awareness, and cognition change. Resonances of all rods and cones integrate to form a smooth continuous vision.

We are aware of integrated rod and cone sensitivities, and we are not aware of individual rod or cone sensitivities. If I saw your face, I would see an integration of skin atoms and not individual atoms constructing your face. At a distance, I see an integrated shape and colors of a mountain not individual leaves.

Low energy, short lasting resonances are not strong enough or last long enough to develop consciousness. However, intermediate levels of mental energy may produce semi-conscious feelings and emotions.

Normal sensations and memories usually guide operation of the brain. Perceived threats develop high mental energy for initiating reactive operating procedures. With normal stimulation, mental operating procedures recall and activate the mechanisms to accomplish desired or needed tasks. The upper brain becomes more prominent in complex reasoning processes. Worry restricts thinking on the past and lessens current abilities.

If relaxed, mental operating mechanisms may integrate more memories, sensations, and contemplations for developing deeper philosophical and spiritual understanding and decisions. God's gift of free will can be very versatile.

The same sensations and events may be perceived as pleasant or unpleasant depending upon moods or distractions. Thinking of, and caring for, the needs of others require a more spiritual process than thinking of and caring for self.

Brains and minds have developed protocols for completing daily and difficult tasks. Mental operations use genetic and learned protocols. Operating our brains and minds at challenging levels builds confidence, joyful accomplishments, and promotes restful sleep. Challenges mean escape to some and attack to others.

I end with a reference to Einstein's general relativity. Size matters. Brian activities begin with the small neuron size level. Neuron relationships are very different from everyday sensed relationships. Scientists have not fully related small quantum models to large relativity models. They must be connected from little to big. The relationship is not linear.

Everybody's crazy to operate their discrete and holistic brains without having short and long term purposes and goals. We should ponder to understand and improve our mental operational processes and work to purge trauma effects that eclipse genetic and learned mental abilities.

Mind Section

Mind

—⚬—

"The mind is its own place, and in itself can make
a Heaven of Hell, a Hell of Heaven . . ."

— John Milton

Our minds are our most important possession. Without them, we are nothing. The brain creates the mind, and the mind recursively controls the brain. The brain and mind control the body. Nerves within the body provide feedback to the brain and mind. The brain is physical. The mind is spiritual. Thinking extends beyond the physical and into the spiritual. God has given us free wills and imagination we may choose to explore and develop.

We should understand our own minds and objectives before trying to understand others' thinking to assist in their objectives. If we have developed solid, reasonable, and spiritual principles, we will always be able to respond positively to others.

Understanding our principles and minds is necessary when praying or communicating with God. He receives our prayers and ideas, and communicates with us at unexpected times. Our souls are part of our minds and a small part of God. We communicate with God through our minds and souls.

A Philosophy of Healing and Spirituality

We take our minds for granted until we experience depression, bipolar disorder, or other adverse mental condition. Then, we realize that thinking can be much less than normal. Minds are horrible things to lose. We must take care of and protect our most valuable possession. Awareness and thinking are God's gifts.

We must frequently evaluate our habits and the habits of those, with whom we associate. If our habits are hurting our health and mental abilities, we should perform an inner study and make changes, or get help if needed.

If anyone is degrading us, we should confront them early on, mentally reduce their importance, avoid them, or get counseling. Allowing abuse and degradation to continue becomes more difficult to correct later on. This was my downfall. Persistent degradation is slow murder.

I know many unhappy divorcees. A trend has been that the less aggressive spouses have allowed aggressive spouses to continue gaining control. Once started, it is difficult to stop. The aggressive spouse continues to think he/she is entitled to get his/her way. He/she develops a feeling of ownership over the less aggressive spouse. After being degraded without counseling, the abused spouse either gets a divorce or acquiesces to live an irrational, unhappy life.

Society, parents, and teachers should be aware of, and prevent, bullying. No one should make anyone feel inferior. Bullying is ignored by inattentive parents. If bullied or mistreated, we should make diverse new friends so no one person or group can dominate, degrade, or isolate us. Never let a bullying spouse isolate you from your friends and family.

Ancestor experiences and memories, preserved through genetics, have given our minds and bodies more intelligence than we will acquire during our lifetimes. Our minds and bodies are integrals of our and our ancestors' experiences. Genetics are the blueprints that define us as humans with human characteristics, thoughts, and needs. We don't think like cats.

Memories are divided into two parts. The first is short term for up to an hour. The second is long-term memory believed to be embedded in brain cell RNA or ribonucleic acid. I theorize that long-term memories are stored as "coded" protein structures within cell membranes.

EMR resonances and mental holograms integrate to create memory and cognizance. Memory is stored within neural membrane RNA as higher spiritual dimensions. Synchronized, coherent electromagnetic resonances write to and read from neural membrane RNA similar to writing to and reading from computer CDs. Models help us understand how the brain constructs the mind and how the brain and mind work together.

Mental freedoms extend beyond spatial and time constraints. We can think of our cat in one moment and the Milky Way the next moment. Minds are spiritual. Light cannot travel that fast. Spiritual waves can.

Rationally organizing helter-skelter baby experiences into memory is impossible for young brains. Early memories must be stored by refined energy levels. Adult memories are stored both by energy levels and relationship criteria important to life's purposes and survival. The brain needs to be reconstructed by briefly experiencing memories at emotional limits. After mental reconstruction, recall becomes easier and quicker.

The mind is constructed by controlling EMR through neuron activations. Neuron activated EMR profiles and frequencies have huge variations for imprinting terabytes of data on neuron membrane RNA. Our brains can store as much information as can the internet. Humans consciously integrate and recall only a very small part of sub-thought information daily.

Mental processes and memories are more holistic and confident when EMR resonances are constructed by greater numbers of neuron activations. The goal is for the brain to work as a whole. Traumas compartmentalize brain functions.

Near two-dimensional commercial hologram surfaces create three-dimensional images. Complex three-dimensional arrays of neural networks store higher-dimensional images and memories. Memory holograms are stamped with emotional dimensions, orientations, relative times, etc.

Eighty-five billion neurons fire with flowing synchronization constructing billions of higher-dimensional hologram resonances. Mental hologram scenarios are the brain's processing tools. We are aware of millions of details in our dreams and vision. Each rod or cone provides one discrete detail within vision.

Two convergent, coherent light sources focused on photographic paper from different angles create commercial three-dimensional holograms. The brain has billions of electromagnetic sources absorbed by brain cell membranes from many angles. Some EMR is coherent and has more influence in imprinting higher-dimensional mental holograms on neural membranes.

Mental functions may be divided into two parts:

1. Physical sensing and reactive processing, which controls routine thoughts and actions,
2. Analytical processing and reasoning, which develops complex ideas, solutions, and skills.

With mental reconstruction, analytical processing improves. Motor-neural networks are re-grown and reprogrammed for improving body control and versatile reactions.

Nerve intensities affect response and memory recall priorities. Hitting a finger with a hammer creates a very high-energy resonance in affected nerves and related areas within the brain. Our minds temporarily lose awareness of other sensations and thoughts. Reactive thinking overpowers creative thinking.

My traumatic expected death awareness from an expected car crash caused "The Flash" awareness of high-energy trauma, emotional memories. "Flash dreamlike" scenario awareness did not include reasoning and relationship dimensions as in normal memories. This explains the lightning fast recall. In this instance, normal energy memories were bypassed and not recalled. Fast high-energy memories prepared the mind and body to react. The lifesaving decision to "whip" the steering wheel to the left was made by recalling and integrating many emotional "Flash" memories.

I estimate it takes one thousand times more energy to say a word than it does to think of that word. In a similar manner, it takes one thousandth as much energy to process a thought subconsciously rather than consciously. We should consciously develop input, but solve problems subconsciously when sleeping, and later consciously review results. It is the energy-efficient thing to do!

Our eyes fail to perceive images that are too quick or stimuli are too weak. Consciousness is not developed. Our conscious resonance limit is not met. Let's distinguish between conscious and subconscious thinking.

Our subconscious minds are unbelievably powerful. We see a view of the mountains. Fifty years later, we recognize the same view. Stimulation activates memory that lets us recognize things once long forgotten.

Subconscious processes search for completion in everything we do. We talk and write in complete sentences. Meeting daily and long range goals gives us feelings of completion. Longer range goals give higher feeling of completion. We become more successful if we learn to logically break long range goals into attainable shorter range goals. By doing this, we have feelings of successfully attaining many goals. If not organized, we have uncertainties without feelings of completion and accomplishment. We may study, exercise, and practice for years to become a champion at some intellectual or athletic pursuit.

Integrated neuron resonances overlay EMR energy on receptive neural membranes until mental holograms become bright creating conscious. Mental holograms must develop a level of completion to meet conscious criteria. Imagination is constructed by the brain and mind integrating, comparing, analyzing, and extrapolating mental holograms to form consciousness.

We like to share ideas with those who accept or support our ideas and activities. There is comfort in repeating and sharing uplifting songs, rhymes, and spiritual rituals. Recitals give us comfort and confidence as we get older. We like to be part of important ideas and activities by repeating them with like-minded believers.

Most of us need to believe in something greater than ourselves. As young children, we grew up believing our parents were our protectors and greater than ourselves. Some of us believe.

God is omnipotent and must be believed in. However, we must be smart and defend ourselves against repetitious and false brainwashing chants. We must learn from others but develop our own reasoning and principles.

Subconscious processes must iterate and converge to form logical conscious ideas. Mental limits define iterative process for mental convergence. Reasoning would consider the entire universe in making decisions, without boundaries or limits. As an example, I want to get the mail. My mind iterates and concludes that I must walk to the mailbox and then pick-up the mail with my hand.

Engineering systems and brains self-destruct when operated beyond design limits. A reconstructed mind accepts wider normal and emotional inputs, and develops more logical, imaginative and decisive conclusions.

Mental holograms, alphabets, and words are building blocks for thoughts and language. Understanding inner processes and writing ideas down improve thoughts and language. Thoughts are initially constructed in "picture or wave language." We must iterate to translate our "picture or wave" thoughts into our best organized words, sentences, and paragraphs.

We may study and mentally reconstruct to improve reasoning abilities. Emotional writing is improved by studying brilliant books and briefly experimenting at mental limits. Analyzing inner thoughts and scenarios enhances reasoning, predictability, and writing. Briefly forcing minds to limits extends imagination to spiritual levels.

Persistent stress overshadows healing processes. We must reduce stress for effective mental healing.

We must build wider mental resonances for more inclusive reasoning and spiritual decision-making. Be creative in lowering stress levels. We are responsible for our own successes and happiness. We must think of and do things that make us and others happy to live long, happy lives.

The limbic system is the brain's rough, fast response system. It has limited reactions to threats. Normal upper brain reasoning is too slow for immediate threats. Higher cerebrum processes relate incoming stimuli to historical memories to develop in-depth thoughts and responses. During normal daily low energy interactions limbic system processing is less active.

The mind consists of synchronized electromagnetic radiation resonances produced by neuron spikes and cultured by neurotransmitters, emotional limits, neuron membranes, and the soul. The mind has an integrated spiritual component. From human prospective, God's spiritual energy and information travels "infinitely" fast. His knowledge of the universe is complete and up to date at each point in the universe. We can pray anywhere.

Human minds send and receive spiritual information through electromagnetic and dimensionless spiritual waves. Mental and spiritual waves synchronize for communicating with God. Spiritual waves within the soul culture spiritual thoughts.

Light consistently transmits truthful information from its sources. In normal brains, inner mental reflections are truthful, detailed, and spiritual. EMR reflections and resonances, throughout the brain, are more important in developing consciousness than all original individual neuron EMR sources. The sum is greater than all of its parts. Inner reflections add mental and spiritual meaning.

Human wisdom includes genetic influences, subconscious activities, memories of emotional and normal experiences, and innate spiritual dimensions. We have precursors to wisdom saved within neural membranes. Neuron generated EMR must interact with neural membranes to construct consciousness. We and the universe exist only due to God's consciousness.

If we understand our minds in greater depth, we will have greater genetic and spiritual sensitivities. People will be more reasonable toward one another. People will like themselves more and think more holistically about others. There will be fewer wars.

Everybody's crazy believing their brains and minds will always iterate and converge to meaningful conclusions. Each of us has some level of disorders. We must work to complete ideas and goals to stay mentally healthy. This work has given feelings of completion.

Memory

MEMORIES ARE THE ESSENCE OF whom we have been and who we are. They contain internal and external histories of our lives, who we've connected with, who we've helped, and who has helped us. Memory is necessary to get to work and do our jobs. Losing memory means losing ability to live independently and do daily tasks. Memory and cognition too often decline with age.

Some memory loss may be normal and not signs of dementia. We should remain active, exercise, accept mental challenges, and mentally reconstruct to enhance memory and lives.

A healthy brain and resilient memory is nurtured by staying physically and mentally active. Walking is a healthy exercise. Reading and writing keeps the mind active. Making predictions with follow-up refinements builds confidence in judgments. However, we must be careful. Judging is based upon previous experience and can be good or evil.

Discussion groups of interest can be healthy mind exercises. The Harvard Medical School has a program to maintain healthy senior memories.

Mental reconstruction is meant to organize subconscious and dream processes for improving memory and cognition. Right-brain and left-brain dominance exercises are meant to synchronize detailed and holistic memories for greater completeness in thought development.

If afraid of forgetting an idea or how to do a needed task, we write a note. We feel sure we will remember to read the note when needed, and recognize and understand the letters and words we have written. Note-taking and other mnemonic tools increase probability of doing needed tasks. We seldom think of assumptions we make.

Does God have memory or always have complete awareness of all activities in the universe over its fourteen billion year history? Or does He have perfect recall? God must have total awareness and understanding of, or be able to recall, all historical activities in the universe for guiding the universe into the future. Without memory, humans have no basis for planning the future.

Humans have greater ability to recall emotional events in our lives. I remember kicking that fifty-yard punt over and over. Recalling good memories is pleasing and relaxing. Healthy minds retain all memories but have hierarchical recall abilities. Talking with an old high school friend may stimulate long forgotten memories that could not have been recalled on one's own. We more easily remember emotional events, which give us feelings of completeness or incompleteness.

We develop mental health warning signs if we recall negative emotional events, and poor decisions too often. We must work to understand the circumstances of these events. Make judgments on why and how they occurred, accept reality, and avoid those circumstances in the future. We must build up defenses early against physical and mental threats. Knowledge is a wonderful for mental healing.

In some way, our college football team winning a game gives us a feeling of completion. Even though we may have graduated fifty years ago, we still feel part of our university and its football program. Parents have a sense of completion when their children attain important goals.

God exists in higher dimensions beyond human vision but not imagination. In difficult times we become more aware of spiritual dimensions and God's presence. What good is awareness if we cannot use it for our or others benefits? We remember our emotional

Memory

spiritual communications. Spiritual awareness gives deep feelings of completeness.

Everybody's crazy not understanding the value of maintaining good memory for reasoning about past, current and future activities. Memory is the foundation of thinking and reasoning. Without memory we can do nothing. Everybody's crazy thinking they sense and understand all of Gods dimensions and abilities. In spiritual dimensions, God is very small and very large.

Trauma

When a fast-acting high-energy trauma is sensed, the brain does not have time to react normally. The reactive limbic system processes highly energetic information and restricts it from damaging the fragile upper brain. The upper brain experiences an information blackout causing a moment of insanity, of not knowing what to do. Sporadic trauma scar activations adversely affect the brain and mind over a lifetime, unless energy is purged through psychotherapy or mental reconstruction.

I distinguish between emotional and trauma events. We can increase control over emotions with emotionally limiting experiments and practices. Subconscious processes react to quick and overpowering events before events become conscious. Events are emotional as long as fast subconscious processes have hope of successful coping reactions. We expand emotional limits to react with more reason and less emotion to challenging events.

If fast subconscious processes have no hope of coping, consciousness reactions are not initiated. There is a brief blackout. A trauma has occurred and a high energy limiting trauma scar has been ingrained within the brain. Trauma limits are difficult to expand. However, similar repeated events may produce only emotions if subconscious processes adapt.

Neck, jaw, and facial muscles tense when reacting to trauma. These reactions are important in understanding reasons for psychiatric "neck" exercises in purging trauma scar effects.

Fast-response neural networks within the neck, throat, brainstem, and limbic system absorb extreme trauma energy from sense nerves. If the energy of a stimulus is beyond emotional limits, the brainstem and limbic system do not forward high-energy trauma information to the upper brain.

When reacting to elevated nerve frequencies, trauma memories are stored within neural membrane resonances in the limbic system. Afflicted neural networks are ingrained with trauma scars that fester within the brain, causing sporadic unsynchronized, unproductive influence on normal brain activities.

Failed reasoning during a brief mental blackout, in stressful times, ingrains a "failure" trauma scar within the cerebrum. Desensitizing therapy may reduce effects and uncertainties of reasoning traumas. Studying and practicing responses to similar scenarios reduces emotional effects of reasoning failures.

Anyone may become overstressed from trauma or persistent degradation, with loss of control, depression, or bipolar disorder. Everyone has their breaking point in severe circumstances. My work builds resistance to stress, depression, and manic episodes.

Energetic conflicting body and verbal languages ingrain trauma scars in innocent victims. Body language is interpreted by the analog right-brain and words are interpreted by the discrete processing left-brain. Quick conflicting gestures and language confuse. Words may be positive and body language negative. Conflict between left and right-brain interpretations develop reasoning trauma scars.

Perpetrators control with mixed and false messages. Some perpetrators may not recognize adverse effects victims incur. They are simply mimicking parents' behaviors. Others become addicted to power by confusing and degrading victims. Power corrupts.

The two conflicting languages are not understood causing feelings of confusion and uncertainty. These conflicts are difficult to counter. Simply saying, "Stop those mixed messages," does not work. The psychological power of conflicting messages is too ingrained.

One might respond, "Your verbal and body languages give mixed messages. Sending mixed messages is a form of lying." "I recognize and will protest your conflicting verbal and body languages until you make them consistent." Mimicking or exaggerating their verbal and body language may cause perpetrators to desist. In any event, recognizing the conflict and letting the perpetrator know you recognize the conflict is healing for you. If continued, over time, mixed messages can be devastating to victims who do not understand the conflict.

I have little respect for anyone who intentionally confuses others, including mixed message perpetrators." We must defend ourselves from traumatizing mixed, controlling, and degrading messages.

Impulsive controllers are as dangerous to victim's mental health as are conflicting body and verbal language perpetrators. Conversations and tasks may seem normal. Then, unexpectedly, an impulsive, controlling voice degrades and demands unsuspecting victims do his or her bidding.

Impulsive commands are degrading, embarrassing and often perpetrated in front of others, adding to embarrassment. Impulsive commands are so quick and demeaning that they are difficult to counter. Perpetrators pounce at unexpected, vulnerable times and places.

Victims usually humbly comply. If this behavior continues, it becomes devastating to the victim's health. Perpetrators get brief rushes of control and power with unexpected, forceful commands.

The solution is to prepare for, immediately question and reject impulsive commands. "What did you say to me? Why did you say that? You will not use that tone of voice with me." Confronting is more effective than just walking away. The perpetrator is caught red-handed. Things will get better.

Perpetrators do not mind embarrassing you. Reject abusive, impulsive commands early on. Impulsive behavior is bullying. Abuse must stop. Victims must reason through abusive behavior and reduce importance of impulsive bullies. One might say, "My spouse has this "impulsive controlling voice that is hurtful to me."

Early trauma scars were caused by high-energy reasoning insanities. Impulsive commands activate high-energy repressed memories that do not synchronize with reasonable responses. Trauma scars are similar to cancers not synchronizing with normal body activities. We need to reduce energy of trauma memories so they will synchronize with normal memories and activities.

Cancer cells do not support normal body functions. Without coordinated purpose their actions becomes to survive and multiply by attacking normal body cells. In nature, simple cells only reflect and reproduce themselves. Cancer cells attack normal cells, which are sensed as having different reflections and purpose. Normal cells reflect each other supporting mutual growth. The importance of building and maintaining a healthy body is more important than the well-being of individual cells. Normal cells have a holistic purpose to construct and be part of an overall healthy body.

Persistent stress lessens the immune system's ability to eradicate cancer cells. If the mind and body are less certain of overall goals, individual cells are less certain of goals.

Impulsive controllers cause stress, mental pain, heart attacks, cancers, and slow murders. If adverse behaviors continue, perpetrators are not worth your time and pain. Be bold, reject bullying behaviors early on. We must make bold actions if persistently abused. I wish I had done so early in my dysfunctional marriage. It would have prevented my bipolar disorder, and possibly nurtured a reasonable marriage. Be proactive! The time is now!

Families must reflect harmony to each member. However, diversity is a wonderful experiment. I like and respect peoples, of all races, who treat me well. I do not like relatives who steal from, degrade me, or vandalize my property.

Everybody's crazy believing they are not adversely influenced by childhood traumas and brainwashing effects. Psychiatry, alternative mental reconstruction exercises, and, possibly, other alternative methods reduce negative effects of localized neural trauma scars within the brain. Everybody's crazy staying in degrading, abusive marriages or relationships. No one should allow continued abuse. Correct abusive relationships or get away as soon as practicable.

Depression

THE BASIC STRUCTURE OF THE conscious mind is to think of, predict, prepare for, and execute future activities. Even thinking about the past is a future activity. If seriously considering suicide, the mind is thinking of ending its future. Subconscious processes slow down to survival mode. Thoughts are no longer human thoughts. Suicide is "unthinkable" but occurs when there is no inner peace and joy, and there is no hope of pain or life getting better.

During my only depression in 1977, I feared and expected imminent death, but also experienced an unusual spiritual presence. God had not given up on me. Suffering and spiritual sensitivities are intertwined. Mental abilities lessened; spiritual awareness increased.

Suffering and depression may have spiritual benefit. Jesus' suffering and death created hope of everlasting life for those believing in Him. Our own suffering may become spiritually helpful to ourselves, those who believe in us, and God. Mental uncertainties and suffering open mind and soul sensitivity to God's spiritual waves that cannot always be interpreted into words. Those who have suffered earlier in life tend to be more spiritual in supporting and giving to others.

If someone shows persistent signs of depression, parents, employers, churches, and spouses should help him understand root causes. So much pain and suffering can be avoided with early understanding. Often the cause of depression is deeply repressed. The patient may be too embarrassed to admit he let gradual emotional degradation cause his depression. If there is no injury or sickness, emotional relationships are the cause. Too often, depression is caused by an abusive spouse, parent, or boss.

I did not receive psychiatric care until I was highly manic and out of control. I do not recall a single psychiatrist asking the cause of my depression and mania. No minister or church leader asked why I was depressed even though I had severe depression symptoms.

Church leaders should be trained to help the depressed understand and express causes of depression. Psychiatrists should continue to probe patients' minds until they both recognize and understand the cause of depression, or stress disorders. That should be the main goal after stabilizing patients. Cause of my depression was frequent deceit and degradation by my former wife.

During depression, physically weak, and mentally limited, I sensed a vague holistic, or general, spiritual purpose. I continued loving my children and parents. Their love kept me alive.

Suffering mental uncertainties and pain while locked in a psychiatric ward, I began frantically writing to understand my distraught mind and save sanity. While confined in this prison, I experienced a strong feeling that babies receive complete spiritual wisdom from God upon conception. At this time, I sensed movement in my brain and fundamental changes within my mind. Shortly afterward, I felt a miracle was needed for a new successful, spiritual life.

I mostly wrote about my clinical depression. I learned that the medical community divides depression into two categories:

1. Reactive Depression is normal profound depression. Temperament becomes negative about self and the future. Emotions vary from lack of responsiveness to profound despair, and even thoughts of suicide. Reactive depression slowly returns to normal moods and thinking without medication.
2. Clinical or Unipolar Depression is a neurological disorder involving an imbalance of neurotransmitters within the brain.

Thinking becomes slow and sometimes painful. The clinically depressed may become so preoccupied over negative thoughts, occurrences, or losses that they appear lifeless without purpose. Extreme emotional lows and lack of attention to family and others are effects of preoccupation over failures, losses, or pain. The clinically depressed experience repetitive thinking and persistent worry without real attempts of solving problems. Solutions seem impossible to the point the afflicted has given up solving difficulties or adjusting to losses for restoring self-esteem.

In depression, the brain and mind linger in abnormal, negative, and sometimes self-destructive moods. Depression is caused by loss of self-esteem, health, a loved one, or exposure to persistent physical or mental abuse. Life becomes confused, hopeless, and dreaded without "any possible" way out. Wherever a depressed person happens to be, never seems to be the right place. Mental pain follows everywhere. After several months, my depression erupted into bipolar disorder.

Depression may be caused by suppressing anger over long periods of time. I continued to praise my former wife and she continued to degrade me. I repressed inner anger for letting myself live such a stupid life. Over time life had less purpose and made less sense.

Praising people was all I knew, and needed, to live in a wonderful country community. My parents, relatives, and friends were always positive to everyone. Continuing to praise someone close to you who is constantly degrading you can be deadly for you.

I knew my former wife's degradation was untrue and dumb, but persistence took its toll. From her parent's alcoholic background, she felt she had to act and "be" superior. Putting down those close to you is the easiest way to act and "eventually be" superior. It happens too often. Such persons are emotionally and spiritually inferior.

Repressed anger turned into depression for letting abuse continue for five years. At the time I did not know how to deal with or correct negative behavior. I was hiding a stupid married life from others. I had been taught not to complain. My former wife was an expert in pushing for control and discontinuing when I began to react. Our marriage was a fraud from the beginning. Her behavior seemed to be of having been sexually abused.

Janet Geringer Woititz's book, *Adult Children of Alcoholics*, 1983, explained my former wife's behavior. I wished I would have read it early in the marriage. With understanding, things could have been better.

Due to childhood abuse by my older brother, I had learned to accept abuse. In the beginning, my former wife's abuse did not seem so unusual. It gradually became more controlling.

I share blame for my disorder. I never confronted my former wife early on for her behavior. It took years after the marriage to understand her behavior. Her deranged mother had constantly criticized and degraded her daughters. My former wife acted to ensure that no one would abuse her. Life was abuse or be abused. What a dumb life we lived?

People may be good to some and destructive to others. My former wife was good to the children, neighbors, and to her coworkers.

In our only psychiatrist's session together, my former wife realized how she had shocked the psychiatrist, and refused to attend future sessions. We should not underestimate damage caused by childhood abuse.

I began wanting a divorce only weeks after marriage; however, I thought a divorce would greatly disappoint my mother. There seemed to be no way out. I was trapped.

In depression "impossible" situations and problems were repeatedly recalled without organizing efforts toward solutions. Chemical changes within the brain slowed thinking. In embarrassment, I retreated from the outside world into a hell of recurring negative, painful thoughts. At one point, I rather had been a fly I saw flying around. The fly seemed to have a purpose. Suicide became appealing to escape the mental pain, and embarrassment of feeling and being less than human.

In the depths of depression, I could not recall a single word or speak. I tried but could not simile. I had lost control of smile muscles. For a few days, suicide was my only pleasant thought.

In my only depression, I was sure I had severe brain damage and would never recover abilities. I had reoccurring thoughts that life is not worth living as a mentally damaged person.

With low mental energy, left-brain reasoning is overpowered by general right-brain negative feelings and emotions. Right-brain rhythm and harmony is lost, but occasionally having glimpses of "Big Picture thinking" and spiritual presence.

At times, caregivers should mention examples of others who have successfully recovered from severe depression. Realistically describe healing from depression as a slow systematic process including re-adjusting self-image and ego for faster healing. Tell patients that depressed minds heal slowly but can fully recover.

Without anticipating any future, I would walk down a hall and freeze. There was no purpose to think, move, or do anything.

The most frustrating aspect of depression is "circular thinking." Worry does not allow sleep to release tensions and renew energy. Without sleeping for weeks, thinking was never conclusive. Negative memories just fly round and round since reasoning limits have been overridden.

Both relaxed and high energy moods activate right-brain dominance for long-range, rhythmic, and holistic thinking. The clinically depressed and manic are drawn to holistic, or "big picture" views without thinking through details. Persistent right-brain dominance precludes detailed left-brain problem solving. Holistic right-brain thinking often becomes spiritual. Healing needs detailed and holistic processes. We need a well coordinated brain and mind.

Mental control can be improved by practicing switching between left- and right-brain dominance using tools such as Holusions. See my "Mental Holograms" essay. This activity releases stress and builds awareness of left or right-brain dominance. Thinking easily bounces between the left and right brains during normal activities.

Family, friends, and caretakers should talk about good, things the depressed has done in the past and realistic opportunities in the future. Show interest in things the afflicted has successfully done in the past to help rebuild self-worth.

Healing is enhanced by encouraging simple step-by-step processes. Caretakers should encourage the depressed to do left-brain thinking by having him do routine chores. Setting the table and folding clothes are simple left brain tasks. Give the depressed an opportunity to help. Don't push. It may hurt the depressed to think or do anything. Even folding clothes may be a challenge.

Humor is never advised, as the depressed will take humor negatively. Depressed minds are predisposed to negative thinking.

Helping the depressed be active heals by redirecting his mind away from hurtful circular thinking. Never push, but leave simple things for the depressed to work on if he chooses to do so.

The depressed needs simple successes to begin thinking positively. Show an interest in him. Be alert, be careful not to bore or insult a depressed patient's intelligence. With your help, the depressed will recover faster. Remember! He will be smart again.

It is important to have counseling together. You both may be able to correct simple things that make both of your lives better.

When someone is depressed or bipolar, mental health providers and ministers must work to understand causes. They should help the afflicted understand and explain root causes. Perpetrators may deny responsibility for causing depression and bipolar disorder. If a spouse is depressed or bipolar, joint counseling is necessary. Marriage means unity for mutual sanity.

Psychiatrists must determine causes of depression and suggest that involved spouses, parents, children, or others be part of counseling sessions. If they will not join, providers must help patients become emotionally separated from perpetrators. It may be a life or death decision. There are too many suicides. I praise the Lord for my parents and Dr. Gene Good in supporting my recovery.

Police should be patient and try to understand why a bipolar person is out of control. They should understand that perpetrators will not admit their involvement in causing another's bipolar disorder. They will be indignant about the out of control person's behavior. Something has caused stress and bipolar disorder. Decisions must be made to protect bipolar patients from abusers. A bipolar victim has been overstressed by persistent abuse or stress circumstances.

A goal of this book is help readers avoid depression, bipolar disorder, and other disorders.

Everybody's crazy letting abusive "significant" others cause depression and disorders. When possible walk away from, reflect and describe effects of, and reject, abusive behaviors early on. Emotionally disengage. Get counseling.

Bipolar Disorder

—ɯ—

A PRIMARY CAUSE OF BIPOLAR disorder is persistent stress and feeling there is no way out. Feeling "trapped" in a degrading job or marriage causes stress, and bipolar disorder to some. Uncertainties overshadow certainties. Uncertainties of not knowing what to do or say cause stress. The mind and body are stressed. Thoughts and responses no longer feel "complete or good enough!"

Bipolar disorder may follow clinical depression and may include thoughts of suicide. Without hope of life continuing, spiritual thoughts emerge. In the depths of depression and the beginning of bipolar disorder thinking was erratic. I had a strong thought: "No human could endure such pain and live. I must not be human."

I was somewhat confident at the beginning of marriage but not prepared for my wife's subtle, impulsive degradations. In 1977 my depression erupted into bipolar disorder, dreaming while awake, and grasping for reality. Persistent degradation destroyed a fairly confident person.

My mind became overactive to find solutions to negative ideas floating in and out of consciousness. In the jump from depression to mania, I briefly became Jesus, but could not trust my own mind. Very quickly I knew I did not have Jesus' love or healing skills. I became a poor confused, sick person again.

Insane thoughts went from suicide to dreams of a Nobel Prize. The manic mind has huge mood and expectation swings. After severe difficulties, we learn our minds are our most important possession. My mind has been my personal laboratory since 1977.

In severe depression, mental limits are breached no longer providing reflections for subconscious convergence to complete thoughts to make intelligent decisions. Beyond limits, minds and machines lose control and may self-destruct.

Persistent stress causes uncertain and disruptive subconscious processes. Mental insecurities caused fast thinking in hopes of recovering sanity. Fast thinking overstresses the brain causing a "chemical imbalance." Abnormal neurotransmitter concentrations cause mood and thinking dysfunctions.

Fast thinking evolves into "big picture or holistic" thinking with little left-brain dominance for detailed every-day thinking. Mania may include irrational dream processes and characteristics.

In the beginning, some manic episodes are degrading and scary with loss of control. However, as some episodes progress, the mind becomes hardened and fearless in desperate efforts to save sanity by racing to various dream goals. It is a tragedy not knowing if one's own thoughts are rational, and relatable to self and those present.

Psychiatrists prescribe medications to correct neurotransmitter imbalances and to reduce mood swings and energy levels within the brain. My mental reconstruction exercises and processes purge excess energy from traumatized neural networks. The brain is easier to control with less energy. It iterates faster to logical relationships and conclusions, with less energy.

High-energy sporadic neural activations interfere with normal brain resonances. Normal brain processes must increase overall energy to overcome effects of sporadic trauma effects. The ability to relax is lessened. The brain and mind remain tense.

Normal neurons produce rather consistent firings to synchronize with other neurons. The brain must increase normal synchronized activations to overcome sporadic traumatized distortions.

Muscle and brain abilities grow when briefly stressed to limits. However, prolonged stress is damaging to the brain and muscles. At limits, subconscious processes are forced to be creative to regain confident processes within limits. After briefly stressing the mind to limits, one must relax allowing subconscious processes to construct wider, more complete limits. Operating the brain above emotional limits for a long time produces illogical thoughts and loss of reality.

Brief mind limit experiments force subconscious processes to widen their limits. Thinking must become versatile to converge and return to complete thoughts. Subconscious processes must work creatively to restore thinking below emotional limits. We become smarter by briefly stressing the mind to limits at times. Broader subconscious limits are developed if "baby" developed mental limits are lessened and replaced with more logical, less emotional limits. Developing more logical subconscious limits will expand thinking and gage emotions for socially accepted reactions. Genetic mental limits will gain influence. The mind becomes less afraid to think at limits, guided by developed, gagged emotions.

Curing bipolar disorder requires understanding causes and effects. Everyday ideas are nurtured within normal electromagnetic resonances. Routine excitement increases mental energy, but the brain and mind quickly regain normal thinking limits. In mania emotional energy often extends beyond limits, and the mind goes out of control.

At the edge of a cliff, a normal person might briefly think of the excitement of jumping off and flying. In mania, such ideas linger.

In high energetic moods, manic-depressives are drawn to high-energy emotional ideas and actions. High energy emotional thinking may occur too rapidly for convergence to reasonable conclusions.

We must reduce stressors if not briefly extending the mind to limits. By reducing trauma effects, we become smarter, more versatile, and spiritual. Our thinking characteristics and limits are influenced more by genetics, or ancestor histories of successful, emotional accomplishments and lifesaving actions and reactions. Our genes also include positive and negative effects our ancestors experienced and learned from failures.

A manic person may decide he needs to prove his sanity. Proving sanity requires thinking smartly. The manic-depressive often races to accomplish "smart" tasks. Accomplishments give feelings of being smart and sane. However, going too fast may raise mental excitement beyond rational thinking levels.

Unfortunately, there are times in episodes when manic-depressives might believe any dream or scam. I pray that anyone preying on the weak, disabled, or elderly receive God's wrath.

Manic-depressives, going out of control often become stigmatized. Once stigmatized, it is difficult to overcome labels and regain respect. If healed manic-depressives have unrelated symptoms, general practitioners, without psychiatric skills, will falsely diagnose bipolar patients of being manic. Bipolar patients can be excited, abused, or even poisoned, without being manic. Being free of manic episodes for 20 years is my cure and monumental success!

Only, I have practiced and tested mental reconstruction methods successfully. I plan on requesting the National Institutes of Mental Health to review my work. I hope to collaborate with a University or other research institute to continue this work.

Schizophrenia occurred briefly in severe episodes. In the heights of one manic episode, I experienced hallucinations. I "saw" trailing images of dancers' legs as in cartoons. This was due to timing adjustments occurring in critical vision areas of the brain. Subconscious processes become aware that vision is not efficient. The brain makes adjustments. I have learned to expect unusual occurrences. Calmness allows time to understand vision and reasoning adjustments.

In my first manic episode and in the backseat of my dad's car, I had a delusion of becoming so light I feared floating out of the seat. Another time, someone or some entity was reading my thoughts.

No one wants their inner thoughts read, fearing loss of thinking freedom.

During this time when outside, I had unusual sensations around the crown of my head depending upon the direction faced. This sensation was similar to my brain being a magnet and affected by an electric field, or the earth's magnetic field. It may be possible for a circular current to form in the brain during extreme mania. A circular current creates a magnet. Delusions may be caused by the subconscious attempting to hide unusual sensations and thoughts.

Sensations and inner thoughts developed an amazing inner reality that interfered with normal activities. After manic episodes, making sense of unusual experiences became a learning experience. In depression thinking and activities were degrading. At the beginning of elevated moods, manic-depressives expect exceptionally good and exciting things. Feelings are somewhat similar to beginnings of alcohol highs. However, eventually, reasoning limits are overridden or eclipsed. Delusions result when the subconscious attempts to reason beyond emotional limits.

If depression or mania negatively affects abilities and behaviors, attitudes of observers toward the afflicted become negative quickly. Some feel superior, others feel sorry, and some want to understand and help. As we recover and become better than ever, attitudes change very slowly. Hurting people hurt others. Blessed are those with self-confidence for helping those in need!

Some may consider love a disorder. It begins with over-active emotions similar to bipolar disorder. Bipolar disorder and love make us vulnerable. First time in true love, one feels differently and thinks irrationally.

True love is caring for and protecting another's safety and happiness greater than one's own. He wants to be honest with her and himself, and share important ideas and goals. He wants to help her to be all she can be within reason and without stress. He wants to form a unit that is greater than two individuals. She wants to help him similarly. Each hurts when the other hurts. Blessed are those living in true love! I can only dream of a love like this. This loving unit may include children to reflect parents' lives and values. Love is crazy if not returned.

Everybody's crazy during manic episodes. With incomplete thinking, manic-depressives lose control and can be easily abused or abusive. Being stigmatized, and abused by predators, makes mental healing more difficult. Everybody is crazy to love emotionally if love is not reflected. Predators take advantage of the vulnerable in love.

This independent story of healing and hope has been mostly kept confidential. I did not want to hear others say: "You can't do this or that" and limit ideas and writing. Many will degrade my work without recognizing long-term benefits. I hope to help readers heal their minds and be healthy and happy. So many important discoveries have been ridiculed and not recognized until years later. I do not claim to be affiliated with any recognized mental health or spiritual authority.

How could a physicist and nuclear engineer let a controlling spouse degrade him into depression and bipolar disorder? He was brainwashed in childhood to accept degrading behaviors in close relationships from his older brother.

Everybody's crazy if not recognizing that life is a miracle, especially, for those surviving traumas and expected death. Everybody's crazy if degrading others without placing themselves in their shoes. God does not like anyone degrading anyone. If anyone needs help bend way, way down to lift them way, way up.

Episodes and Insanities

XLIV

One need not be a chamber to be haunted,
One need not be a house;
The brain has corridors surpassing
Material place,
Far safer, of a midnight meeting
External ghost,
Than an interior confronting
That whiter host,
Far safer through an Abbey gallop,
The stones achase,
Than moonless, one's own self encounter
In lonesome place,
Ourself, behind ourself concealed,
Should startle most;
Assassin, hid in our apartment,
Be horror's least
The prudent carries a revolver,
He bolts the door,
O'erlooking a superior specter
More near.

— Emily Dickinson

WILL (Excerpts)

There is no chance, no destiny, no fate,
Can circumvent or hinder or control
The firm resolve of a determined soul.

Why, even Death stands still,
And waits an hour sometimes for such a will.

—Ella Wheeler Wilcox

Initial Manic Episode

Depressed in 1977 without sleeping for months, a tortured, slow death was permeating mind and soul. Anxiety, stress, and fear of death forced a depressed mind into erratic fast thinking in search of lost sanity. My thoughts seemed stuck in molasses, and my life seemed frozen in a tragic play.

My former wife's abuse had built up distrust over the years. I would not respond to her during manic episodes. My mind was reactive with feelings stretched between deceit and truth. She had two separate behaviors. She had a degrading, deceitful one when we were alone, and a reasonable one at other times. She seemed to have a split personality. A healthy person does not become a severe manic-depressive unless severely deceived, controlled, and abused.

During my first episode, she recruited my parents to get me psychiatric help. I trusted my parents. They took me to an emergency room, and I ended up in a psychiatric ward. My psychiatrist said that my former wife overreacted to my manic uncertainties, adding to my anxiety.

In a psychiatric ward, a thought occurred to me. How could any person endure so much mental pain and live? "I must be Jesus Christ!" Hallelujah! I yelled to mother and dad, "I am Jesus Christ!" To my surprise mother did not seem pleased with my new discovery. She gently forced her face directly in front of mine and calmly said, "Hugh, you are not Jesus Christ!" For the first time in my life, I did not believe my mother. Emotional feelings and excitement were too strong.

I went out into the hall, and at my first opportunity, proclaimed to a poor elderly lady: "I am Jesus Christ!" She responded with raised hands, a bowering of her head, and a "Praise the Lord." This response made me feel genuine, for a brief moment.

Surprisingly, a not-so-manic thought occurred. If I am Jesus Christ, I have a responsibly to this lady, mother, dad, and my children. With this thought, I knew I was not Jesus Christ and did not have His love or ability. I immediately became a tired, sick, lost person again and retreated to my hospital room. With some coaxing, I accepted a tranquilizer and resigned to give up a hurtful life. The next morning I felt better and was more reasonable after my first sleep in months.

During this first manic episode and hospitalization, I began emotional writing while locked in a psychiatric cell fearing insanity, permanent confinement, and death. Writing was the most stabilizing thing I could do. I wrote about physics and my injustices to prove my sanity and save my life. I could recall physics equations more clearly than in my normal state of mind. Writing added reason and purpose to my life, gave a sense of sanity, and cleansed my soul.

Unfortunately, I was prescribed Haldol, drugged, numbed, and released. After a week, Haldol produced horrendous side effects that nearly killed me. I could not swallow and muscles cramped all over my body. I again thought death was imminent. After this battle for life, I have always felt as if living on borrowed time. In prescribing new medications, psychiatrists must monitor helpless patients frequently for side effects. I never saw, or wanted to see, that psychiatrist again.

Severely depressed or manic patients are not able to explain ills and side effects. This time I knew I needed emergency treatment. I was assigned to Doctor Gene Goode and taken off Haldol. I returned to being a normal manic-depressive, if there is such a condition. Doctor Goode gave me hope and confidence in psychiatry.

During episodes in this early time period, my parents and aunts and uncles were so helpful and encouraging. I trusted my family. My children were young.

My former wife was a taker and never encouraged me. In divorce, she tried to take everything she could. However, years later, after our divorce when she thought I was wealthier, she tried to get back together again even after she had caused me so much pain and loss of health. I no longer had feelings or respect for her.

Adult children of alcoholics have insatiable need for security. When married, my former wife frequently said she needed a high level of security. Of course, this was always at my expense.

1988 Episode

At work in Phoenix, Arizona, there was an atheist who frequently told me: "It is so stupid to believe in God." After some time, I told him, as a Christian, I relied on Jesus and God. He was reactive and rude after that time. Without believing in God, he seemed to believe he was the highest intelligence in the universe. Stress during this conflict led to a manic episode.

A few weeks later, manic thinking turned inward, and I could not respond to others normally. I tried to appear normal but absolutely knew my thinking was not normal. I became reactive.

I became obsessed with drug dealers who ruin innocent lives. Unfortunately, I thought anyone looking suspicious was a drug dealer. I was put in jail for one night for my own protection. I experienced being handcuffed in my manic attempt to save the innocent from drug dealers.

I found myself in a large holding cell with about 15 tough looking prisoners. Unfortunately, many of them looked like drug dealers. I was on a mission with no fear or mental limits. I yelled at them for ruining lives. One prisoner came up and swung at me. With a reactive mind I dodged. He looked rather sheepish because he had missed. I had no fear. I beckoned him to come back. Luckily for both of us he walked away. In my normal state of mind, I am not a fighter. I try to reason through differences.

After that incident I was more reserved. That night was long with no place to sleep. The next morning I was too preoccupied to listen to or answer exit questions. I thought of myself as a protester against drug dealers. A blind friend had protested several causes. I was a protester against drugs. For that reason I signed out of jail with his signature. I could remember exactly how he signed his name. Finally, I'm free, or am I?

I walked out of jail that morning with absolutely no idea where I was or how to get home. I felt I could not call anyone so I walked and walked. I walked through some of the roughest streets in Phoenix all night without fear for my safety. Finally, adrenalin was wearing out. I was tired the next morning as the sun rose. I noticed street signs enough to find my way home. I had walked for miles.

Hours of weary walking allowed some sleep. I had been fearless for days. But apparently a chemical that suppresses fear ran out. Little things began to have great importance. People on a nearby balcony were spies. TV programs seemed directed to me. I was uncertain as to whether to react. I became afraid of almost everything. I told my story to the police. They suggested I stay in a nearby Holiday Inn.

I must have slept some, for the next day I was concerned with the outside world. I drove home, remembered I was prescribed Thorazine and lithium, and took medications. I called my Phoenix psychiatrist and told him of my ordeal. Surprisingly, he did not suggest an appointment.

Things started getting better. I became aware of missing work for several days. It was difficult explaining why I had missed work and not notified anyone. I told the truth that I had gotten my nights and days mixed up. Things slowly became more normal. I have dream-like memories of this episode. Some things made sense and others did not.

This ordeal was important to me. I learned I could find my own way back to sanity without a doctor's assistance. However, if I ever have similar difficulties, I will seek a doctor's help. This episode was way too risky.

1994 Episode

This manic episode was milder than previous episodes. I was able to function quite normally but became sensitive to unusual feelings when turning my head left or right. My explanation was that my brain was affected by electric or magnetic fields from utility wires or by unusual sensitivities to the earth's magnetic field. The brain is electrical and can be affected by electric and magnet fields.

A chemical imbalance may have affected my melatonin levels. From Oprah.com/health, December 18, 2013, the following article, seems to support my odd sensations when rotating my head. Research by Darren Lipnicki is similar in nature to my experience. My melatonin levels must have been affected.

From *The Planet's Gentle Pull:* Research finds a connection between magnetism and melatonin: The fewer fluctuations in the earth's magnetic field (geomagnetic activity), the more dream-inducing sleep hormone the body produces. Inspired, Darren Lipnicki, a psychologist formerly at the Center for Space Medicine in Berlin, recorded his dreams for eight years—he then looked up the records of geomagnetic activity closest to where he lived and found a statistical correlation. After two or more days of an unusually calm magnetic field—and (presumably) higher melatonin—his dreams were much more vivid and bizarre than they were following stormier phases (when melatonin may have been suppressed.)"

Mania includes forceful ideas including dreamlike qualities. "Strong" forced manic ideas demand attention and, too often, cause inappropriate actions and reactions. Waking and dreaming processes become confused. Mania may include schizophrenia, bizarre dream images, and displaced characters. Manic episodes are more difficult to understand than dreams.

Manic-depressives may follow their dreams with little reasoning. Imagination soars. Manic minds become creative and spiritual with few constraints. Mania may be described as dreaming while awake.

My manic episodes were caused by early sibling abuse and an abusive, deceptive former wife, influenced by her two alcoholic parents. The abused turn negatives into positives. Minds can rebound from depression and bipolar disorder.

Everybody's crazy and insane during severe manic episodes. This work makes sense of life not making sense. Should we do this or that? We must learn from mistakes. Everyone's crazy for not discovering, confronting, or avoiding who or what is causing stress, depression, or mania.

Mental Limits

—⚹—

We may exceed, expand, purge, and re-grow mental thinking limits. Mental limits usually do not change significantly during lifetimes unless highly emotional occurrences or traumas stress our minds beyond childhood emotional limits. Emotional and trauma limits restrict thinking abilities. Brains need mental limits to reflect electromagnetic radiation from neuron spikes to create resonances or iterations for converging to conscious ideas for decision making. Our minds must be able to focus on itself and our bodies and environments for us to survive and thrive.

Mental limits and IQ's usually do not change much during normal lives. IQ's are related to how well mental, EMR resonances can iterate and converge to consciousness.

High energy emotions, during mania, breech childhood developed emotional limits. The mind loses control when emotional limits no longer reflect sense and memory EMR waves for creating resonances and conscious abilities. Childhood traumas and highly emotional failures originally ingrained our early and later mental limits. Mental reconstruction processes are meant to re-grow wider, kinder mental limits. A goal is to gain reasoning and creativity during highly emotional challenges.

We may choose limiting challenges, and limiting challenges may choose us. The brain is limited by genetic structures and early ingrained emotional experiences. Social customs and restrictions normally limit thinking, emotions, and actions before trauma or genetic limits are encountered. Normal activities and conversations usually flow without meeting limits.

Stress can send the mind to limits. At times, let yourself experience moderate levels of emotional and physical stress. This increases ability to stay calm and reason through real stresses. Reasoning through difficulties reduces stress, and develops confidence and a sense of well-being.

Weight lifting or exercising at limits and then relaxing gives an inner sense of accomplishment and control. With patience, innovation, and brief limiting exercises, we can better understand and expand emotional and physical limits.

Praying and thinking holistically about life reduces importance of brief adverse incidents. Each of us is important to existence and God. We should think of healing ways to confront or reason with degrading people or avoid them.

Mental limits are ingrained within our neural membranes and minds during severe stresses. We re-experience the emotions when ingrained mental limits are stimulated. Listed are some occurrences that may ingrain emotional thinking limits within the brain:

- Expecting death when severely depressed to the point of not being able to think in words or of "freezing in place."
- Expecting death.
- Failing an important undertaking that negatively affects self and important people.
- Failure in crawling, walking, or riding a bike.
- First time crawling, walking, or riding a bike.
- Accomplishing or failing difficult mental tasks.
- Accomplishing or failing difficult physical tasks.
- Being severely degraded or embarrassed.

- Being severely injured or in severe pain.
- Elation after unexpectedly solving a long, difficult problem.
- Being left out causing loneliness or feelings of abandonment.
- Thoughtless or careless activities or responses causing deep feelings of guilt.
- Fulfilling, or failure to perform, or abusive, sex.
- Finding true love.
- Losing a loved one.

If we experience emotions from traumatic experiences beyond those of related childhood trauma limits, two things happen. A new limit is engrained that further limits thinking, or the early trauma limit is breached making it easier for mania to occur with the mind going out of control. If limiting traumas occur and we are able to understand and control our reactions to them, we build wider, more rational thinking limits.

Care is taken in my Psychiatric Exercises and Mental Reconstruction Chapters/Essays to understand the effects of exercises and processes on the brain and mind. With understanding we expand mental limits. Without understanding, stress is harmful and may restrict thinking that, in frustration, may lead to disorganized manic episodes.

The brain and nervous system respond to activated senses and recalled memories for making decisions. Highly emotional or manic reactions to "perceived threats or threats to status" develop higher priority than social and custom limits. The manic mind is less socially restrained. Genetic survival responses may cause extreme behaviors. Normal reasoning is overridden. If trauma and emotional energy are lessened with mental reconstruction, original trauma memories become more normal causing less loss of control.

With good parents, young minds are active and free. Adult minds become more constrained from daily or limiting stresses. Genetic, mental, and physical limits restrict thinking and behaviors. Social limits normally affect behaviors before mental limits activate. Social and physical limits restrict creative thinking. With mental and physical exercises we can expand mental limits.

We do not need to be as reactive as caveman needed to be for survival. However, caveman's thinking and survival reactions formed early genetic structures for our mental and physical abilities. We think like humans not like cats.

I model mental limits as overstressed collections of nuclei membranes, which have absorbed extreme energy and repressed recall of high emotional memories. Nuclei react together with unique resonances and common purposes. These overstressed neurons react strongly when stimulated by frequencies similar to original ingraining trauma frequencies caused by extreme emotional events. Mental limits are constructed by reactions to early and later trauma experiences, and by ancestor genetics.

Repeated neuron activations build thicker, faster acting axons and dendrites. The brain is constantly changing from new experiences. Neurons are constantly building memory holograms within membrane structure. As various neuron membrane structures change or "grow," neuron reflective properties change. Reflective properties of nuclei membrane structures change as mental hologram scenarios and memories are integrated within them. Traumas have the greatest affect on nuclei membranes that construct trauma thinking limits.

Depending on EMR angles, frequencies and energy, neuron membranes may develop several reflecting limits for maintaining subconscious and possibly conscious resonances. The mind is complex. From my view point, there seems to be only a few reasonable alternatives for modeling the mind and consciousness.

Human bodies have limits. Our bodies cannot tolerate very hot or very cold temperatures and survive. A gentle touch soothes the body and mind. A hard hit can break bones. If there is too little light we cannot see. If there is too much light we are blinded.

Everybody's crazy not briefly stressing their minds to limits, at times, to reconstruct minds and muscles. If we have developed solid principles and understand our mental limits we have more control of our normal, emotional, and creative thinking. Purging repressed trauma energy builds resistance to stress.

Mental Holograms

—⁂—

MENTAL HOLOGRAMS AND ALPHABETS ARE building blocks of human thought and language. Comparing and integrating mental holograms is the subconscious "picture" language for constructing conscious thought. Modeling inner processes for understanding improves thought, language, and health. Occasionally, we become aware of mental hologram scenarios upon wakening from dreams, and in expected death situations.

Repeated thoughts make related mental holograms brighter and clearer. Similar hologram scenario memories are stimulated by similar sensations, and mental resonances they develop. EMR energy and resonances are absorbed by neural and glial membranes at many angles. The EMR profile of each firing neuron is unique for imprinting unique mental holograms within thousands of neural membranes. Coherent EMR has greater influence in imprinting mental holograms for subconscious and conscious processes.

Pondering in-depth ideas over long periods of time develops longer neural network resonances for absorbing and integrating mental hologram memories. Einstein pondered for long periods of time on similar concepts resulting in his prestigious discoveries. His mind developed integrated, detailed, and specific mental holograms into a holistic vision, called general relativity.

Complex distributed three-dimensional neural membranes construct higher dimensional mental holograms that have some similarities to two-dimensional commercial hologram surfaces and their three dimensional holograms. EMR imprints mental holograms on complex arrays of neural networks. Neural membranes are the brain's photographic paper.

Each firing neuron constructs a vague hologram as it imprints EMR energy and information on near and, to a lesser extent, far neuron membranes. EMR follows a complex path as it is transmitted, reflected, and diffracted by a labyrinth of three dimensional brain membranes and other brain tissue.

Integrated together, EMR from millions of synchronized neuron firings imprint bright detailed holograms on distributed brain cell membranes. Successive generations of high-energy synchronized neuron firings create mental hologram scenarios, consciousness, and memories.

Three-dimensional electromagnetic radiation, from neuron firings, constructs virtual higher-dimensional spiritual holograms. Mental hologram dimensions may include holistic, integrated "color" tinting dimensions representing levels of truth, emotion, depth of belief, and so on. Mental and spiritual holograms may blend together. There is not be a precise dividing line. Any awareness that becomes greater than the sum of its parts is spiritual.

We can do varied experiments to understand our minds. When un-focusing and looking through a large scrolling text file on a computer monitor, all letters are seen holistically or equally when the right-brain is dominant. There is a feeling of understanding the text without reading individual words. We may improve reading with right-brain dominance.

When a baby is very young, vision is processed with his holistic right-brain. He evaluates all non-threatening images with equal importance. Later, he learns to focus on parents, moving things, and pleasant and frightening things. High-energy actions are scary to baby, often ingraining trauma scar, repressed memories. To recall repressed memories, we must stimulate the mind to similar energy levels while thinking in similar areas.

Early right-brain dominance explains why we do not easily remember early childhood. Right-brain memories, like dreams, are easily forgotten. Babies think spiritually with right-brain dominance. When weak and in pain, adults also become spiritual.

In practicing Holusion exercises, I have sensed left and right-brain dominance transitions. Vision changes from up-close, left-brain two-dimensional Holusion images to and from more distant right-brain virtual three-dimensional images. We gain left/right brain dominance control.

We remember up-close important details and goals with the left-brain. Destinations are specific and remembered. Individual steps toward destinations are not remembered. Discrete, up-close left-brain dominance for discrete thinking and memory develop later in baby's brain.

A bipolar person experiences incomplete and out of control thinking, and does inappropriate things at times. However, there are benefits. Right-brain, creative, and spiritual thinking becomes more important. Normal abilities are eclipsed by more exciting creative abilities and spiritual presence.

Everybody's crazy not realizing that mental holograms are a major part of memory and thinking. Remembered dreams are semi-conscious and conscious mental hologram scenarios. Creative and spiritual thinking eclipse everyday thinking.

Alternative Mind Healing

—⁕—

SPORADIC TRAUMATIZED NEURAL NETWORKS INTERFERE with normal brain activities causing stress, uncertainty, and pain. Most of us have endured inner stress from repressed memories for so long we are mostly unaware of it. Inner stress has become part of our lives. Some have more and some less.

When experiencing headaches, local tensions within the brain cause local pain. Psychiatric exercises release localized repressed tensions.

A headache can be from stress and pressure in one area of the brain. It is a cramp in the brain. Glia cells tense. The normal reaction is to frown. Frowning keeps the brain tense and does not encourage relaxing. Resisting frowning, broadening the face, and relaxing the body may ease headaches quicker. Get medical help for severe or persistent headaches.

Focusing long distance and broadening the face broadens and relaxes the brain. With a relaxed brain, blood flow increases and stress is dissipated throughout the brain more easily. After relaxing the face and brain, pain may worsen briefly, but dissipates quicker. The brain influences the face, and the face influences the brain. We may smile our headaches away.

Closing eyes during meditation sometimes initiates facial awareness. Tightening feelings extend from around the forehead to cheeks and, sometimes, under the chin. After tension eases, the face and mind feel relaxed. This awareness has occurred only after years of mental reconstruction. It may take years of work to awaken these sensations.

Waiting patiently in prayer, with eyes closed and focusing long distance, I have received spiritual feelings that God is omniscient and dwells within my and human minds and souls. In prayer, we must reduce energy of normal waking thoughts to become aware of low energy spiritual communication waves.

Neck exercises stimulate overstressed neural networks to release repressed stress energy. Alternative mind healing has been exciting and mostly pleasant. Alternative processes have taken years of work but have been rewarding. We cannot continue to do the same things and expect healing results. We must experiment with our minds and decide what we like and dislike.

Advanced imaging of the brain, throat, and neck may identify high-energy and overstressed neural networks for precise treatment and shortened psychiatric healing times. Manic-depressives with severe, frequent, or cycling episodes may benefit from new focused healing technology.

Precise advanced lasers may stimulate overstressed neural networks to limits releasing their excess energy. With reduced energy, once traumatized networks resynchronize to make brain activities more normal and holistic. The more the brain works as a whole; the smarter we become.

In my case, chiropractic vibrations have opened nerves in my back at emotional limits by releasing repressed trauma energy. With less tension, these nerves have become more capable in passing signals from the brain to muscles in my arms and wrists.

Readers must evaluate their afflictions before choosing to mentally reconstruct. Mental reconstruction processes are long and must be chosen wisely at readers' risk.

Everybody's crazy believing alternative physical exercises cannot heal the mind in many cases. Physical exercises can briefly extend the brain to limits releasing repressed trauma energy from afflicted neural networks. Muscles and the brain grow only when briefly stressed to limits. Extended stress is never beneficial to body or mind. Reasonable, brief mental and physical exercises are good for the mind and body.

Healing Vertigo and Arthritis

—⁓—

I LOOK FOR EXERCISES, PROCEDURES, and meditation, not medications, for healing the mind and other ailments. I had a fall and trauma to the back of my head that caused a concussion and vertigo. I researched the internet for solutions. Below is the rather simple procedure I used that healed my vertigo. I also have been working to develop a solution for arthritis in my knees.

I have included these procedures thinking they might be helpful to readers. It is wise to talk to your doctor before engaging in any medical procedure.

The Epley Maneuver, named after John Epley, M.D., is an accepted treatment for benign paroxysmal positional vertigo (BPPV) that aligns the ear crystals (otoconia) within bodily balance systems. I needed to use this exercise only once. It immediately healed my vertigo. At the end of the process, I heard a faint crystal tingling sound. The Epley procedures are given below:

The Home Epley maneuver when the left side is affected:
1. Perform this exercise in quietness. Place a pillow on your bed so when you lie back your shoulders will rest on it and not your head.

2. Sit on the bed, legs extended, and feet together. Place hands on either side to support your upper body, keep the back straight and in an upright position.
3. Turn your head 45 degrees to the left and slowly let your upper body fall backwards over the pillow taking care that your head hangs down less than 20 degrees.
4. Remain in that position for 30 seconds.
5. Turn your head 45 degrees to the right and remain in that position for 30 seconds.
6. Roll onto your right side and lie there for 30 seconds.
7. Slowly return to the starting sitting position as noted in Step 2 and sit for one minute.
8. Repeat Step 2 through Step 7 for a second cycle.
9. Repeat Step 2 through Step 7 for a third and final cycle.
10. Repeat this exercise once a day for one week, if needed.
11. If vertigo becomes worse for more than a few hours, you may try the procedure below for an afflicted right side.

As this process first works, you may sense or hear a faint sound of tiny crystals tingling together within the inner ear. You need quietness to hear this sound.

The Home Epley maneuver when the right side is affected.
1. Perform this exercise in quietness. Place a pillow on your bed so when you lie back your shoulders will rest on it not your head.
2. Sit on the bed, legs extended, and feet together. Place hands on either side to support your upper body, keep your back straight and in an upright position.
3. Turn your head 45 degrees to the right then slowly let your upper body fall backwards over the pillow taking care that your head hangs down less than 20 degrees.
4. Remain in that position for 30 seconds.

5. Turn your head 45 degrees to the left and remain in that position for 30 seconds.
6. Roll onto your left side and lie there for 30 seconds.
7. Slowly return to the starting sitting position as noted in Step 2 and sit for one minute.
8. Repeat Steps 2 through 7 for a second cycle.
9. Repeat Steps 2 through 7 for a third and final cycle, if needed.
10. If vertigo becomes worse for more than some brief period try the left procedure or see your doctor.

If necessary, repeat the most effective exercise once a day for one week. When this procedure first works, you may sense or hear faint sounds of tiny crystals tingling within the inner ear. You need quietness to hear this sound. Some may sense a release of tensions with a feeling of clarity for balance.

A lady called me in January, 2014, having frequent nausea, severe vertigo, depression, and insomnia, for over a month. She had fear of falling. Her life was miserable. She appeared drained and weak.

She had been taking medications for her nausea and vertigo but had not performed the Epley maneuver. I told her of my success. I assisted her with the maneuver.

Immediately after the procedure, her nausea and vertigo were better. The next day she felt like having experienced a miracle. Her sleeping was better. She regained control over her life and continued professional therapy to reduce vertigo for certain movements.

Healing Arthritis

I have had a football knee since high school. X-rays showed arthritis and the need for a knee replacement. I began thinking of ways to heal my arthritic knee. My son-in-law, Dr. Andy Hawkins, said I was not fully exercising my knees and was losing strength and muscle. My knees hurt when going up and down steps.

I began an exercise adventure. I worked out on the treadmill and on weight machines, but my focus was on the stationary bike. I adjusted the seat and resistance so my knees were bent farther than before during pedaling. I increased resistance and bending as, knee joints, muscles, and stamina allowed.

My theory is that arthritis creeps into cartilage and bones of joint surfaces that are not being exercised or used, and that my deep knee-bend biking would break up the arthritis. With exercises, climbing steps became easier. My applied physics was working again.

I went to my orthopedic surgeon expecting a knee replacement surgery date. After X-rays, Dr. Gondi said I did not need a knee replacement but prescribed an injection and Voltaren Gel. This gel, when rubbed on the knees, is absorbed quickly and seems to reduce knee pain.

Conclusion

I have refined exercises and writing to help readers heal, and caretakers care for loved ones. In developing healing processes, I have frequently extended thinking below and above routine energy levels to receive spiritual feelings. Spiritual beliefs and outlook assist healing. Words cannot adequately describe my spiritual experiences. When spiritual, minds think beyond words and worldly thoughts. My work has been successful for my healing.

Everybody's crazy not believing physical exercises and processes can heal vertigo and help heal arthritis. A self administered Epley maneuver healed my vertigo on the first attempt. Perform this procedure at your own risk. Arthritis exercises have delayed knee replacement. If having difficulties, see your doctor.

Psychiatric Exercises

―⚏―

"True enjoyment comes from activity of the mind and exercise of the body; the two are ever united."

— Karl Wilhelm Von Humboldt

"In the beginning, psychiatric exploration and mental reconstruction were bold and daring, but, after years of practice, have become routine."

— H. Fulcher

Readers will not find these unusual psychiatric exercises and feedback sensations in current medical practices. However, they have been instrumental in healing my bipolar disorder. I have experienced progressive healing sensations for twenty years. Psychiatric exercises have been significant for healing my disorder, and may be most helpful to bipolar suffers and the overstressed who have lost emotional limits.

For fourteen years, psychiatric sessions and prescribed medications had not been working. I continued to endure sporadic manic episodes. I decided to do something different. I could not continue doing the same things and expect different, better results.

Unique psychiatric exercises were fundamental for mental reconstruction, healing my bipolar disorder, and expanding creative thinking. Exercises purge repressed energy from emotional and trauma memories promoting alternative healing. Exercises have been effective in healing my disorder. It may be difficult to believe inner sensation and reaction changes from the same psychiatric neck exercises over twenty years, unless experienced. Sensations are somewhat predictable in the short term. The brain is complex and takes a long time to heal.

Trauma and brainwashing effects corrupt and limit thinking. I have developed technologies to release energy from overstressed neural networks. My non-conflicting and conflicting neck exercises are my most important tools for reconstructing and healing the brain and mind. Unusual exercises heal inner processes and expand mental limits so the mind responds more rationally to emotional and trauma events.

To heal and expand the mind we need to think beyond normal processes. Experiencing reasonable levels of uncertainty, at times, are helpful in reducing mental energy and expanding the mind. When relaxed, pray to become imaginative and spiritual. Develop your healing path.

Each of us has different levels of understanding. Many of us specialize to be experts in certain areas. With study, models of complex things give feelings of understanding and confidence. We should work to improve our minds and lives. It is important to be bold but also important to be comfortable with ourselves.

Near death experiences and bipolar disorder have stimulated unusual sensations and have led to developing psychiatric exercises. I describe healing processes and sensations as truthfully as I can, and have developed bold theories to explain healing sensations and reactions.

From my research, older persons I have spoken with also experience inner release sensations in the neck and lower brain areas. Sensations indicate releases of stress energy from the neck, throat, and brainstem. My goal became to release inner stresses from the brain and mind through exercises and mind models. A calm less stressed brain creates a rational mind.

Psychiatric Exercises

Psychiatric exercises, at mental limits, release trauma tensions from overstressed neural networks to reduce emotional and trauma tensions throughout the brain. After releasing ingrained trauma energy, afflicted networks become less rigid, more elastic, and re-synchronize with normal brain functions. Thinking becomes more holistic and versatile.

I talked with a friend who was in some of the toughest fighting in Vietnam. Soldiers who survived had trauma scars. Years later, they are haunted by fears and images of killing and dying. Trauma memories were recalled when least expected. This effect is called Post Traumatic Syndrome, or PTS. Soldiers have experienced severe erratic trauma memories years later.

Most repressed emotional memories are caused by baby and childhood traumas. Even with psychiatric care, inner tensions in the brain and neck remain. Psychiatric exercises and mental reconstruction purge energy within repressed memories to reduce their irrational influences.

Young babies react to new and unexpected events, incurring trauma scars in innocent little brains. Early and later trauma scars construct subconscious processing limits in the brain. Emotional processing limits remain throughout our lifetimes unless we purge their excess energy through psychiatry or my psychiatric exercises and mental reconstruction.

We have lived with trauma scars and their effects for most of our lives and are mostly unaware of their restrictions. Some mental limits are obvious. We have learned not to stand in front of an oncoming train or at the edge of a cliff. Other mental limits are less obvious. Should we speak up or remain quiet? Who should we respect, or avoid? Who can we love and trust? Is it healthy to love someone who does not love us?

During my manic episode in 1990, I became aware of unusual localized, discrete energy release sensations in the upper neck and, to some extent, in the brainstem. I was initially afraid of the brain degrading and losing sanity.

Later, I felt sure sensations were discrete stress releases within the upper neck, throat, and brain. I thought I had discovered a method to relax and heal the brain and mind.

I was afraid to tell my psychiatrist or anyone about these sensations. My psychiatrist would have increased medications and turned me into a thoughtless zombie.

In 1992, fifteen years after my first and only depression and after several sporadic manic episodes, I began exercising my neck to purge these inner neck sensations. Sensations were more active and prominent during and after exercises. I began experimenting with neck and other mental exercises. After exercises and processes, my last episode occurred in 1994.

I continued to exercise my neck in various ways to increase sensations and release tensions. After a month, I theorized that sensations were caused by releases of localized energy from neural networks.

In a few months, I could sense energy-release sensations slowly migrating to and from the back of the upper neck, the upper throat, and the brainstem. Sensation migrations were predictable for a few days after exercises. Predicting gave some confidence of understanding of these unusual inner sensations or sounds.

Healing sensations were not unpleasant, exciting to some extent, and yet gave feelings of relaxation after exercises. Thoughts felt light and versatile after exercises. Releasing energy from repressed trauma memories increased freedom of thought and creativity. Trauma scars have slowed thinking over a lifetime.

After a few months, neck, throat, and brainstem sensations felt like having less energy. Alternative psychiatric exercises promote "brain adjustments," that are somewhat similar to chiropractic adjustments, but release much less energy.

Chiropractic sensations were important in understanding brain and mind healing sensations. I had experienced chiropractic energy-releases earlier when joints snapped back into their normal, least stressed, positions. Manipulating joints into least tense positions puts related nerves in less tense positions.

Slowly, I sensed feeling more relaxed and confident. Brains must be in their least energetic, less tense states to be efficient and relaxed.

After several months of neck exercises, I referred to localized neuron energy releases in the neck, throat, and brainstem as **S**naps, **C**rackles, **A**nd **P**ops or SCAPs. The more I exercised, the more SCAP sensations occurred during similar exercises. I proposed that SCAPs resulted from energy releases from overstressed or traumatized neural networks, segments, or even, individual neurons.

If my theory was correct, SCAP sensations would migrate within the neck, throat, brainstem, and to a lesser extent within the upper brain. This seemed reasonable since the neck, throat, and brainstem tense when reacting to trauma. After several months, I confirmed that sensations had slightly less energy over time.

I felt confident of understanding and modeling energy releases and their healing effects on the brain and mind. My theory and prediction seemed to be true. I felt it was possible to purge excess energy from all traumatized neural networks. I defined a mind free of all trauma effects and cleared of restrictive emotional compartments as the "Clear Mind." The brain should work as a whole system.

Releasing trauma energy from the brain is an ongoing process. The clear mind is my goal. I am unsure of clear mind abilities, but am certain of positive changes occurring during this long effort. The brain and mind work better with healthy levels of certainty and uncertainty.

I began to research ways to speed up inner sensations. I needed additional exercises to stress the mind briefly to limits to stimulate release of remaining trauma effects. Unique resistance or conflicting exercises sped up trauma energy releases from neural networks.

After several months, I settled on a set of conflicting neck exercises:

I used resistance with the right-hand for the following repetitive exercises: head-down & back, chin-down & back, head-down and right & return, head-right & return, head-back and right & return, and head-back & return.

Similar left-hand exercises were alternated with right-hand exercises. Exercises used resistance of one hand such that neck muscles are tired after 100 repetitions. These conflicting exercises stimulated more trauma energy releases than normal or non-conflicting neck exercises.

SCAP sensations were analyzed to determine exercises that released the most repressed trauma energy. Additional repetitions were performed with exercises releasing the most sensations.

Psychiatric exercises appear odd, so I practiced in private to avoid adverse attention until methods become more widely known. Conflicting exercise illustrations are shown in Figures 1 – 3 at the end of this chapter/essay.

During the first listed conflicting exercise, neck muscles pull the head down and a thumb pushes the chin and head up creating a muscle and mental conflict that forces traumatized neural segments to limits. The highest related energy neural networks are stimulated to limits releasing their excess emotional energy. With energy released, traumatized networks become less brittle and resynchronize with the brain's normal symphony of activities. In general, anything overstressed becomes brittle.

Neck, throat, and facial exercises are the most effective exercises in purging trauma effects. Effectiveness is judged by the number of energy-release sensations, SCAPs, during psychiatric exercises. Exercising muscles closest to the brain releases the most repressed energy.

After completing conflicting exercises, calm the mind and relax the body for a few minutes allowing subconscious processes to understand changes and make overall adjustments. The mind works better with less energy. Lamaze breathing may help calming the mind and body after healing exercises.

A basic model of the mind is that low-energy thinking is high-level thinking. High-energy thinking, such as anger, is low-level thinking. In anger, we can think of only a few options to degrade or injure someone. With low-energy thinking, we can think of many creative options.

After a few months of practice, exercises could be performed quickly. Sensations from resistance/conflicting head-down exercises feel different with different hands. Left and right neural processing paths are different.

There are differences between normal and conflicting neck exercises. I perform "normal" neck exercises briefly several times a day. During non-conflicting neck exercises, stiffening the neck and throat, in various ways, releases SCAP energy. Infrequently, energy release levels approach those of conflicting exercises. In conflicting neck exercises there is no stiffening of the throat as concentration is on conflicting neck and arm muscles and tensions.

The healing effect of conflicting neck exercises is that subconscious processes become aware of the strange conflict of neck muscles pulling the head down and hand and arm muscles pushing the chin up. This conflict adds uncertainty and energy to subconscious processes. Conflicting energy stimulates repressed trauma memories within overstressed neural segments to limits, releasing emotional energy. Emotional memories become more normal.

Trauma memories are localized with high energy. Normal slower events create memories with less energy and more time to be disseminated more evenly throughout brain or related brain components.

There is a relationship between trauma effects, repressed memories, and neck tensions. This relationship allows us to perform neck exercises to release energy from traumatized neural networks and expand emotional limits.

After psychiatric exercises, the brain and mind become more capable for handling higher stresses. It is better to experience brief pulses of high level stress than endure low levels of stress for long periods of time. Persistent stress is a killer.

My healing processes are much like vaccinations. I stress the mind to limits. The brain and mind are then better prepared to react to real stress.

Some people never relax their faces and brains even while sleeping. Their faces remain narrowed and frowning even while sleeping. In the beginning, relaxing the brain and mind before sleep may be frightening, fearing disturbing memories or night mares will emerge. Some may be afraid to discover their inner selves. Stressed minds stress hearts causing heart attacks and other health issues. If we relax the face and mind, the heart will be more relaxed and last longer for us.

Some people continually frown when not communicating. Briefly broadening the face, and opening the mind, sometimes, allows repressed trauma memories to be recalled. Fully recalling repressed memories releases their excess energy, lessens mental uncertainties, and is much better than letting repressed memories sporadically fester near consciousness for years. A smiling face builds self-esteem, shows acceptance of others, and is sociable.

In repressing trauma memories, the limbic system protects the fragile upper brain. Reactions to pain and trauma normally remain in the limbic system. However, with psychiatric counseling, mental reconstruction exercises, or significant emotional events, trauma memory energy can be released. With less energy, former trauma memories can be accessed and reasoned about by the upper brain.

The primitive limbic system develops quick, rough evaluations and reactions for fight or flight. We need quick defensive reactions in trauma situations.

The right time to deal with repressed trauma memories never seems to happen. Stimulated recollection of trauma memories seems threatening at first, but becomes less threatening and more normal over time and practice. Trauma memories limit thinking over a lifetime unless stimulated to limits for releasing their energy and negative effects. Trauma memories contain feelings of inadequacy, being in the wrong place, and having no way out.

I have proven it is not harmful to purge trauma energy. However, the process is so long that it may not be feasible for most people to pursue. I look for others to improve my methods in the future.

Results from psychiatric exercises are like bodybuilding. There is little change in sensations during the first months of exercising, but they become spectacular over the years!

My goal is for everyone to release all repressed trauma energy to attain the "Clear Mind" and think as minds were designed to think.

Caveman's strenuous daily activities at limits, fears, and deep yells cleared his neck, throat, and brain of trauma effects. Cavemen had "Clear Minds." They were smarter than we are today. They could travel miles into forests and find their way back. Today, we need maps when traveling on roads.

I have a theory on how caveman navigated his environments. In one manic episode, I had different feelings in my brain when I turned my head from north to east, and in other directions. I could only conclude that unusual energetic EMR activities in my brain had essentially created a magnet within my head that was sensitive to the earth's magnetic field. Normal activities in the brain are electromagnetic. Electrons flow due to neuron firings.

From this experience, I theorized that effects of speech and suppressed guilt had overridden this lost directional talent. Caveman had this talent to navigate his environments. Subconscious processes sensed and remembered feelings of directions and distances. I expect, only manic individuals or those with "Clear Minds" may be able to experience this phenomenon. This amazing awareness lasted for only a few days. Even though, we do not have responsibility for traumas, we still have guilt for not being able to avoid them.

Animals may still have this directional "instinct." Humans are directionally limited.

I have practiced facial exercises:

Broaden the face and forehead and horizontally rub muscles between, and just below, the eyebrows with some pressure. It is important to focus long distance to activate right-brain dominance during this exercise. We can relax the brain more when focusing long distance. The brain and forehead are closely connected. When massaging the forehead, including between the eyebrows, we are massaging and relaxing the brain.

Broadening and relaxing the face with positive ideas free creative processes. A relaxed mind is smarter.

After practicing this facial exercise for several years and humbly waiting, the crown of my scalp tightens with exciting, pleasant "electric-like tingling" sensations at times. The brain is making holistic adjustments.

At times, I take both hands and gently broaden the forehead and cheeks. I practice smiling a little more and less. Flush sensations around the crown of the head vary with slight facial adjustments. The brain is connected with and sensitive to facial muscles. Relaxing facial muscles and smiling release inner tensions improving self-image

SCAPs are sensed as near point sensations. Crown sensitivity is a smooth flush wide-spread tingling feeling. Flush feelings have become more prominent over the last few years of mental reconstruction and can be increased by with slight changes to facial muscles.

Perform the following exercise only with healthy lungs. If readers have concerns, ask doctors before practicing. Breathe in as far as practicable. Hold your breath for about two seconds and then breathe in a little deeper. Breathe out as much as practicable hold it for two seconds and breathe out a little more. Begin a little at a time to slowly extend breathing limits. I suggest repeating this exercise a few times a month.

Briefly extending lungs to limits expands stamina and abilities. This exercise activates and cleanses extremities in the lungs not normally used. In cleansing the lungs, some fluid may be discharged causing brief coughing. Discontinue this exercise if coughing is excessive. The subconscious mind reacts to limits.

This exercise extends the diaphragm and other lung related muscles to limits and increased oxygen stimulates the entire body. When muscles are extended to limits, related neural networks release energy, heal, and support greater abilities. The diaphragm becomes stronger, and the lungs become more efficient. This exercise may help induce sleep.

When surprised, we take deep limiting breaths. With mundane lives, we breathe less deeply than earlier generations. Diaphragm and lung abilities are reduced.

Tense neck muscles under the chin to limits for a few seconds to tighten muscles and skin. Perform this neck exercise a few times a week. Over time, appearance improves. These exercises were, performed after years of mental reconstruction. Healing sensations may differ with experience.

This next exercise uses my only mental healing tool. I practice left and right-brain dominance with a Holusion. Figure 4, given at the end of this essay, is the Holusion: "Wolves" by Nvision Grafix, Inc.

Focus long-distance through the surface of the Holusion. Subconscious vision processes become active. The right-brain gains dominance and senses all small detailed images within the two-dimensional hologram holistically, or with equal importance. The right-brain integrates the two-dimensional detailed images into a three-dimensional image deep within the Holusion surface.

I see a three-dimensional image of wolves. As I move my head, the wolves move relative to their background. This is similar to viewing a three-dimensional hologram or viewing an up-close moving person and his distant background.

I practice left-right-brain dominance by alternating between the two- and three-dimensional images. I have viewed the Holusion while moving up and back and to the left and right to discover subconscious processing limits. With practice, dominance switching is sensed within the brain.

Criteria, for readers to practice psychiatric exercises and mental reconstruction, have not been determined. The decision is difficult since individual situations vary and processes require years of patience and dedication. Practicing exercises and procedures has given me purpose and hope over the years.

Bipolar individuals may more readily purge trauma energy. If readers are pleased with their thinking abilities and are happy, I do not recommend practicing this long exercise procedure.

Purging excess trauma energy from neural networks is similar to purging excess energy from nerves near the spine with a chiropractic vibrator. Adding vibration energy to overstressed nerves, near the spine, breaches limits and repressed energy is released or dissipated. I have had amazing results from this chiropractic procedure. Immediately afterward, I had a significantly increased ability to rotate my left hand and forearm. This procedure is referred to as: "opening the nerves." Energy releases, from overstressed neural networks, are similarly stimulated with psychiatric neck exercises.

If readers practice exercises and processes, benefits may be similar to, or different from, those I have experienced. I present my work for readers to make their own decisions, at their own risk. Healing sensation feedback is critical in adjusting exercises to be performed.

Mental healing sensations, creativity, and spiritual awakenings, are difficult to believe unless experienced. Healing processes and exercises require dedication and patience. This mind adventure has been worth my considerable effort.

Everybody's crazy not believing conflicting psychiatric exercises can release repressed trauma and emotional energy from overstressed neural networks, and their memories for healing the mind. Briefly extend the mind to limits to clear disruptive trauma effects for it to think as it was designed to do. If performing exercises, go slowly. Be versatile, and get to know your mind.

Psychiatric Exercises

Figure 1 Head Down Resistance Exercise

Neck Muscles Pull Chin Down, Thumb Pushes Chin Up

Figure 2 Head Down & Left Resistance Exercise

Neck Muscles Pull Chin Down & Left, Thumb Pushes Up & Right

Figure 3 Head Left Resistance Exercise

Neck Muscles Pull Head Left, Hand Pushes Head Right

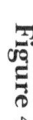

Figure 4

Wolves Holusion

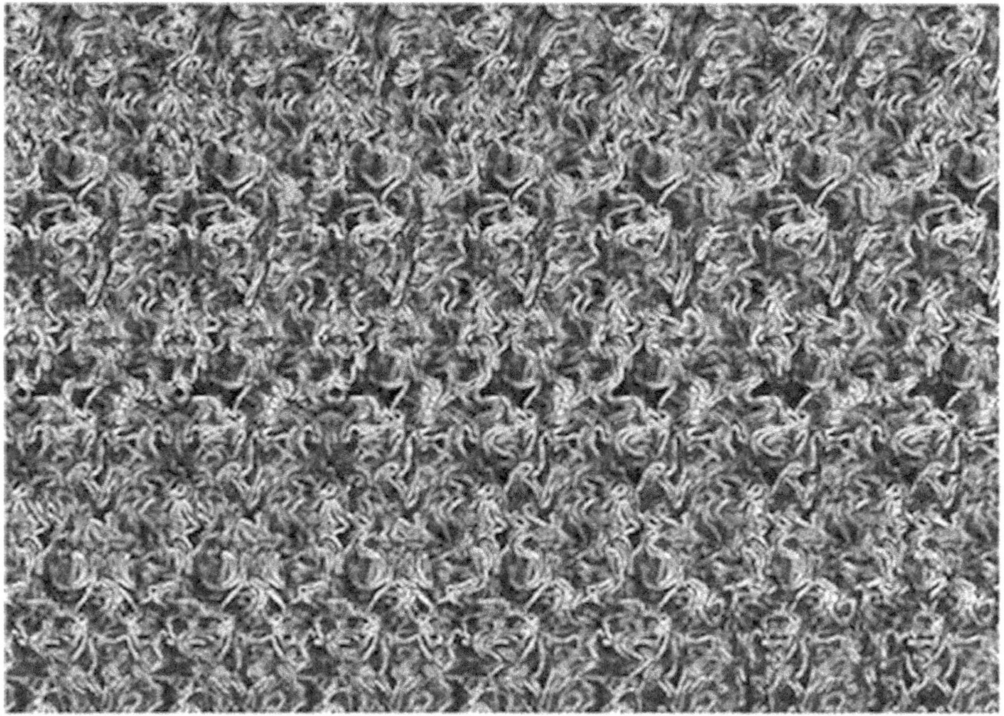

Inner Trauma

—⁂—

I EXPERIENCED MENTAL HIGH-ENERGY RELEASE events in 1988 and 1989. Energy releases from these two events were much greater than "normal" SCAP energy releases.

A high energy reverberating "Inner Metallic Sound" occurred while playing tennis in Phoenix, Arizona in 1988. My knees began to buckle. I recovered before falling. The reverberating sound was deafening, but was over quickly. This energy release must have occurred in the primary sound processing area of the brain.

The number of neurons exceeding energy limits does not need to be great if releases are in the most important auditory formations. When auditory neural networks exceeded energy limits, synchronization was lost. Energy releases caused auditory processes to re-synchronize. This inner metallic sound occurred a second time a few months later, with significantly less energy.

In 1989, I experienced a "Mental Nuclear Explosion" while sleeping. Visual neural networks, within the occipital lobe of the cerebral hemisphere lost synchronization. Traumatized networks in the most important areas of visual formations exceeded limits. Realignment caused a "Mental Nuclear Explosion" resulting in an inner "Flash" of extremely bright yellow light.

As I awakened, my awareness was engulfed in powerful yellow light exploding outward from within my mind in all directions. I thought I would not survive to see normal things again. The powerful light subsided in a "very long" two seconds. I became conscious of sitting up in my bed and sweating profusely. I was in disbelief that I survived this mental trauma.

There was no sound during this inner light explosion. After walking around for about thirty minutes trying to understand what happened, I was exhausted, went back to bed, slept, and went to work the next day.

My explanation was that I was overwhelmed by a highly unusual phenomenon. Traumatized networks lost synchronization in the most important area between the reticular formation and aminergic cluster in the brainstem. These two areas are important in determining waking or sleeping dominance.

When the energy release occurred, both the reticular formation and the aminergic cluster were competing for dominance. Earlier mental reconstruction had reduced communication boundary energy level differences between reticular formation and aminergic cluster activations. The Mental Nuclear Explosion occurred as an adjustment between these two important brainstem "nuclei." Both "nuclei" fired simultaneously at full speed. This unusual occurrence caused the "Mental Nuclear Explosion."

Both systems frantically fired full speed for dominance. I briefly lost hope of life. However, I have not recognized lasting negative effects.

Do you think I told anyone about these two extreme events? No! Everyone would think I'm crazy! Inner energy releases were so unusual that I did not tell anyone until I had some explanation for these occurrences. No one including psychiatrists would have understood such events. I write to share and make sense of these traumatic experiences. Readers may have less worry later if they experience similar events.

In January, 2015, new psychiatric higher-energy brainstem and lower cerebellum release sensations nearly rivaled those of chiropractic joint releases. Cerebellum energy releases may improve sight processing. Sensations were certainly not neck joint adjustments. Releases had less energy than my "Inner Metallic Sound" or the "Mental Nuclear Explosion".

These recent sensations have occurred with normal, and, more so, with conflicting, neck exercises. I describe sensations and feelings as precisely as I can to assist readers, and possible future research.

Everybody's crazy believing such dramatic sensations cannot occur to them. It may be difficult to believe such dramatic inner events can occur without lasting negative effects.

Mental Reconstruction

—⚊⚋⚊—

"We can all reprogram our brain's responses by
putting ourselves into new, initially uncomfortable
situations. We'll learn fear might not mean 'stop';
I've come to believe fear usually means 'go.'"

— Frances Moore Lappé

Mental reconstruction research began with three assumptions:

1. Localized sensations, within the upper neck, throat, and brainstem were trauma energy releases from overstressed neurons or neural networks. From my research older adults experience inner energy release sensations when exercising their necks.
2. I predicted that sensation locations would migrate within the upper neck, throat, and brainstem and slowly become and feel less energetic. With less disruptive, sporadic trauma energy, the brain will become more efficient and easier to control during emotional events. My goal became to exercise my neck until all trauma energy was purged.
3. Traumatized or overstressed neural networks store repressed trauma memories that mostly remain subconscious. They are sporadically activated by stimuli similar to that of the initiating

trauma. Releasing energy makes trauma memories more normal and the mind becomes less over-reactive.

The brain and mind become highly energetic during manic episodes that may activate repressed memories, initially ingrained from reactions to traumas. Conflicting exercises release disruptive emotional energy from traumatized neural networks.

With trauma energy lessened, increased subconscious mind control has prevented my bipolar episodes. Freedom from mania for over twenty years is proof of my theories.

For mental and physical health, we should maintain a relaxed mind and body when not exercising or competing. Meditate for a minute or two a few times a day. Lowering energy of the brain and body promotes subconscious freedoms for creative processes.

Most of us have had headaches. We become aware of locations of the pressure and pain. I have experienced few headaches during mental construction. Mind healing sensations are mostly pleasant and migrate between the neck, brainstem, and the upper throat with some sensations migrating to the cerebrum.

During emotional and trauma reactions, the neck and throat stiffen ingraining trauma scars. This is the reason most energy releases are sensed in the neck and throat.

Our minds consist of integrated and flowing EMR resonances from billions of neuron activations. Without neuron EMR synchronizing and integrating long enough to form resonances, there is no consciousness. Subconscious processes integrate related sub-ideas or resonances to form complete ideas. The mind is greater than the sum of neuron activations. Integrated EMR resonances create the mind and its spiritual dimensions.

Normal neural networks are elastic, supple, and "bend" with conflicting exercises. They normally accept and release energy from exercises and normal reactions as they should. Overstressed neural networks become rigid and do not bend. Traumatized neural networks store energy up to limits and then release their excessive energy, sensed as SCAPS.

Early repressed non-verbal trauma memories are thought to be the majority of trauma memories. Early trauma memories include pain of birth, the first breath, wordless fears of being left alone, loud noises, hunger, falling, injuries, etc. Everything is new and frightening to new babies, except nursing and cuddling.

Repressed trauma memories, semi-consciously activated, create bizarre dream distortions. After trauma energy is released, dreams become less distorted and more supportive of waking activities. When practicing psychiatric exercises, recalling trauma memories is not needed to purge trauma effects. Conflicting energy breaks down trauma energy release barriers.

When trauma scars are purged, normal subconscious processes no longer need to avoid them. Reactions become more appropriate in emotional situations. With less trauma scars, less total brain energy is needed to override these disruptive mental cancers. Traumatized neural networks do not synchronize with normal mental rhythms. These mental cancers have their own identity and react independently from normal brain activities.

After trauma energy is released, traumatized neural networks re-grow and function more normally as part of the brain's symphony. With continued exercises, subconscious processes become more adept at re-growing creative neural structures.

Writing promotes feelings of excitement and helps build and understand complex ideas. Predicting future complex events is difficult. I have been able to predict short range SCAP changes but not long range changes. Thinking and writing about the brain, mind, and God stimulate mental reconstruction sensations.

I have not felt discomfort from SCAP releases. They have become increasingly pleasant, greater in number, but with less individual energy released over the years. A basic premise is that pleasant feelings are positive signs of psychiatric healing.

After several years of conflicting exercises, SCAP, release sensations feel almost normal. Releasing mental energy relaxes the brain to its more efficient, natural state. Nature, including brains, loves energy efficiency.

If nerves and neural networks are tense, they restrict blood flow within the brain and face. Thinking becomes less efficient. We are able to sense when people are doing things efficiently. Runners look efficient when running smoothly.

Repressed trauma energy releases, and SCAP sensations have been released in shells. At times after neck exercises, I would experience only a few SCAPS. Thoughts were that mental reconstruction was nearly complete. However, a day or two later while performing similar neck exercises, another shell of trauma scars would rupture, releasing another flood of SCAP sensations.

Traumatized neural energy is stored and organized by shells. I suspect memories are also stored and organized by shells.

A few very active energy releases have caused my hair to stand on end. I delayed talking about healing processes, exercises, and sensations until I had developed models to explain sensations.

When overstressed neural networks are ruptured, other neural networks compete for influence. Less used neural networks become more active. Affected axons and dendrites grow thicker and become more efficient the more they are activated. They channel neurotransmitters faster and develop greater influence in their specialized processes.

Mental reconstruction builds communication between conscious and subconscious processes. Some subconscious processes become more conscious. We develop more control of our minds with more confident ideas. Every conscious idea has numerous supporting subconscious processes or sub-ideas.

There is a frequency and energy barrier between subconscious and conscious processes. Reducing the energy of the brain lowers the conscious energy barrier. More subconscious processes support construction of conscious ideas.

The reconstructing mind both deepens and expands decision-making options. With expanded mental limits, previous emotional challenges become more normal. Becoming comfortable with our minds and limits is part of the cure. Understanding more about subconscious processes and feelings improves confidence and creative thinking. With less trauma energy, earlier traumatized networks work in harmony with the rest of the brain.

The brain and mind make fundamental processing adjustments only when stressed to emotional limits. For a full life, we must get to know our minds at limits. Excessive stress can cause a number of problems including disorders. Stressing the mind to limits for too long hurts more than heals he mind.

We practice physical and mental activities to develop confidence for performing them in real life events. We must review repetitive mental and physical activities, at times, to understand and improve inner processes.

Challenges, at limits, keep the brain flexible and creative. Otherwise, the brain becomes rigid and only performs routine tasks. The mind feels more integrated and complete after successes followed by relaxation.

When surprised, we automatically inhale. There is slightly less pressure on the brain. Options for quick reactive thoughts and actions become greater. On the other hand when angry, we hold our breaths creating higher pressure in the brain. With increased pressure, we can think quickly but can only think of a few aggressive thoughts and actions. The brain is sensitive to slight pressure variations.

When reacting at emotional limits, responses become uncertain and out-of-control. Subconscious processes evaluate incoming trauma information and work frantically to stay within emotional limits. From experience, we learn to control emotions, and broaden physical and intellectual skills at expanded emotional limits. Healing fragile bipolar minds requires living, for brief periods, at emotional limits.

Severely stressed minds become compartmentalized. Disasters may be so stressful that minds develop separate conscious compartments for escaping trauma fear to cope. Mental reconstruction breaks down any compartmentalization for the brain to become more synchronized and function as a whole. Brain compartment healing feels similar to experiencing significant emotional events. There are feelings of a new direction and confidence.

When mental reconstruction is complete, the mind will be free of trauma restrictions and process as a complete, whole system. Minds become reborn. There may be a connection to being reborn in the biblical sense.

Continuing the same activities usually has the same results. However, continuing the same psychiatric exercises delves deeper into diverse repressed memories, releasing changing inner sensations.

Increasingly pleasant sensations are easily explained. As energy of trauma and emotional memories are purged by exercises, awareness of normal, pleasant memories and feelings become more prominent. Sensations may include a brief renewal of the face and scalp.

The face and brain are closely related. When the face tenses, the brain tenses. Glia cells contract and neurons become slightly closer together. EMR waves and resonances from synchronized neuron firings become slightly shorter with increased energy for making fast responses.

When feeling normal, relationships between the face and mind are mostly subconscious. If focusing on facial muscles, subconscious processes iterate to strengthen consistency between the brain and face.

Concentrate on facial nerves transmitting sensitivities to the brain. Envision nerves firing toward and within the neck, brainstem, throat, limbic system, cerebellum, and the upper brain. Considering relativity and light, ideas developed throughout the brain integrate into unchanging spiritual points and infinite existence within the soul. Spiritual ideas become independent of physical space and time.

A relaxed brain allows greater blood flow within the brain. A healthy brain and mind need to be relaxed except when experimenting, preparing for challenges, or actively thinking through routine and greater challenges.

For years, I have not feared experiencing fast thinking or mania. After twenty years, trauma energy release sensations were sometimes followed by brief ecstatic feelings.

With a less tension, more blood flows to the brain and face. There is more oxygen for neuron activations and neurotransmitter flow. The brain supports a smarter mind and healthier body. The face will be and look healthier. It may even develop a slight shine

Increased blood flow explains flush sensations around the crown of the head when relaxed. Mental reconstruction slows wrinkles and aging. However, as we "grow" older, we have less blood flow and oxygen to the brain, face, and body. They wrinkle.

The mind is amazing. It is difficult to imagine that so many complex activities in the brain can integrate for the mind to focus on one thought or vision.

Minds heal and creative lives begin when extending thoughts and activities beyond comfortable behaviors and to emotional limits. Making healing models has increased confidence in my work. Mental reconstruction has been a long, lonely process.

Religion and faith build inner confidence and have had huge influence on my mental reconstruction, healing, and health. Religions that require excessive memorization and promote rigid thinking will make mental reconstruction difficult.

Everybody's crazy believing overstressed neural networks cannot release repressed energy to become more normal and creative. Normal brain processes no longer need to override sporadic, high-energy neural network activations.

Inner Sensations

SOME ANALOGIES MAY HELP READERS acknowledge inner sensations. If having experienced chiropractic adjustments, readers are aware of "click" sensations when joints are returned to their correct, least energetic positions. Chiropractic adjustments release stress from neck and other joints. Without having experienced chiropractic adjustments, some may doubt the existence and character of sensations.

Readers may sense neck, throat, and brainstem sensations when exercising their necks. Inner sensations have less energy than joint release sensations. They have decreasing energy and become more pleasant over the years.

Reducing stress in neck, throat, and facial nerves renews facial muscles. The face becomes tighter and less wrinkled. Unfortunately, muscles below the chin do not seem to tighten. Perhaps normal body exercises would help.

Stress causes joints to slip out of their normal less energetic positions, which affects nerves, pain, and mobility. Ingrained stress and trauma energy within memory neural networks affect mental abilities, emotions, anxieties, spirituality, and cause levels of residual pain. From my theories, excess emotional energy must be stored in tensed axons, dendrites, neuron bodies, and glia, or support cells. Tense muscles and nerves store excess energy that is transmitted to the brain.

If not having worked out for some while and then exercising regularly, the body and mind feel more relaxed and pleasant. In exercising, muscle cells are torn down and then rebuilt. Neck exercises tear down overstressed brain cells by releasing emotional energy. They are reconstructed to function more normally. The mind, brain, and body become more connected. To some extent, each thought affects every cell in the brain and body. Muscles and the body feel more pleasant with an exercise program.

Hunger hurts and the mind and body feel tense. If we have been very hungry and then eaten, we sense pleasant feelings and strength returning throughout the body. The mind thinks more normally without hunger dominating the mind.

If readers have never been really hungry or had a dramatic improvement from exercise practices, readers may be unaware of "healing" sensations. To initiate changes in our minds and bodies, we must experiment and do activities beyond the normal. Mental reconstruction is similar to body building. Repeated exercises build faster and stronger muscles and brains.

If we have been sleep deprived for a long time and finally have restful sleep, the brain and body relax. Neuron and glia cells are cleansed of toxins, the brain becomes more creative, and the body becomes less stressed. The rested mind and body feel more pleasant.

Everybody's crazy to believe that mental reconstruction does not stimulate pleasant inner sensations. With patience, psychiatric exercises may be beneficial to readers. The brain is complex and takes a long time to heal.

Consciousness Model

SCIENTISTS DEVELOP THEORIES TO UNDERSTAND principles of nature for human benefit. They suggest experiments to prove their theories. If we understand more of our consciousness, we can, and help others, think better and more creatively. I am unaware of other theories explaining consciousness. My work is separate from established research.

Firing neurons within the brain synchronize creating electromagnetic resonances. Resonances that last beyond some time threshold and with energy above competing resonances create consciousness.

Resonances must last long enough to create vision. We do not see a bullet passing through the scope of our vision. The time the bullet is within of the scope of vision is too short for conscious resonances to be developed.

If activations of eighty billion neurons or subsets of neurons can focus to construct one conscious idea or image, individual neuron activation EMR must integrate to form consciousness. The brain is continuously integrating information from activating nerves with recalled memories to develop comparisons, reasoning, and consciousness. We do not become aware of individual rod and cone activations. We become aware of integrated rod and cone activations for vision.

If nerves receive high energy activation levels, they activate faster and promote shorter, higher energy, EMR resonances in the brainstem and limbic systems. Pain, anger, and extreme desire create high primitive energy resonances in the brain.

A Philosophy of Healing and Spirituality

Our TVs and radios receive electromagnetic waves or signals from many different stations. The same air is filled with different radio waves or frequencies without them interacting or distorting each other. We can tune the resonance of our radios to receive the one station we wish to listen to. We normally wish to listen to one station at a time.

With millions of rods and cones and other sensors throughout the body, millions of synchronized neurons are stimulated to produce numerous coherent EMR resonances within the brain. Coherent EMR resonances create subconscious and conscious mental holograms. We have proof of mental hologram scenarios from dreams.

We have thousands of mental holograms, with different frequencies, within and overlapping one another in the same space. With slight variations in energy, the mind switches from one hologram scenario to the other. Many three dimensional hologram resonances or scenarios "live" in the same brain space. With limited abilities, humans develop consciousness of only one mental hologram at a time from many overlapping mental holograms.

The brain has ability to focus on each point of vision within so many coexisting three dimensional mental holograms. Like snowflakes, neurons and neuron activation profiles are different and are sources for constructing so many unique mental resonances or holograms at the same time.

An activated neuron explodes EMR outward in characteristic directions depending upon its membrane shape. Its original EMR is a reference source for reflected, refracted, and possibly diffracted EMR from its own membrane and membranes of other cells with focusing angles to create one neuron's resonance or hologram.

Individual neuron holograms integrate and overlap other neuron holograms having similar profiles and frequencies creating integrated holograms for developing human vision and other sensations. Reflected, refracted, and diffracted EMR are focused to create a recursive detailed mind and brain. Neuron resonances depend upon brain cell membranes and their angles and surfaces for focusing EMR back to the original, and to other activating, neurons. Membrane resonances matter more than distance.

Each point of a commercial or mental hologram medium or membrane reflects continuous differing angles of images at continually differing viewing angles. Mental scenario images vary with stimulation and time.

Each mental hologram has distinct frequencies. One mental hologram produces conscious from many "viewed" angles. Depending upon stimuli thousands, or perhaps millions, of mental holograms can exist together within the brain's space. Slight variations in hologram frequencies allow mental holograms to integrate. Stimulated and integrated EMR resonances, cultured by reflections, refractions, and diffractions from many neurons and cell membranes within the brain create dreams and mental holograms for consciousness.

The brightest and most energetic mental, conscious hologram reflects spiritual waves throughout the brain and universe in spiritual dimensions. Subconscious hologram scenarios do not create spiritual waves. Humans are only responsible of conscious ideas and activities.

We may develop an experiment to identify mental resonances, with activation or deactivation, using electromagnetic sources at various angles and frequencies. Source angles and frequencies should be similar to those of firing neurons, neural networks, or brain components. Patients, describing negative or positive effects, could provide information to support mental healing technologies.

If simple thoughts become difficult at certain EMR source placements and angles, it is an indication that conscious resonances are being disrupted or overridden. By slightly varying wavelengths, sources could account for EMR having to pass through the skull.

With coherent EMR sources from one neuron expanding in discrete directions, EMR resonances or mental holograms are supported by billions of small parallel membrane segments from its own and other brain cells. With eighty billion neurons and billions of glia cells, there are billions of small parallel membrane segment surfaces reflecting EMR and each constructing very faint details of mental holograms. Resonances with the same or similar frequencies are integrated to form the dreams we become aware of.

With parallel and near parallel reflections from small membrane segments, one might reason that mental holograms are somewhat quantized. Each reflection and refraction adds hologram detail. Membrane absorptions and refractions add to membrane memory and mental structure.

Several experimental sources may be introduced at the same time and at different angles searching to isolate and prove conscious structures. Detecting source absorptions may determine mental resonances within the brain. Focused, higher energy EMR may detect and release energy from localized trauma memories. Neuroscientists may define further experiments.

The goal is to discover reasons and corrections for patients having difficulties in certain types of thinking. Introducing certain brief, low energy waves may activate areas of the brain to improve thinking, and even body control. Continued applications may be helpful.

The brain is complex. I have given a scenario that may contribute to understanding consciousness. Readers are free to develop more.

Everybody's crazy, if believing a physicist and nuclear engineer cannot develop useful theories for understanding consciousness.

The Clear Mind

—⚎—

"The Clear Mind" has been my goal since 1995. In this model, the brain is cleared of all adverse trauma effects and emotional processing compartments. The clear brain and mind process holistically. There are no longer trauma energy releases, or SCAPS, from psychiatric processes. Ideas will seem to fly. More subconscious options are integrated and promoted for each conscious idea. Thinking feels and is more confident. With inner confidence, one becomes more empathetic in caring for self and others.

From 1977 to 1982, I had several severe manic episodes stemming from an incompatible, degrading marriage. I had only a few disruptive manic episodes from 1983 to 1994. Since 1994, I have not had a single manic episode. I no longer worry about becoming manic and going out of control. This is my major accomplishment!

Without disruptive trauma effects, brains and minds work as God designed them to do. Trauma afflicted neural networks are scarred, brittle, and activate sporadically disrupting the normal symphony of brain activities. Normal processes must increase activations and energy to overcome repressed trauma memory disruptions. Activated repressed memories do not become fully conscious but fester as threatening, uncertain feelings and emotions. Without trauma memory effects, the brain's creative resonances bloom into full-blown orchestras.

With stimulation, the brain and mind become able to understand and heal their inner processes. There is better communication between the brain, its DNA, memory, mind, and soul. Longevity genes are activated for a longer life. The brain processes with lower energy when performing stressful activities.

The mind thinks faster and is able to simplify complex thoughts and designs. Complex designs are integrated into an understandable wholeness of purpose. Dreams are organized by more precise energy levels and appear more life-like. There is less inner conflict. The mind is more creative and confident. Recall improves. Desire and ability increase to build self- and others' confidence.

With trauma effects dissipated, communication between the mind and soul become clearer and truthful. Trauma effects have eclipsed communication with the soul. With lower mental energy, spiritual communication is received more consciously.

The brain and mind construct a complex recursive system. Mental reconstruction has come a long way toward achieving the clear mind. I have worked for twenty years toward this goal. Healing and spiritual accomplishments have been amazing but my clear mind goal remains elusive.

Most of us have compartmentalized brains and minds to greater or lesser extents. Activations of highly emotional overstressed networks divide the brain into different subconscious, and sometimes conscious, compartments. Compartments are integrated into one thinking structure practicing psychiatric processes

My mental reconstruction exercises and processes purge excess energy from overstressed neural networks that have divided the brain into compartments. When excess energy from all overstressed neural networks is purged, the brain and mind become free to process as a whole. As of this writing, I am not certain what final "Clear Mind" improvements will be. My hope is that final results will prove mind healing processes and even prove God exists.

My life's journey has been an odd one. Creative and spiritual inner activities are not believed unless experienced. I am willing to work another 20 years to accomplish the Clear Mind. I am not certain of effects readers might experience if practicing processes.

The clear mind only has genetic restraints. Reasoning and creative processes are expanded. Subconscious processes perfectly recall memories and consider many options in making decisions.

I expect continued pleasant inner sensations toward achieving the Clear Mind. The creativity of dreams will integrate with waking abilities for a higher reality. Achievements require dedication and work for constructing a new mind.

Clear minds will prove bipolar healing and spiritual wisdom. Clear minds will improve praises and benefits to God for receiving His blessings.

Christian leaders preach that we need only to believe in and surrender to Jesus for everlasting lives. Some believe and surrender with ease.

Clear Minds may recall the spiritual wisdom of conception and early life. My spiritual walk has been influenced by my science background. We learn about God by studying His universe.

I have taken a path less traveled. It would have been easier to join the crowd but that was not my calling. Jesus took a different and difficult spiritual path. He was the spiritual rebel of His time.

In 1995, I received an amazing, unexpected inner voice seemingly coming from all directions that penetrated my very soul: "Don't Leave God Out!" This inner voice interrupted the completion of my first healing book and extended writing into spirituality. This message had a holistic effect on my spiritual path for twenty years. I search for spiritual completeness.

I have never felt qualified to write spiritually. However, I felt compelled to obey! Harmonic reverberations, from God's amazing message, have stimulated creative ideas for 20 years. I can only use the knowledge and skills that I have to interpret and write about healing and inner messages.

Everybody's crazy if believing minds cannot be cleared of all childhood and later trauma effects. The mind is complex and requires a very long time to be cleared of adverse effects. The Clear Mind aspires to reach toward perfection.

Evil and Evil Minds

Serenity Prayer

God, grant me the serenity to accept the things
I cannot change, Courage to change the things
I can, and wisdom to know the difference.

— Reinhold Niebuhr, Theologian

"Sin is disobeying any of the Ten Commandments."

— Billy Graham

"A child who is allowed to be disrespectful to his
parents will not have true respect for anyone.

— Billy Graham

"The world is a dangerous place, not because of those who
do evil, but because of those who look on and do nothing."

— Albert Einstein

Evil in the Bible:

> "Even though I walk through the valley of the shadow of death, I will fear no evil, for you are with me; your rod and staff, they comfort me. You prepare a table before me in the presence of mine enemies. You anoint my head with oil; my cup overflows."
>
> — Psalm 23:4-5, Disciples Study Bible.

> "Complaining against God is called evil."
>
> — Numbers 14:27

MANY OF US DO NOT talk about evil until they endure life threatening circumstances, or there is significant theft or damage. If someone is evil to us, we experience guilt without doing wrong or having blame. We may feel guilt because we were in the wrong place at the wrong time.

Evil is when someone intentionally hurts, swindles, degrades, or kills someone for their psychological or financial gain. Drugs and alcohol produce selfish, evil minds. Some parents cannot let their daughters or sons in their own home because they steal things to buy cocaine. Parents feel guilt with or without fault. How could my child go so wrong?

Most authors write about positive experiences and lives until they observe or experience serious physical or mental abuse, conspiracy and/or other evils. This essay gives examples of evils against the author.

Evil, self-centered men deceive innocent young women into substance abuse to take advantage of them. Many once beautiful young women become prostitutes to pay for their drug habits. Drug addicts steal to pay for drugs. Evil perpetrators often go unpunished.

Evil and Evil Minds

Evil, prejudiced people degrade and feel "superior" because of wealth, appearance, strength, skills, sex, race, size, or sexual orientation. Some prejudices have been engrained over generations. Prejudiced people are supportive to many but evil to the vulnerable. A seemingly wonderful minister may abuse his wife.

Drunken men and women feel so "high and mighty" that they abuse the "weak and unworthy" including parents, spouses, children, and friends. A police officer may be wonderful at helping people on duty, but after drinking abuses his wife. Bar women, are in the minority and learn to control and abuse men.

Womanizers lie to and abuse innocent women. Shortly, they are on to their next conquest. Attracting women for quick sex and ego becomes more important than building lasting relationships. Womanizers develop huge egos. They have no respect for women, their wellbeing, or their husbands. They take pride in attracting and abusing other men's wives or girlfriends. They destroy relationships and lives.

Some good intended, mild mannered parents let older siblings physically and psychologically abuse younger siblings. Some severely abused younger siblings become limited or non-functional. Later, younger siblings may blame, and rebel against, parents for not preventing abuse.

Sibling bullying is more damaging than high school bullying. The abused has constant fear without an escape.

Big companies, stock exchanges, banks, and real estate agents lie, intimidate, and manipulate to steal from the innocent working class. Their lobbyist influence lawmakers to make laws allowing them to legally steal to increase their control and profits. American laws are made by and biased toward the rich making it easy to hide white collar evil. Madoff's Ponzi scheme was an extreme evil. Many were devastated by his scheme. Financial institutions and Wall Street have a license to steal!

A worse evil is when a child is emotionally and sexually abused. As an adult, that child may sexually abuse innocent children and adults.

Sexual abuse is a tragedy for perpetrators and victims. Without intervention, sexual abuse becomes ingrained and may continue generations. American psychiatry does not intervene until atrocities have become extreme and widely recognized. Only severe perpetrators are punished.

We must evaluate who is being good to us and who is not. Criteria should be who is helping us be independent, giving us confidence to do good things, and helping us be creative. Hopefully, parents and teachers are doing these things.

Evil tears down and destroys creativity. Creativity means having new, positive structured thoughts that are helpful to self, others, and God. It takes creativity to understand and receive spiritual communications.

We should praise those who are good to us but hold those who are evil accountable. If criminals continue stealing without being caught, they feel entitled to continue. Most of us try to understand and love everyone, but we do not need to love those who scheme to destroy us. I pray for God's guidance in resolving evil.

EVIL AGAINST MY PROPERTY AND ME

I lived peacefully on my farm until 2004. Things were never stolen from, vandalized, or misplaced in, my home. Peace and harmony changed in 2004.

A lady I loved asked me to sell her grandson some land. I sold him three acres at an edge of my farm, on her account, in 2004. I did not know her grandson well but was looking forward to having him and his family as neighbors. I expected to care for him and his family.

This lady's grandson was always pushing for more and more, and never thanking me for the things I did for him. After I agreed to a favor, he would say nothing and arrogantly turn and walk away. I put up a fence to keep him from encroaching with his landscaping on my land. After putting up the fence in 2006, I never talked to him again.

It is everyone's responsibility to report evil. Otherwise evildoers feel entitled to continue. We must never let threats keep us from reporting evil.

For ten years, someone has broken into my house and vehicles steeling and vandalizing valuable property, and steeling or hiding personal property to frustrate. I have changed locks several times. For years I have had to bolt my doors from the inside at night. My Britta pitcher was poisoned.

This neighbor has intruded my privacy by placing cameras at property boundaries. He is a sophisticated bully and criminal.

When inspecting my fence at the border of my rogue neighbor's property, wires were sometimes cut. If he was within view, he avoids eye contact or acknowledgement and retreats into his house. Anyone would recognize the guilt on his face and in his body language. However, when I am away from my house, he is bold and feels entitled to break in and steal. My tennis racket was recently stolen.

Bullying continues over generations. A few years ago this rogue neighbor's mother seemed to think it was funny that she was involved in my older brother's bullying when we were young. Bullying is catching.

I have called the sheriff many times. There are GPS devices and phone taps criminals can purchase to know when victims are away from home. Alarm system blocking devices can be purchased.

My only person of interest for breaking in my house beginning in 2004 is Jean Paul, "Jay," Coulson III who moved next door in 2004. He continually returned my goodness with evil.

I have worked to understand such an evil person. On Dr. Phil's show on September 22, 2014, he discussed evil persons' behaviors, they:

1. Infiltrate your life.
2. Create Conspiratorial Confidents - to persuade others to abuse victims
3. Misdirect and Obfuscate

4. Has Arrogant Entitlement – feel entitled to degrade and steal.
5. Lack Empathy – Do not feel bad when degrading and hurting victims.
6. Has No Remorse/Guilt – justify their evil. Only getting caught will stop their evil.
7. Thrive on Drama
8. Brag About Outsmarting – victims
9. Isolate to Destroy Credibility – of victim
10. Lie – to attain selfish goals.
11. Frauds/Cheats/Steals – destroys and steal things in houses.
12. Give dishonest History – to override victims credibility

In my view my person of interest fits all of the above traits. I was raised in a wonderful country environment and taught to love everyone. Unfortunately, this is no longer true for me. I had to develop principles to protect and be true to myself.

Spiritual principles do not change. However, unwittingly, churches give comfort and false worth to evil attendees that lie and do evil to destroy others. Church going is not synonymous with spirituality. Some of the most evil doers hide in churches. In the news, a sexual predator acted normally outside his home, went to church regularly, but imprisoned and tortured three beautiful women as sex slaves for ten years.

We cannot continue supporting those who are perpetrating evil against us. We are being untrue to our inner principles. If continuing, we will lose self-respect and health.

I aspire to love, care for, and be good to everyone I can. However, for my health and wellbeing, I can no longer continue to be good to those who degrade, lie about, and conspire against me. Evil doers destroy so many who are different or weak. So many criminals go unpunished.

Everybody's crazy believing evil could not happen to them or in their neighborhoods. Some lying evil perpetrators have not been caught for years. Criminal minds continue evil until caught.

Spiritual Section

Nothing before Time

Introduction

During my first manic episode, I became preoccupied and amazed with inner, spiritual thoughts. Importance and confidence in normal thinking lessened. I felt empowered to reason through everything. It was the beginning of my "Nothing before Time" model.

It became important to model God's Own Creation so He could then create the universe. Has God existed forever in primordial or pre-spiritual time before creating the universe and physical time? Spiritual time is very different from human sensed physical time.

Before time, it was uncertain if and when the universe would be created. My primordial model continues into the Big Bang creation of physical time, space, and energy. I have assumed that Heisenberg Uncertainty limits existed in primordial time. It was the best principle for explaining my Nothing before Time model that exploded into God and then the universe.

Genesis Model

Before developing my creation model, let's briefly relate Genesis to science and cosmology:

On <u>the first day</u> of Creation in Genesis, God separated Light, Himself, from complete darkness, or "Nothing before Time." Infinite primordial space-less, imaginary dimensions had consistent indeterminate energy throughout primordial existence. The first day of the Genesis model has similarities to cosmological creation models. In a small fraction of a second, God created and separated all atoms and physical dimensions from Himself and His spiritual dimensions.

On <u>the second day</u>, waters were separated from waters. This may refer to initial uniform hydrogen gases separating to form galaxies and stars. It may also refer to the cooling of dry land and the oceans separating from the molten core of the earth. These concepts would have been difficult for biblical writers to interpret with the knowledge they had. The earth was flat. We, humans only receive spiritual wisdom we are prepared to receive and interpret.

Readers are free to interpret the first two and remaining days of the Genesis Creation model.

Nothing before Time

My primordial model must be simple but sufficient to create God and then the universe. Primordial, pre-spiritual existence had no measurable differences, awareness, or primordial history.

Scientists believe they will never be able to calculate existence before the Big Bang, mathematically. Cosmology equations become asymptotic and develop an infinite singularity when calculating backwards in time to the Big Bang. The Big Bang was a singularity. Spiritual dimensions and properties have not been addressed in cosmology. Through God, all things are possible.

If God is omniscient, He is conscious of all things and actions. He will know how He came into existence and may reveal primordial information. God is holy, independent of space, and the same in Virginia, Hawaii, and on the North Star, Polaris - 430 light-years away.

What caused the "Big Bang?" Primordial time leading up to the "Big Bang" was negative. Nothing became more organized in negative primordial time. Entropy became zero at the initial moment of the

Big Bang. Entropy is a physics term for measuring disorganization. Overall entropy of the universe continually increases as the universe becomes more disorganized.

In pre-existence there was no "spatial" difference between a primordial point and infinite homogeneous primordial dimensions that were perfectly organized, as primordial oneness a moment before the Big Bang. Each imaginary primordial transition between the primordial point and primordial infinity created a pre-quantum of primordial pre-energy or negative energy.

I give an example of transitioning between a point and space-less infinite existence. I close my eyes and imagine one idea or infinite ideas existing in one point within my darkness. Then I imagine one or infinite ideas existing throughout my "infinite" darkness. I have no idea how my infinite darkness is structured. I have not thought of physical space. Readers can believe or not believe that my non-spatial, transitional thoughts existed. Nothing before Time existed, and God originally existed, without physical space, as ideas exist. Nothing before Time and the spiritual existed before the physical existed.

Primordial negative pre-energy became so great that an additional primordial-quantum of negative pre-energy made no difference creating primordial infinity. "Identical" primordial reflections exploded exponentially flashing into positive spiritual energy and dimensions, creating God and relativistic spiritual time.

God then created the universe, relativistic time and space, and virgin wave energy as the beginning of the Big Bang. Virgin "Light" is directly from the Big Bang and not created later from atom excitations.

In a fraction of a second later God created all atoms in the universe. He separated holistic spiritual existence from detailed physical existence. Spiritual dimensions perfectly record histories of all physical events in the universe.

Physical time and space allow organizing and disorganizing activities. Gravity integrating hydrogen atoms into stars is an organizing activity. Freezing water is organizing. Melting ice disorganizes.

For the singularity of Creation to occur, negative, imaginary primordial time must have converged to zero. For God and the universe to be created from nothing, an opposing negative existence must have been purged. Some refer to this negative existence, with emotional needs to recombine with, or destroy, God and Heaven, as the Devil and Hell. These negative forces had rather be nothing.

In the moment before the Big Bang Creation, Nothing before Time uncertainty limits were exceeded. It became certain that God existed with potential to create a universe. For events to occur physically, mentally, or spiritually, there must be uncertainty and freedom or the universe would only be homogenized, holistic, and predestined. There are levels of uncertainty in everything we think or do.

In assuming Heisenberg Uncertainty limits existed before time and using the mass of the universe, we can estimate the very fast primordial, imaginary transitions that created very fast spiritual waves and God.

Let's consider the frequency of primordial vibrations multiplied by primordial energy. When their product exceeded Heisenberg Uncertainty limits, spiritual existence became certain. Primordial energy became so great that an added pre-quantum of primordial energy was so small, that is was negligible. A primordial change must have occurred for the Big Bang to explode into God and then the universe. The total primordial energy of Nothing before Time became infinite. God was created with infinite spiritual energy. Adding a quantum of energy, or anything, to infinity is still infinity.

Scientists discover physical relationships within the universe with successful, repeatable, and provable experiments. We learn about artists by studying their art and about God by studying His universe. Activities in the universe continue to create physical history and God's wisdom. The current physical configuration of the universe and current light focusing into spiritual waves construct God's continuous conscious wisdom and abilities.

Current configuration of the brain, incoming sense information, and EMR activities from firing neurons focus to create memory and the mind. The mind is spiritual.

Nuclear engineers sometimes model nuclear reactor cores, without cumbersome spatially dependent calculations, for determining preliminary nuclear reactor fuel and other materials for core design. Meaningful calculations can be made without modeling spatial differences. Calculations model homogenous concentrations within infinite reactor core dimensions for approximations of reactor core designs. Nothing before Time with infinite homogeneous properties may be either a real or imaginary model.

In nuclear calculations without accounting for spatial differences, a model may be either an infinite or a point model. Similarly, Nothing before Time may be considered either a point or infinite model, without spatial differences possible.

Cosmologists spend little time theorizing about "Nothing before Time," the DNA or blueprint of God and the universe, and the seed for matter, energy, space, and time.

Cosmology calculations become infinite, indeterminate, and unreliable at the instant of Creation. Scientists believe they will not be able to calculate or model existence before the Big Bang Singularity Creation of the Universe. Extreme physical events, such as the Big Bang, lead to mathematical singularities, which are not easily modeled. Our best hope of understanding primordial existence is if God reveals it to us.

God was created in the first moment of the Big Bang as pure oneness with Self-awareness. His Virgin spiritual wave energy was too great to be stable. In 10^{-35} seconds of His existence, He created all atoms of the universe from within Himself. God has continuous knowledge of all physical and spiritual things He has created. Physical time in the beginning of an extremely dense universe was very different from earthly time today. Since God was created before physical time, He has existed forever.

God was created as perfect symmetric waves within spiritual dimensions, heaven. Physical dimensions are integrated with God's spiritual dimensions. We might think of the universe's physical dimensions as God's body. Spiritual freedoms allow human minds to converge to social and spiritual truths or diverge to falseness and evil.

After God created atoms, the universe had differences that could be measured. He has awareness of each quantum of space within the universe. Fourteen billion years later God nurtures human minds toward His Truth. Humans have an inner awareness when not being truthful.

Scientists have not recognized any remnants from Nothing before Time. Primordial history is lost or never occurred.

To understand God, in greater depth, we must understand Einstein's General Relativity for understanding galaxies and other big things throughout the universe. God is bigger than the physical universe.

To model properties of the universe, cosmology calculations require six or seven additional dimensions to integrate quantum mechanics models (small things, atoms) with general relativity models (big things, galaxies) into one calculation framework. God is relativistic to the physical universe. These additional dimensions must be spiritual relationship and integration dimensions.

Physical dimensions and laws control and expand the universe in an orderly fashion and are the backbone of the universe. God makes or reacts with holistic changes throughout spiritual dimensions. Consciousness and other brain activities holistically affect brain structures.

The Unified Field Force, including gravity, was initially repulsive that caused the Big Bang explosion. From cosmology, in a small fraction of a second, a repulsive gravity force reversed polarity and became an attractive gravity. The "Heisenberg Uncertainty Principle" essay provides a rough calculation for the final primordial frequency that initiated the Big Bang explosion and created very fast spiritual waves.

God and the universe have a recursive relationship. Physical activities in the universe create God, and God controls the universe. Brain activities create the mind, and, recursively, the mind controls the brain. Humans and God form a recursive relationship. God created humans for them to worship and influence Him.

Nothing before Time supports my omniscient and omnipresent spiritual model. Primordial existence must have been a building structure with uncertainties for the Big Bang to have occurred.

Conclusion

There is no awareness or thought without uncertainties. God has certainties and uncertainties, and perfect knowledge of all physical and spiritual history. God and humans must have uncertainties, or they cannot make decisions. The greatest human accomplishments are when a scientist or hero makes the greatest uncertainties, certain. Without uncertainties, God, the universe, and humans would be predestined. No "real" decisions could be made. God and humans have uncertainties, make decisions, and are not predestined.

A goal for God and humans is to build spiritual certainty from physical uncertainty. No decisions could occur if absolute certainty were accomplished. However, the evolving configuration of the universe constructs God's perfect awareness of all history.

This essay is meant to give readers a feeling of existence before time, God, and the universe. Readers may be as imaginative as they like.

Everybody's crazy for not searching to understand the origins of the universe and human life. We can learn from simple models that develop feelings of existence before time.

Creation

Philosophers and cosmologist ponder the universe's initial and current structures and behaviors. Some ponder the existence and structure of God and heaven. In His beginning, God needed structure to define His existence and ability. There is no energy or power if everything is the same. He created the universe, of His own free will, with structural differences to support His spiritual structures, energy, and time.

Manic-depressives may receive strong spiritual messages during manic episodes. Some spiritual messages have given feelings of Creation. After initial amazement, spiritual messages feel as if known for a long time.

I have worked to recall and write spiritual messages received during depression and mania to continue spiritual models. My philosophical and spiritual models are based upon science, the Bible, and spiritual messages received.

My experience in modeling nuclear reactors has given some confidence in modeling. My Creation model began with my model of "Nothing before Time." Primordial pre-quantum, pre-waves between the pre-spiritual point and pre-spiritual infinite homogeneous existence, were the bases of my "Nothing before Time" model.

After God's creation, as the beginning of the Big Bang, He existed completely as higher dimensional spiritual waves and resonances as all of existence. Spiritual time began somewhere between zero and infinite primordial time. There was no physical time until God created the universe. God's spiritual energy was too emotionally powerful to control. He released, from within Himself, 10^{82} confined vibrations, or atoms with discrete energy in less than 10^{-35} seconds to create properties of the physical universe.

Scientists estimate the number of hydrogen atoms in the universe is from 10^{78} to 10^{82}. I use the higher number since I believe scientists are not able to model or predict the entire universe.

Initially, God was completely spiritual waves. He released "Light - EMR" energy and then matter energy to create an expanding universe. Spiritual waves were and are shock waves from the initial Big Bang explosion.

Spiritual waves resonate between the origin and the expanding boundaries of the universe. As the universe expands, spiritual waves expand in length at the speed of light. "Nothing" beyond the universe is completely uniform or homogeneous and devoid of energy. Nothing resists change by absorbing and reflecting virgin light and spiritual waves.

Light from the other side of a very big universe has not reached earth yet. Since space itself expands at large distances from galaxies, scientists may observe light from far-away galaxies as traveling faster than the speed of light we measure on earth.

Spiritual waves travel much, much faster than light as they vibrate between the Big Bang center and the expanding boundaries of the universe in much less than a second. God's wisdom of the entire universe is always up to date.

Why did God create the universe? God was created spiritually perfect and the same everywhere. He, as all of existence, was perfect. Perfect cannot change! Everything was perfectly organized; there were no uncertainties. Then God, with a perturbation, created the universe with uncertainties to have something to nurture, grow, and reflect His Love. Similarly, parents have a need to nurture their children and mold them into reflections of themselves.

God created time and space allowing discrete changes in the universe and holistic changes throughout heaven. Energy is continually shared between Light, (God,) and matter within the universe.

We must be careful in defining perfect. God observes and manages physical disorganization to become more perfect in spiritual time. The universe becomes less organized with time and God becomes more organized to understand and record all activities in the universe and in heaven. The universe has physical and probability uncertainties. God responds consistently to physical, mental and spiritual activities and challenges. God is perfect independent of physical time.

God created the universe with uncertainty and conflict. Conflict between light, EMR, and matter continues. There will always be conflict between God, evil, and negative, disorganizing forces. Will existence end as completely "Light" resonating with spiritual freedom or as dark motionless "frozen" matter?

God is aware of and perfectly records all activities in the universe. He created perfect unchanging physical and probability laws to organize His universe. Allowing uncertainties, God's loneliness turned to emotions including Love. He created Man on earth and possibly beings on other planets for them to receive and reflect His love back to Him, of their own free will. Good parents set grown children free but want them to reflect their training and love back to them.

God constantly communicates with, and controls, the universe. Man is controlled by gravity, light, and other forces, but has free will to think independent of God and His spiritual laws. With uncertainties and Man's free will, God has never been lonely.

Pets have minds of their own and give humans something to care for and love. Pets keep us from being lonely. Even beautiful flowers do not give us the loving feeling that pets can give us. Humans were created to love pets, others, and God. My cat's purring is very relaxing to me.

At times, philosophical questioning provides direction for scientists to research and understand more of the universe. Scientific experiments sometimes prove philosophical conjectures and theories as facts.

Light energy is created by accelerated charged matter with freedom to travel throughout the universe at relativistic speeds. Matter energy is confined energy. God is always traveling at the speed of light, and is aware of all activities within the universe.

"Perfect" spiritual books are interpreted differently by various congregations and cultures. For a spiritual life, we must reason about spiritual books to separate enlightenment from control. See my essay on "Thomas Jefferson's Beliefs."

With enlightenment, one reasons about and feels comfortable about earthly and spiritual completeness. One isolates himself from outside influences. Only God matters. Enlightenment may last, or only be brief.

Spiritual models are meant to provide a sense of understanding and adventure. Models of God will improve with science research, interpretations of traditional spiritual books, and current spiritual messages received and documented. God's complete wisdom is available everywhere when we are prepared and sensitive enough to receive it. Our prayers are recursive. We only receive spiritual information we are able to understand. A fundamental human goal is to learn, and reflect, God's Truth.

Since traditional spiritual leaders have founded a spiritual basis, we are able to recognize spiritual messages from God today. Inner healing sensations and spiritual messages are intuitive. They develop awareness differently than human to human communications. Scientists also learn about God by studying and analyzing His universe.

Everybody's crazy if believing humans cannot learn about the universe and God from science, and receive important spiritual information directly from God today. The Bible and scientists have different versions of creation. However, Genesis is proof that ancestors were interested in understanding and recording the universe's and human origins thousands of years ago.

Soul

—⌇—

THE BRAIN CONSTRUCTS MILLIONS OF light/EMR resonances from synchronized, integrated neuron activations to create the mind. The soul compares the integral of mental resonances to God's truthful, holistic higher dimensional resonances.

Integrated spiritual hologram resonances within our souls have perfect communication with God's infinite Hologram resonances. The soul contains all thoughts and activities during life for judgment at the moment of death.

Spiritual communications to and from our souls are disrupted by trauma memories and unspiritual thoughts and actions. However, during high emotional energy of expected death trauma, spiritual wisdom within our souls breaks into consciousness. Our souls always have perfect communication with God.

Depending upon spiritual resonances integrated from thought and action resonances, the soul is either spiritual or void of spiritual wisdom. Spiritual values are multiplicative. A very evil action may negate many spiritual thoughts and actions. For example, the worst evil action may have a value of: $1/1,000,000$. The best spiritual action may have a value of 100. It would take many spiritual activities to overcome that one horrible act and its small fraction diminishing spiritual truth. In this simple model, final integrated spiritual ratings must be one or above for individuals to be accepted into heaven.

We have a guiding light to live by when spiritual wisdom is constantly reflected from God to our souls. Trauma effects within the brain eclipse spiritual communications. We must reconstruct our brains for our minds to be reborn and communicate freely with our souls. Newborn babies, without trauma scars, have pure communications with their souls and God.

The soul absorbs wisdom within spiritual dimensions independently of physical space and time to be spiritually complete or holistic throughout the universe. Spiritual communications consist of truthful relationship information from the mind, soul, and God. High energy trauma reactions beyond emotional limits are absorbed directly into the soul through the fast acting limbic system. In severe trauma, we surrender our control to God as young babies naturally do to parents. "Flashes" are spiritual communication.

Normal mental energy levels are for acting with, and reacting to, physical activities and events. With very low and very high emotional mental energies, the mind has greater spiritual communication abilities. Many of us lower emotion energy to pray.

Human actions have physical constraints. Thoughts may depend on physical objects and activities or be independent of physical restraints. We can visualize ourselves crawling and, in the next instant, flying to the moon in a spacecraft. Mental holograms have freedoms beyond simply reflecting physical images and scenarios.

God is not as interested in specific things we do but is more interested in the spiritual relationships we share with others and Him. He is interested in loving and sharing attitudes. With low mental energy, our souls become connected with our right-brains. We do not get to heaven by works of righteous but by righteous attitudes and God's grace.

God receives our prayers and reflects spiritual messages back to us through our souls. If we nurture spiritual awareness, we can reflect truthful spiritual communication to and from God. When clearing all trauma effects, we can have a recursive relationship with God.

Receivers must truthfully translate God's holistic spiritual "wave" resonances into words within our fragile words and languages. God's spiritual wave or resonance language can be received and translated truthfully in many languages. Words and minds are never perfect but the same spiritual message may be translated similarly if receivers are honest and unbiased. False prophets twist spiritual communications for their own and their followers' benefits.

Mental reconstruction is important for freeing minds to communicate with their souls and God. Every thought we have is only a model of physical and spiritual reality. We are human with limited physical and spiritual senses and abilities.

For God to be everywhere and instantly know everything about the universe, higher dimensions must exist beyond Man's understanding of light, space and time. God's awareness engulfs each atom in the universe and transmits spiritual information about it instantly throughout the universe. God knows each atom and each hair.

The soul consists of truthful current and historical spiritual information. Upon physical death, the soul's wisdom is accepted and absorbed by God's higher dimensional Hologram, independent of space and time.

The soul integrates positive attitudes, feelings, and relationships beyond mental abilities into spiritual wisdom. Good deeds and thoughts are multiplied within the soul. The soul communicates our good thoughts and deeds as gifts to God, creating our spiritual identities.

Our sense information, processed by the brain, mind, and soul, construct awareness of self and environments. If nurturing spiritual awareness, we may reflect, and react to, God's blessings and commands. Our souls and God are part of everything we do, except when we think or do evil. We separate ourselves from God when we think or do evil.

We will be judged heavily by intentional words and actions that have damaged the helpless. To be spiritual, we must be good to everyone we meet, if possible.

A Philosophy of Healing and Spirituality

No scientist is arrogant enough to believe he can sense or understand all of God's dimensions. Our souls contain our truthful, spiritual histories in higher dimensional spiritual waves. Our spiritual histories cannot be changed. Our souls cannot lie. God's dimensions are not sensed by man's inventions but sometimes by our minds through our souls. God knows our integrated spiritual value every moment.

We sometimes hear that someone is "soul searching" to make spiritual decisions. We must relax and get our minds out of the way. Relax the mind into being void to thoughts, and, eventually, the soul responds with confident ideas that are better than we thought we could have of on our own.

Upon death, the soul escapes the mind and body to become integrated within God's Infinite Spiritual Hologram Dimensions. God has ability to reflect our soul's resonances to loved ones for influencing their minds, mostly, when they are in need.

To be spiritually successful, we must develop truthful souls. Being worldly successful makes it more difficult to be spiritually successful. Egos get big and, essentially, make the poor slaves.

Everybody's crazy not believing our souls are part of God within us, and that they extend to the edges of the universe. Our soul's spiritual waves travel across the universe as a vague spiritual hologram image within God's infinite Hologram in a small fraction of a second. If accepted as everlasting spirits, in heaven, our spiritual resonances are much more real than brief mental resonances and physical bodies.

Mind, Heart, Soul

Saying or hearing, "Have a heart!" has deep structure meaning. Old sayings that have endured over the centuries have deep meaning. In recent years, two men have been exceedingly evil to me - one breaking in, stealing, vandalizing, and hiding things in my house, and the other lying, threatening, including assault and battery. Experiencing evil helps us appreciate love and joy more deeply.

Generally, my mental healing experiments began with a positive outlook. Even while psychologically abused in marriage, I continually hoped abuse would stop and life would improve. I am fortunate as I have been abused by only a few individuals in my life. Many men and women have been abused and tormented frequently.

The phrase, "Have a heart!" means continuing positive thoughts even when experiencing negative behaviors from others. Let God judge and punish. Vengeance is God's option.

Negative thoughts and anger restrict thinking and blood flow within the heart and brain, and degrade health. Hence the term: "Cold Hearted." Persistent negative thoughts and actions cause heart pain, and eventually heart attacks. An evil mind is damaging to its heart and soul. The heart and soul are connected.

Positive thoughts are mostly right-brained, spiritual, and open to options. Be open and honest with, and good to, others, and you will be good to your heart. You will live happier and longer.

In earlier centuries, philosophers and the medical community thought the heart was the center of cognition. The heart, brain, and mind are connected physically and emotionally. "Open your heart" means open a caring heart and mind. "Cold hearted," refers to low blood flow in the heart and a rigid, self-centered mind that is closed to listening to and helping others. "Warm hearted" means an open heart, with unrestricted blood flow, and an open mind that is caring and helpful to others. Long existing descriptions about the heart is part of our deep structure language with spiritual meaning.

Everybody's crazy thinking the mind, heart, and soul are not connected. Good mental resonances built wisdom within the soul. Deep emotions affect heart health. Persistent negative emotions are adverse to heart health.

Beliefs

Religious Beliefs: Strong belief in a supernatural power or powers that control or affect human destiny.

IN HIGHER MENTAL STATES, WE may become aware of the existence and characteristics of a deity or deities that intervene in the world and human lives. Religious values and practices are usually centered on teachings of a spiritual leader or leaders. Religious beliefs and practices are usually systematically organized with strict dogma.

Christian beliefs, documented in the Bible, have existed for over two thousand years and its truthfulness is not questioned by Fundamental Christians. Even though some Christian dogma has been disproven by science, fundamental Christian leaders go to great lengths to continue believing that the entire Bible is God's perfect word.

Throughout the years, Christian scholars have decided what should be, and not be, in the Bible. Humans, their decisions and words, are never perfect. God is consistently perfect. Meanings of words depend on individual experiences and change over time. Meaning is lost in interpretations and translations.

Before traditional religious eras, imaginative people created and believed in many gods that had to be worshipped and obeyed. Early worshippers felt they could deceive their gods. People have received emotional spiritual messages and worshiped idols, leaders, and events they did not understand.

Without checks and balances, it is human nature to exaggerate to gain influence and power over others. Still today, people tend to believe greater lies more easily than small lies; remember Madoff, who scammed investors out of billions of dollars.

Christians believe in Jesus and one God. Today, Christians are supportive of and help others believing in different religions. America with its Christian heritage supports humanitarian needs throughout the world, regardless of their religion.

During this writing, Russia has invaded Ukraine. What is Russia's humanitarian contribution to the world? What are Vladimir Putin's spiritual beliefs? With communications available today, could he not negotiate with Ukraine and the West to find a political solution without bloodshed? Russian citizens seem to support Putin's aggression with little regard to human life. Putin lied about invading Crimea. All war criminals lie. Putin lied just like Hitler lied.

Without principles, people lie and exaggerate for their own benefit. In the future, scientists will find certain, current science facts and spiritual beliefs untrue.

Philosophy: the rational study of fundamental and general problems, including knowledge, reason, values, existence, and language. Philosophers, such as Socrates, Plato, and Aristotle thought and acted based upon rules of practical wisdom. They were "lovers of wisdom."

Philosophic Beliefs: Things people believe in.

People's beliefs are affected by their genetics, histories, experiences, moods, and emotions. With different abilities, moods, and emotions, each person has developed their beliefs from different experiences. I might think a person is wonderful. With different experiences, others might dislike that person.

Some Christians think of God as a fatherly figure while others think of God as a brotherly figure. Early beliefs are indoctrinated and affect long term understanding of, and interactions within, the world.

As children, most of us had faith and believed our mothers and fathers would take care of us. As adults, we believe in physical laws and our abilities to navigate and control our environments. Many of us believe in God for a better life and blissful existence after physical death. We only live according to our beliefs.

I have faith that God and my loved ones, who have passed on, hear my prayers even though I do not understand spiritual time and communications. We only live according to our beliefs.

Most of us believe in science knowledge and engineering application. Our cars, planes, electricity and phones would not be possible without science and engineering. With testing and refinement, engineered devices make life easier for us.

Our beliefs in ourselves and our environments allow us to do everyday activities. Spiritual beliefs give us feelings of being loved and cared for, even after death. Humans often search for self-worth and meaning that extends beyond physical life.

We believe we can walk and talk and do many things. Without beliefs, we cannot even do daily tasks. Integrated beliefs build abilities to do complex things.

Some of us become brainwashed and follow good or bad leaders who demand adherence to their dogma. We must distinguish between spiritual leaders and false spiritual leaders. Many of us believe a powerful God is watching over, and caring, for us.

Science Beliefs: About two-thirds of scientists believe in God, according to a survey that uncovered stark differences based on the type of research they do. Recent studies appear to debunk the oft-held notion that science is incompatible with religion. Those in the social sciences are more likely to believe in God and attend religious services than researchers in the natural sciences.

Science Facts: An observation in nature that has been repeatedly confirmed through experiment as true and a fact. In science, a fact is never final.

The scientific method: A way to ask and answer scientific questions by making observations and doing experiments. The steps of the scientific method are:

- Ask a Question
- Do Background Research on Social or Natural Sciences
- Construct a Hypothesis of What You believe to be True
- Test Your Hypothesis by Doing an Experiment or Study
- Analyze Your Data and Draw a Conclusion as to whether your hypothesis was true or false
- Communicate Your Results and the expected use of your results

We should search for, learn, and practice the truth in everything we do. Traditionally, philosophy did not include religion. This is understandable since governments in many countries were, and are, ruled by religious leaders. Religious leaders would not allow philosophers or scientists to question their beliefs or authority. Many religions have declared that their Spiritual Leaders and Books were and are perfect. Manmade words are never perfect and are interpreted and translated differently by people with different experiences.

Religions should search for, and question, the truth in today's spiritual books and teachings. Science and religions should search for the truth together. Knowing and practicing the truth attracts God's blessings. We should use science and technology to improve spiritual communication skills for proving science and spiritual beliefs. Science and technology are only discovering truths that God has given us 14 billion years ago.

The scientific method has done wonders in developing "truthful" technology for advancing human lives. Thomas Jefferson applied science to interpret Christianity. We should reason about spiritual messages we receive. As in science, we should truthfully communicate expected benefits to us and others.

Jesus taught his followers spiritual technology when he taught them the Lord's Prayer. (See Matthew Chapter 6.) He taught Christians many spiritual beliefs and technologies.

God gave us independent minds with free wills to choose our own worldly and spiritual destinies. If believers analyze their religions as scientists have done in science, the world will become a safer place. Many have interpreted religions for their benefits, to the detriment of other believers.

One of the most important things in life is continuing to learn and admitting when and where we are wrong. This applies to science and religion.

If a traditional religion gives spiritual comfort and confidence, that is wonderful. However, controlling religions ingrain false superior dogma in followers' minds. One drastic dogma encourages killing all believers of different faiths. They have brainwashed, ingrained false ideas in rigid minds.

I initially attempt to love everyone. However, it is difficult to love those who want to degrade, hurt, or kill us. Some with deep prejudices want to do so without even knowing us. If we believe we are spiritually superior, we are spiritually inferior and without God's purpose.

We can learn God's Truth from true religions, and from spiritual messages directly from God. We must continue learning spiritual wisdom for salvation.

In John 14:6, Jesus tells His disciplines He is the only way to heaven. Other religions do not believe this. To Christians, Jesus is the best way for acceptance by God. After His resurrection, Jesus continues to save lives of those believing in Him.

If one does not wish to reason beyond traditional religions, Christianity is a wonderful, peaceful option. Beliefs and life styles are important for mental health, peace of mind, and eternal life. Spiritual leaders, their doctrines, my interpretations, spiritual messages received, and physics models of the universe and creation, have framed my spiritual beliefs. Each of us should interpret and reason about our religion. Searching for truth and beliefs in religions is the most spiritual thing we can do.

Everybody's crazy for not distinguishing between science facts and spiritual interpretations and beliefs. Science facts allow us to learn about and structure the physical world for our benefit. Religions help us think beyond physical lives for comfort in believing our lives somehow, and will always, matter to an all powerful, all knowing God. We seldom think of how this happens or may happen after physical death.

Thomas Jefferson's Beliefs

—⚏—

AFTER SUCCUMBING TO BIPOLAR DISORDER, and having experienced "expected" death, I questioned my mind and beliefs. I needed to integrate my new spiritual awareness with my Christian beliefs.

In the summer of 2011, I visited Thomas Jefferson's summer vacation home, Poplar Forest, in Forest, Virginia, near Lynchburg. Its design is much like Jefferson's Monticello home in Charlottesville, Virginia.

America has advanced in science and technology primarily because Jefferson insisted on separation of state and religion in the United States Constitution. At that time it was unusual for governments to be separated from unchanging, rigid religious dogma. Americans have had freedoms to discover and express creative ideas. Freedom to search for science or God's physical truths has given Americans so many freedoms and rewards.

I purchased a site book: *The Words of Thomas Jefferson*, which includes quotes by Thomas Jefferson on religion and separation of state. This book helped me culture spiritual thoughts. Thomas Jefferson's quotes are over two hundred years old:

1. "... our civil rights have no dependence on our religious opinions any more than our opinions in physics or geometry."

   An Act for Establishing Religious Freedom, 1786

2. ". . . all men shall be free to profess, and by argument to maintain their opinions in matters of religion, and that the same shall in no wise diminish, enlarge, of affect their civil capacities."

> An Act for Establishing Religious Freedom, 1786

3. "Believing with you that religion is a matter which lies solely between Man & his God, that he owes account to none other for his faith or his worship, that the legitimate powers of government reach actions only, and not opinions. . ."

> To the Baptist Association of Danbury Connecticut, 1779

4. "The whole history of these books [the Gospels] is so defective and doubtful that it seems vain to attempt minute inquiry into it: and such tricks have been played with their text, and with the texts of other books relating to them, that we have a right, from that cause, to entertain much doubt what parts of them are genuine. In the New Testament there is internal evidence that parts of it have proceeded from an extraordinary man; and that other parts are of the fabric of very inferior minds. It is as easy to separate those parts, as to pick out diamonds from dunghills."

> Thomas Jefferson, letter to John Adams, January 24, 1814.

5. "In every country and in every age, the priest has been hostile to liberty. He is always in alliance with the despot, abetting his abuses in return for protection to his own."

> Thomas Jefferson, letter to Horatio G. Safford, March 17, 1814

6. "Priests...dread the advance of science as witches do the approach of daylight and scowl on the fatal harbinger announcing the subversions of the duperies on which they live."

   Thomas Jefferson, Letter to Correa de Serra, April 11, 1820

7. "Among the sayings and discourses imputed to him [Jesus] by his biographers, I find many passages of fine imagination, correct morality, and of the most lovely benevolence; and others again of so much ignorance, so much absurdity, so much untruth, charlatanism, and imposture, as to pronounce it impossible that such contradictions should have proceeded from the same being."

   Thomas Jefferson, letter to William Short, April 13, 1820

8. "And the day will come when the mystical generation of Jesus, by the Supreme Being as his father in the womb of a virgin will be classed with the fable of the generation of Minerva in the brain of Jupiter. But may we hope that the dawn of reason and freedom of thought in these United States will do away with this artificial scaffolding, and restore to us the primitive and genuine doctrines of this most venerated reformer of human errors."

   Thomas Jefferson, Letter to John Adams, April 11, 1823

With his science and philosophical approach, Thomas Jefferson did not believe all information in the Bible was true and fought against religious control of governments. He criticized motives of Christian leaders of his time.

I have had thoughts in attempting to model and understand God. God is Light, electromagnetic radiation, gravity, and integrated higher dimensions. God's spiritual forces surround and cuddle humans and living beings. Higher spiritual dimensions are separated from physical dimensions by the speed of light.

Light is the intermediate medium between physical dimensions and very, very fast spiritual dimensions. We should not judge God by our simple physical and spiritual understandings. Complex general relativity equations model very large activities in the universe beyond normal human sensitivities and understanding.

Modeling large things in the universe with General Relativity is a small beginning to modeling God in depth. Modeling and understanding God is more involved and difficult.

From my spiritual messages received, we should question science and religions. I do not think we should blindly follow any spiritual leader or book without questioning his/its reasoning and background. Self-promoting scientists, spiritual leaders, and writers are human and, with opportunity, often become power seeking over those they think they can control for their own benefits.

America has many good spiritual leaders who are dedicated to God and their followers. My criteria for spiritual leaders are: Are they nurturing and appealing with love, reason, and gentile spiritual guidance, or are they emotionally controlling with selfish purposes? Are they building truthful mental and spiritual confidence in their followers? Are they helping their followers to think and reason?

If we believe God is omnipresent, existing everywhere, and omniscient, knowing everything in the universe, there must be a dimension or dimensions that receive information from every point in the universe, integrate that knowledge, and spread all that integrated knowledge back to every point in the universe at a speed much faster than the speed of light. We must develop reason and logic in forming beliefs. Will religions ever become as precise as science?

Philosophers question current and historical thoughts and activities. Why do we experience such pain, uncertainties, and struggles on earth for possibly attaining a blissful eternal existence after physical death? The high mental energy of pain and uncertainty synchronizes with spiritual resonances. Jesus suffered.

How can a few moments of physical life be worth God caring for us forever? From within our souls, our very vague spiritual resonances, spiritual holograms, are absorbed throughout heaven in spiritual dimensions as a very small part of God's infinitely detailed, brilliant Hologram, or Mind. If we have lived spiritual lives, we become part of God. Jesus' beautiful, bright Hologram has been integrated within God, and the Holy Spirit, to form a Holy Trinity. Hopefully, we will become part of that Trinity.

God, existing throughout the universe, is perfect and needs our discrete human-sized spiritual experiences to make Him more perfect. God is always perfect in spiritual time but can become more perfect in human physical time. God learns from human free wills.

Spiritually perfect means God is truthfully the same throughout all spiritual dimensions and the entire universe. Pain and the high mental energy it causes may be helpful in purging repressed trauma effects facilitating communication with the soul and God.

Humans and human writing are never perfect. Time destroys all physical things.

Jesus is integrated within God in higher dimensions. This explains the Trinity, or Three in One – Father, Son, and Holy Spirit. Let's not limit God to Man's frail senses and reasoning abilities.

Philosophers ask questions that cannot be answered. Religions have answers that cannot be questioned. We should question religions, philosophers, and scientists.

Science has been so beneficial to man because scientists have learned to question and prove or disprove one another's experiments and theories. Without questioning nature, man would still live in caves.

I have faith in Jesus, but question biblical writers. It is clear that many self-proclaimed spiritual leaders have been more interested in power than in enriching the spiritual quality of followers' lives and in guiding them to salvation. It is difficult to always be truthful in writing. A slightly different word can change the meaning of a spiritual communication.

Thomas Jefferson was a brilliant thinker, writer, and politician. His writings have influenced many governments throughout the world and my own thinking. His questioning of the Bible, religion, and government is worth study. We are free to reason and believe or simply accept what others tell us.

Everybody's crazy not believing that Thomas Jefferson was the major influence separating religion from our American government and promoting freedom of religion in the United States. Freedom of religion and thought has allowed America to be the most inventive nation on earth. Religions often promote compliance and suppress individual creativity.

Christianity

Most readers are familiar with Jesus, the Bible, and Christianity. There are two basic approaches:

1. Fundamental Christians believe the Bible is the perfect Word of God, even though it has had many translations, and believe it cannot be added to or subtracted from. They believe every word and sentence is perfect and all anyone needs to find eternal life.
2. Progressive Christians just as strongly, believe in Jesus but believe in the spiritual intent of the Bible.

I believe in the spiritual intent of the Bible, and believe interpreted and translated manmade words are never perfect. My belief is that loving Jesus and following His principles and values develop an acceptable path to heaven. I often wonder what Jesus would think of the New Testament that was written sixty or so years after His crucifixion. I do not pretend in any way to be a biblical scholar. However, I experiment with different mental energies and ideas for spiritual feedback.

I present a few ideas and quotes that have influenced my beliefs. Early in my life, I was introduced to and believed in the United Methodist doctrine. This doctrine is important to me today. After manic episodes, expected death traumas, and messages from God, I have often questioned and analyzed my own beliefs.

Christians believe we must be born again to receive everlasting life in the higher dimensions of heaven. I believe being "born again" means we must purge our minds of "negative" trauma effects. This may happen during life or in the dying process. If we purge trauma effects earlier in life we may acquire spiritual understanding that may be helpful to us, others, and God.

Jesus said, ". . . You must be born again." John 3:7. This means believing in and surrendering minds and souls to Jesus and God. The mind is freed of trauma effects, or ingrained sins, when we are born again.

Trauma scars are sins, ingrained by genes, when we were young, and, to some extent, later in life. We have inherited early sins without having fault. Sins are responsible for our selfish ideas and actions. We were born perfect without sin.

Evil memories stored within our ancestor genes, mimicking ingrained behaviors from childhood, and our deliberate evil behaviors activate embedded sins that isolate our minds from interacting with our souls.

Jesus said, "For God so loved the world that he gave his one and only Son, that whoever believes in Him shall not perish but have eternal life," John 3:16.

Fundamental Christians believe that if they love Jesus first they will be more able to love their spouses, children, and others. This is a fundamental Christian idea. Both spouses looking up to, loving, and praising Jesus, will have egos in check to love each other more deeply.

Paul wrote: "Do not conform any longer to the pattern of this world, but be transformed by the renewing of your mind. . . ." Romans 12:2

Trauma experiences, and messages from God, have influenced my spiritual beliefs. Releasing trauma effects awakens spiritual sensitivities. My mind has been reborn through mental reconstruction and God's grace. My spiritual rebirth has required years of humility and hope. Some believers need only to acknowledge Jesus as their personal spiritual savior and path to heaven, to be reborn. My path has been more involved.

I experienced wonderful spiritual changes and believe I have been reborn. However, humans do not know anything with absolute certainty.

Jesus said, "No one has ever gone into heaven except the one who has come from heaven – the Son of Man," John 3:13.

Was Jesus saying no one has gone to heaven except Him, unless believing in Him? During His life, He taught followers about God and His path to heaven. What has happened to those blessed folks who never heard of Jesus? There were spiritual leaders and followers before Jesus' time. Was Jesus speaking only to followers who were present when He spoke? Jesus is the foundation of my spiritual path but I believe there are other paths to heaven. Over many centuries, God has spoken to so many in need.

I have worked for years to receive and interpret messages from God. I try to document His Truths I have received. Humans cannot perfectly understand and write about God's higher dimensions and truths using manmade words, but we can make models to help us understand and live spiritual lives.

Christians believe the most important spiritual thing is to be saved and attain eternal life in heaven. They believe that, with a few scant years on earth and believing in Jesus as their spiritual savior, they are worthy of everlasting, blissful lives in heaven with God, Jesus, and the Holy Spirit taking care of them for billions of years, and then forever. God must be gracious and powerful to give believers eternal life.

Christians believe Jesus was perfect even when experiencing severe pain on the Cross. Pain and suffering are often thought of as necessary for salvation. Jesus suffered on the Cross to give Eternal Life to those who believe in Him and His Teachings.

Christianity is a gentle, loving religion. Arrogant false religions may destroy the world in attempting to rule all of humanity. They brainwash children early, and others later, in life. Their believers have been taught to spread their beliefs and rituals even by killing those who will not worship God in their way.

Christian leaders do not explain why there is little record of Jesus' life from thirteen to thirty years of age. My thoughts are that Jesus became bipolar from high expectations and challenges in developing spiritual communication skills. Bipolar disorder and its uncertainties may be beneficial in preparing to serve God.

Manic-depressives have long, difficult paths to understand, organize, and redeem their minds, and to share their suffering, healing, and spiritual experiences to benefit others in need and God. Bipolar uncertainties may have a spiritual purpose. Our purpose in life is to reflect our spiritual lives to God. A few manic-depressives I have talked with have had spiritual thinking and experiences.

Christians espouse that Jesus lived a perfect life free of sin. Having bipolar disorder is not a sin.

I believe Jesus developed extraordinary spiritual communication skills in overcoming bipolar disorder. In Jesus' times people looked down on mental disorders. That may explain why there were little records of Jesus' young life. This makes sense since manic-depressives gain spiritual skills but lose social skills.

If manic-depressives present their strong inner spiritual messages to Christian leaders, they will degrade us and do everything to protect their power and influence over us and their followers. Humans are human. Imagine, what Jesus was up against during His three years of teaching? He was the "progressive," spiritual radical of His time. Established leaders seldom voluntarily give up power, unless there is a strong constitution for sharing or giving up power.

Many Christians believe God inspired biblical writers so their writings were perfect. Humans have little idea of what perfect means. God inspires spiritual writers today, but their writings are never perfect. Were King James' writers perfect in writing their version of the Bible?

If it was perfect, why are there newer versions? Word uses and meanings change.

Ministers I have talked to have been inspired by God to join the ministry. There are good ministers who get little attention. Some have written spiritual books and have developed communication skills to influence and nurture wide audiences.

Scientists have experimented and determined that dinosaurs lived millions of years ago. Fundamental churches still proclaim that dinosaurs lived six to ten thousand years ago. Some Christian leaders hire questionable scientists to "prove" false history and that the Bible is perfect. Christian and other religious leaders have disclaimed science advances for centuries. They fear science will destroy their "perfect belief system." A problem is that "Perfect" is unchanging.

Religions must be flexible to incorporate proven science truths. They should be looking for God's truths. Science searches for God's physical and relationship truths. The New and Old Testaments are absolutely amazing for the understanding writers had at biblical times.

Praise builds caring and love for God and spiritual value for worshippers. God desires our praise. Praising others helps us develop perspective in ourselves, others, God, and the universe. Asking for help admits vulnerability. Christians must admit weaknesses and be humble to be reborn. If we find others needing help, lean way, way down to pull them way, way up. It is the Christian way.

The church is important for believers to think and work together, to integrate beliefs, and share concerns and praises with God, and with Jesus integrated within God. Sharing beliefs with others strengthens beliefs.

Everybody's crazy not believing that surrendering to Jesus is a path for everlasting life. We can learn about communicating with, and praising, God through Jesus and science.

God speaks to us through His perfect spiritual waves. Words are manmade and can never translate God's Waves perfectly. Everybody's crazy believing religious books are the "perfect word" of God. There are no "perfect words." "Perfect Words," espoused by fundamental religions, have gotten the world into the conflicting mess it is in today. Unless belief "in perfect" changes, there will continue to be hatred and wars.

Atoms communicate consistently and perfectly with other atoms through gravity and electromagnetic waves. Light waves communicate information truthfully and perfectly though vacuum. Absorptions and distortions of light through matter are consistent and understood through physics. Both of these information carrying waves have God's perfectly consistent physical characteristics.

Since light (or EMR) and gravity waves transmit information perfectly, I conclude that God's spiritual waves transmit perfect spiritual information to spiritually open minds. Humans only receive perfect spiritual wave information they are open to and able to understand. Humans can only interpret perfect spiritual wave messages with imperfect human words. However, written words have a spiritual quality of not changing or being constant.

God rules the universe. Who can believe that words from earthly languages create God's perfect language? Humans cannot translate anything without bias. I have never heard of a spiritual leader say that a different people or race is more spiritual.

God's spiritual waves are perfect. There are no perfect manmade words. However, the "Word of God" is a shortcut for God's perfect spiritual waves.

Everybody's crazy believing if any one scripture in a religious book is false then the entire religion is false. Only a controlling zealot would say such a ridiculous thing. Evangelizing perfect beliefs is meant to control and brainwash, and is dangerous to humanity. Just look at the world today.

Born Again

FROM RESPONSIBLE, HEALTHY MOTHERS, HEALTHY embryo brains grow with spiritual completeness. Little brains function in complete spiritual harmony. Babies learn holistically as fast as dreams. Unfortunately, traumas encountered in adverse physical and psychological environments, compartmentalize the brain. Thinking becomes distorted and incomplete. Some even develop separate personalities as in the 1957 movie, *Three Faces of Eve*.

Many people have compartmentalized their spiritual beliefs and practices from everyday life. Few of us are able to keep God in our thoughts as we perform careers and daily activities. There are too many details and distractions.

God gave us senses and abilities to engage in physical activities. Much of our thought addresses physical and psychological needs. However, we should weave spiritual thoughts and praises into our daily lives at times. God and good parents do not expect us to think of them all of the time.

Since my last manic episode in 1994, I have been interested in the meaning of rebirth and the renewing of the mind. The Bible includes several passages concerning rebirth and renewing the mind. I was apprehensive and waiting in a doctor's office for minor surgery. While preoccupied, I unexpectedly recalled spiritual ideas. Ideas were similar to the following passages from my Disciple's Study Bible:

I. Do not conform any longer to the pattern of this world, but be transformed by the renewing of your mind. (Romans 12:2)
II. For you have been born again, not of perishable seed, but of imperishable, through the living and enduring word of God, (1 Peter 1:11:23)
III. Jesus said, "You should not be surprised at my saying, 'You must be born again.'" (John 3:7)

Being reborn is a mental and spiritual rebirth and not a physical rebirth. Being reborn is to trust in Jesus and His gentle, loving ways, surrendering to God, and being thankful for our gift of life. We must distinguish between high energy physical thoughts and low energy spiritual feelings and thoughts.

Excess trauma energy, within neural networks, normally accumulates over lifetimes. Sporadic high-energy neural activations disrupt normal, synchronized mental processes. God's refined low-energy spiritual wave communications are eclipsed. Releasing excess repressed trauma energy allows afflicted neural networks to resynchronize with normal brain functions. The overall energy of the brain is lowered. The brain and mind become less compartmentalized and more holistic for receiving God's Holy Truth.

The brain is complex. From my experience, it takes years to purge excess energy from trauma networks and associated memories for them to become resynchronized with normal brain functions. When mental reconstruction is complete, the renewed, reborn brain and mind will again have the spiritual harmony of a newborn baby's brain and mind. A renewed mind spiritually receives.

There are several ways to purge excess energy from traumatized neural networks. A simple way is pleasant thoughts, broadening the forehead and face, and smiling. Frowning and worry increase the energy of the brain. Calming the brain with meditation reduces energy throughout the brain. Some methods of activating and releasing energy from trauma memories are:

1. Working with a therapist to recall and understand high-energy repressed memories
2. Modeling the brain and mind to understand and release tensions. Models of the brain and mind do not need to be precise to promote inner healing.
3. Think of real or imaginary conflicts that briefly stress the mind to limits. Mental exercises can stimulate overstressed neural networks to limits for them to release their excess emotional energy.
4. Reacting to psychiatric exercises, the highest overstressed neural networks release trauma energy, before less stressed networks release their energy.

Think through emotional processes to reduce trauma effects. <u>Brief</u> stress exercises prepare the mind for real stress later on.

When all trauma effects are purged, the brain and mind work together as a whole. The Clear Mind is one path to become mentally and spiritually reborn!

Everybody's crazy not believing in the need to be mentally and spiritually renewed or born again for eternal spiritual existence. Mental reconstruction is an important part in being mentally and spiritually reborn.

Prayer

Spiritual ideas received are like diamonds in the rough. They have deep hidden beauty and meaning. We must cut and polish them for them to sparkle and reflect our spiritual ideas through words to share with others. Spiritual ideas have deep structure resonances that reflect and awaken inner truths and values. We must use our mental power to lower our mental energy for opening our minds to God. God is omnipresent and always within our brains and minds. We become spiritually awakened. God's blessings are always present. We must prepare to receive them.

When depressed and giving up on life, we no longer focus on earthly goals. Our holistic right-brains become dominant for communicating with, and surrendering to, God. Humble prayer sends low-energy higher-dimensional spiritual waves throughout the universe to be accepted and absorbed by God within His Perfect Hologram. Our prayers aren't accepted by only a nearby part of God but holistically by God throughout the universe in higher dimensions.

God gave humans and living things free will. We think with free will for achieving daily tasks. We can do this or that. God does not normally override our everyday free will thinking.

With free will, it is spiritual to think of, help, and give confidence to others. Nurturing and loving our children and spouses is spiritual. Praising God for what we have and enjoy is spiritual.

It seems unreasonable to believe God creates humans to have them kill one another if they worship Him differently. At times, God demands humans to do things for Him. However, most of the time, we have freedom to accomplish our and His purposes.

The more we learn about prayer technology the better we can communicate with God. In depression, brain and mind energy levels become lower than normal free will energy levels. With lowered energy levels, we are more in need of communicating with God. God is influenced more with humble, low mental energy or extreme emotional energy. Normal energy levels are for normal daily activities.

Babies and children are brainwashed by demanding high-energy verbal and body languages. Demanding spiritual leaders brainwash rather than teach or lead. Brainwashing destroys free will and limits normal and spiritual thinking. The abused become prisoners within their own minds. Many religions brainwash children at very young ages. Brainwashed individuals regurgitate memorized dogma rather than reasoning about their spiritual lives.

During extreme trauma, high energy nerve and mental resonances are stimulated. Expecting death, "Flash" responses are initiated. Highly emotional reactions initiate subconscious prayers. God senses our high emotions and saves us from "impossible" situations.

Surrendering to God in prayer is important for receiving His blessings. We and our souls are helpless without God's love and care. He even loves us when we are unlovable, waiting for our surrender and reflections of His love.

Many of us love to repeat those old spiritual hymns over and over. They help us praise Jesus and God. God "senses" our praises and reflects them throughout the universe and back to us.

God responds to our prayer needs from His spiritual time and space dimensions. If we do not recognize God's responses, He has enriched our souls for later. Sometimes, we may re-evaluate our needs with less selfish, more holistic prayers. We should question our prayers to determine if they also serve God's needs. He needs us to praise Him for He has prepared the universe and heaven for us. Praising God might be similar to how we should praise our mothers and fathers for all the good things they have done to prepare us for life.

Clocks measure physical time. Mental time can be faster than observed physical time. Spiritual time is faster than our fasted mental time. We live on earth such a short time. Heartfelt prayers may have great importance in Eternity.

Spiritual time is integrated time. Memories of new events throughout the universe are integrated within memories of previous events. Current physical configurations of the universe and spiritual structures of heaven depend upon their entire histories. God's awareness includes all present, and historical, occurrences in the universe and heaven. God's omniscience is complete or holy in spiritual time.

I meditate in darkness. Details of the universe no longer matter. I become aware of God's consistency, or omnipresence. My face comes alive with tightening feelings. Usually later, in God's time, I receive spiritual feelings or messages.

In prayer I "tell" my revered deceased parents, uncles and aunts, heroes, Jesus, and God They are "Wonderful." I ask for their blessings. Loved ones, integrated within God's Infinite Hologram, certainly hear our prayers.

Everybody's crazy not believing prayer technology can be improved. Spiritual waves, from our souls, travel throughout the entire universe and God in a very small fraction of a second.

Religion

"It is an overwhelming thought to realize that as we degenerate in morality, we increase in force."

— Dr. David Jeremiah,
"The Handwriting on the Wall,
Secrets from the Prophecies of Daniel," 1992

"Children must be taught how to think, not what to think."

— Margaret Mead.

The quote above by Dr. Jeremiah fit fiery sermons I heard when young. Some sermons back then might be described as "Hell Fire and Brimstone" sermons. Sermons were scarier and more controlling the more forceful they became.

Normally, we should appeal to reason without high-energy emotional voices, except in emergencies. Encouraging voices build love, concern, and confidence.

Forceful speakers engrain emotional scars in young listeners' minds. Youth remember the speaker's power and force more than his words. Emotional decisions usually do not have long lasting benefits.

Powerful speakers may arouse our own selfish emotions to control us. Later their ideas and interests become more important than our own.

Religious leaders often refer to their founders as perfect to influence and brainwash followers. Followers are taught that other religions are imperfect and should not be believed. Their own religion cannot be questioned and is the only to path to heaven for everlasting life.

Look how Hitler emotionally built up the German people as superior inspiring them to believe they should conquer the world. Religions espousing false superior spiritual attitudes have caused so many wars. No one wants to feel inferior or spiritually inferior. Any spiritual leader who espouses spiritual superiority is spiritually inferior. Only God judges spiritual lives.

We should not be afraid to share spiritual messages we have received. Truthfully writing down and sharing spiritual messages refines their accuracy and importance. Share spiritual ideas with calmness and reason.

Spiritual feelings received may be as important as words. Spiritual feelings provide a broader, holistic purpose in life. Feelings and words may be refined later to define spiritual meaning.

Humbly present spiritual messages without feeling or acting above or below listeners. Care, and show you care, about listeners' wellbeing when presenting spiritual truths. Ask if they have spiritual experiences to share? Be sure they know they have free will to believe or disbelieve interpretations. We should be patient in presenting or accepting shared spiritual messages. Spiritual needs occur at different times and ages, and in different ways. People have different levels of spiritual understanding at different times in their lives. Expected death experiences heighten spiritual needs.

Traditional spiritual leaders emphasize traditional or historical teachings and dogma. Traditional spiritual leaders give spiritual messages recently received little importance. Spiritual words received today can provide guidance toward God's truths. We must reason carefully before sharing God's Truths. The more we know about God's Truths the more spiritual we can become.

There was so much violence in the Old Testament. Were God's chosen people more spiritual than others? Did God play favorites? It seems so. Did Biblical writers write the perfect, unbiased truth? Humans are self-centered and write differently about the same occurrence.

Christians believe Jesus was not completely human. He was conceived by God's spirit within Mary. Thomas Jefferson did not believe this. I believe God can do miracles. The Bible states we are to believe God's miracles.

Traditional "superior religions" have caused wars, and continue to cause wars that may end civilization. If humans are to survive, believers must resolve interpretations of God's Truths. God is Holy, His Spirit applies to all. However, everyone and all minds are different and are reflected differently by God.

Cultures must work together to build spiritual technology for an integrated spiritual future with opportunities and freedom for all. With communication technology advances, hopefully, spiritual distrust will cease and develop heaven on earth.

Imagine how great the world could become if everyone worked spiritually and physically together. Everyone would feel spiritually equal to everyone. World social, economic, and spiritual accomplishments would be many times greater. There would be no hunger and an earthly and spiritual purpose for everyone.

Cultural experiences differ. We are not perfect today and our parents and ancestors were not perfect. Older generations taught their children to strictly adhere to their authority. This was necessary to keep children working in the fields.

Children are not as readily brainwashed today. With the internet today, children learn new important things faster than parents do.

One dream is for people of all religions to rationally, with less emotion, learn about God and His universe, and integrate science and spiritual beliefs into facts for sharing every day and spiritual truths.

With open-minded reasoning, there will be less religious conflicts, violence, and murders in the world. We should distinguish between beliefs and facts in everything we do.

We should reason about all religions. Jews were God's chosen people. Jews wrote and believed that. No one can go to heaven without believing in Jesus. Christians wrote and believed that. Christians are not saved by their good works but by God's Grace. Muslims believe only they go to heaven. All others are soul-less infidels. Muhammad wrote that. And so on.

Why do religions degrade others with different beliefs? It is to make their followers feel superior so they can be both united and controlled.

Religious superiority is false and destructive to their believers and outsiders. Fundamental religions were based upon old clannish protective thoughts and behaviors. With today's communications, we have an opportunity to think as peoples of one world.

From religious conflicts, either God has changed His opinion over time, given mixed messages, or biased writers have misinterpreted His messages for their culture's benefit. Spiritual and government leaders have always been biased toward themselves and their cultures.

In earlier times, it would have been difficult for a new "anointed" spiritual leader to excite people about equal opportunity for everyone on earth to achieve heaven. It was easier to inspire believers to feel superior by degrading some "inferior" group or culture. Hitler was an example of this.

Why doesn't God just speak loudly and the same to everyone? Why aren't all good people chosen to receive "strong" messages from God? There are so many unanswered questions. God speaks constantly to everyone but high-energy mental trauma scars eclipse spiritual communications. We and God live in different dimensions. Humans must learn to communicate in God's dimensions.

Religions should open spiritual communications to reduce uncertainties about God, life, and death. Religious services help us think about God, others, and to be less selfish. We become selfish if we stay to ourselves. God encourages spiritual communication in congregations.

Religious leaders claim knowledge about God beyond earthly and science understanding. They use spiritual wisdom to control, inspire, benefit, heal, and give hope to, followers. Throughout centuries, religious leaders have motivated believers to evangelize their religions.

Accepting uncertainties is of great importance to remain healthy. We need certainty and uncertainty. Even after religious leader atrocities, followers continue to believe and worship in the same way, and at the same church.

Religions do not have built-in checks and balances, too often, resulting in false spiritual leaders. Thomas Jefferson, James Madison, and America's founding fathers recognized this shortcoming and included checks and balances in the American Constitution, to prevent religious tyranny.

Many of us have been brainwashed by religious leaders early and later in lives. We believed we would have no life after physical death unless we believed as we were taught. We learned that it was important to prepare for and have a spiritual life after physical death, and then we will experience everlasting bliss. Some believers spend so much time preparing for heaven that they never enjoy life. Loving and making others happy is preparation for heaven.

Scientists are discovering benefits from understanding God's universe and are having greater influence on our lives. Some scientists disavow religious beliefs, when they different from scientific facts. By studying religious books and science, we can unite spiritual truths. The best thing science and religions can promote is the truth. Most religions today promote biased, "perfect" dogma while having pride in feeling superior, righteous, and above differing believers.

The worst Christian is spiritually superior to the best Jew and Muslim. The worst Muslim is spiritually superior to the best Jew and

Christian. The worst Jew is spiritually superior to the best Muslim and Christian, and so on. These beliefs need to change to bring the world together. Everyone should search for spiritual truths. Religions, that don't change, will not be able to compete in an educated, changing world. We can receive guidance from current spiritual messages.

Brainwashed believers, with ingrained dogma, will not change but try to dominate and control differing believers. Brainwashed individuals think everyone else is the problem, and needs to change. People who will not change hinder worldly and spiritual progress. God gave us free will to learn and adjust.

Narrow-minded and brainwashed people only want to hear ideas that support their beliefs. They are especially close-minded to new spiritual ideas. These strict believers live in a mental cage.

Some followers surrender to their spiritual leaders and some to God. We should only surrender to God. Jesus is integrated within God and is a part of God. All accepted souls become integrated within God, and exist holistically throughout the universe in heavenly dimensions.

To some extent, believers should develop principles from their own experiences and not lose self-identities. They should integrate social, science, reasoning, and received spiritual messages into feelings of spiritual wholeness. With all the things we learn, we should still value our individuality. Accomplishments, social acceptance, and spiritual beliefs develop self-worth. Religions should guide, not control our beliefs, decisions, and lives.

The worst sins have been committed by spiritual leaders. The Inquisition by the Catholic Church executed heretics who believed differently from them. Pretending to follow God's calling while abusing and killing others for psychological gain and power is the greatest of sins. What could be worse than causing people to doubt and fear their own minds and spiritual beliefs?

Many religions teach children to memorize their spiritual books and dogma and forbid doubt. Without uncertainty and doubt, humans do not learn to reason. Personalities and creativity are suppressed.

Efforts, in memorizing protracted scriptures, increase importance of successful memorizers. Memorizing promotes submissiveness to leaders, power over others, and deadens creativeness.

Philosophers work to discover truths about nature and life. Everyone should study and reason about their religion. Do scientists have an obligation to disprove false beliefs?

God gave us reasoning abilities. With patience and humbleness, we can extend reasoning to communicate with, and learn from, God.

All churches work to maintain and expand their influence and power. Leaders use psychology, entertainment, and spiritual leadership to meet personal, social, and spiritual needs of their followers.

Religions promote their spiritual beliefs and prophecies. Traditional religious founders have claimed they have received messages and guidance from God. Some of their messages and prophesies conflict with modern science. Religions must develop procedures for considering science truths.

Traditional religious writers may have done the best they could with the knowledge they had. Their way of writing and their number system was different than that of today. It may have been impossible for them to understand and write a number as big as 13.75 billion years, the current science estimate for the beginning of the universe.

Hopefully, religions will become more open and accept science discoveries. With more common structure, religions would become more supportive of one another.

We can meet someone new to discuss and reason about science. We can agree and disagree on science opinions. It is more difficult for most of us to meet someone new and discuss and reason about religion. Philosophers and religious scholars can discuss religions objectively.

Many spiritual messages have seemed so personal that receivers believed they were only for them and their people. Humans can only interpret God's perfect spiritual waves. To be human is to error. Many receivers have corrupted God's unchanging and ever-present Holy messages for selfish purposes.

Some believe God speaks in perfect English. If so God must speak perfectly in all languages in the universe. I do not believe God bases his perfect communications on imperfect words and languages.

God is Holy and His message is the same to all beings in the universe. Human languages are interpreted and translated differently by different readers and listeners. Different words mean different things to different people depending upon experiences. Human languages are not perfect.

My interpretation of my powerful message from God: "Don't leave God out!" was instant and precise. My mind and soul instantly understood this astonishing spiritual message in "words." I have had to work to choose the right words for less forceful spiritual messages.

The powerful "instant" message I received seemed to come directly from God. Jesus and other spiritual leaders must have received "many" powerful spiritual words directly from God. However, I believe powerful spiritual waves overwhelm normal thoughts creating an abrupt spiritual consciousness. Gentle spiritual messages emerge like diamonds in rough giving us freedom to mold them with our skills.

God told me what to do but not how and what to write. He gives us a seed and free will to write using our own experiences and creativity. I have difficulty believing a perfect God speaks in imperfect human languages.

Jesus may have made the best possible word interpretations of God's perfect spiritual wave communications. However, Jesus' apostles wrote differently about His work. Today, ministers' inflections cause different interpretations.

Religion

    The speed of light in vacuum, the force of gravity, and God's spiritual waves are consistent and perfect. Holy means complete and equally applying throughout the universe to everyone.

    Everybody's crazy believing religions are perfect. Humans can never be perfect or write perfectly. Dogmatic, perfect religions have caused more wars than all other causes. The word, "perfect" is often used to control rather than support and heal.

Spiritual Model

If we are doing, or thinking about doing, physical activities, our minds are constructed within the limbic system and left-brain. Talking or thinking about words, physical activities, or environmental interactions are left-brain activities. Left-brain activities, insecurities, and fears are based upon avoidance of pain, self-preservation and procreation.

Reminiscing about successes and failures, and hopes for the future when no immediate action is expected becomes right-brained and sometimes inspires spiritual contemplation. It is spiritual to think about where we are in our lives, the good we have done, and hope to do.

Viewing long distance scenery without thinking in words and without thoughts of physical activities or interactions is appreciating God's work and is spiritual. Loving and giving to others is spiritual. Praising God is spiritual. Words often get in the way of spiritual thinking. Humbly thinking holistically, with the right-brain and forgetting about our bodies, words and discrete things, and time, we transform into spiritual awareness. Our mental waves develop resonances within our souls to synchronize with God's spiritual waves.

Spirituality is based upon close relationships and emotional integration of thoughts. Building loving relationships is necessary before building a relationship with God. We must develop loving and caring feelings and principles. We must interact with and love those we can see and touch before we can love God, who at first we believe cannot see.

God is not the physical universe, but is the reflected image of the universe. God is not the physical earth, but is the reflected image of the earth. God is not the physical tree, but is the reflected image of the tree we see. God is Light and through Him we see everything. God and the physical universe are closely related.

Most people, including spiritual leaders, are self-centered toward their livelihoods and investments in effort and money. Spiritual leaders are human and like most of us do selfish things when under pressure.

Spirituality is communicating with and praising God to receive spiritual direction, benefits, comfort, and understanding. Religions are structures to guide spiritual beliefs.

When very young, individual worth is wrapped up more in dad and mom's expected attention than in independent self-worth. Much of our self-worth should be in receiving God's attention. At times, we feel God and the entire universe loving and cuddling us.

Mental reconstruction feelings are localized and discrete. Spiritual reconstruction builds wider, more general feelings for encouraging spiritual surrender.

No one is spiritually superior. Upon conception, each of us was perfectly spiritual. Acting superior with verbal and body language degrades self and others mentally and spiritually. From my experience, those less accomplished are more likely to show "false" superiority. No one needs to be degraded or to feel inferior.

If we choose our own path of spiritual enlightenment, most religious leaders will degrade our efforts. Dogmatic religions believe they are too superior to reason about current spiritual messages.

If ideas initially seem new and exciting but after some time feel like we have known them for a long time, they are spiritual gifts from God. Over time, spiritual messages deepen in meaning.

Emotional, selfish ideas may be deceptive and mistaken for spiritual ideas. If exciting ideas seem to apply only to us and our spheres of interest, they are not spiritual ideas.

If ideas seem directed to "all peoples" and later feel as if known for a long time, we have received a spiritual message. I have felt God's presence and received unexpected ideas that were better than I thought I could have had on my own. These ideas flow throughout this book.

Awareness is different from consciousness. For example, we are aware of knowing someone's name, but not conscious of that name. We may have awareness of knowledge, but we may not be conscious of that specific knowledge at a particular time. We may recall it later. We are aware of God's presence but are not always conscious of His purpose for us. When humbly caring for others, we feel God's presence.

I briefly became conscious of God's purpose when receiving His astonishing message, "Don't Leave God Out!" Often I have received unexpected spiritual ideas, which I felt were harmonics to God's astonishing message.

When writing throughout the years, spiritual ideas sometimes slowly rise to consciousness when I am relaxed and thinking about similar or even opposing things. Spiritual messages include a sense of caring for all of mankind with feelings of certainty. Feelings of receiving spiritual ideas are similar to just solving a difficult problem and then being able to relax.

Spiritual information may become more real than physical or mental information. Spiritual information is reflected, multiplied, and integrated within higher dimensions throughout the universe in spiritual time. Physical energy is additive and influences local physical environments. Humans must have and use local physical energy to survive environments and have energy to think.

God travels at the speed of light and is relativistic to man and the physical world. Focused light, EMR, within human minds, create spiritual waves and resonances for communicating with God. God is the focal point of spiritual waves.

Humans need physical and spiritual energy for awareness, thinking, and attaining everlasting spiritual life. The soul integrates, stores, and reflects spiritual energy and information. Reminiscing and reflecting good memories to God develops a spiritual communication path

Prayers while alone can be as important as shared prayers. In shared prayers, we lose individual identities to become a part of others with God.

Spiritual ideas have little or no physical energy, but when reflected by higher dimensions, become integrated within God, and shared throughout the universe and heaven. Shared spiritual ideas and activities make God's hologram brighter, extending throughout the universe. With dedication, goodness and truth, we can be more important to God.

In church, children learn of goodness, kindness, and fitting into something greater than mother and dad. Feeling part of a church or extended family, lessens thoughts of self, and builds holistic, right-brain feelings and memories. Group spiritual activities encourage right-brain thinking for looking beyond self. Most of us desire to fit in and become part of groups having similar interests. Selfish thoughts are lessened in groups. We learn to think of others.

Written words remain constant and independent of time, whenever read. God's love for mankind and control of the universe is constant. We could not live without God's constant physical laws.

We hold on to early-learned beliefs and thinking structures until we experience a significant emotional event. This event may be a relationship with Jesus, another spiritual leader, or an emotional, expected death event. We look to God for guidance and consistency when lives are hectic, fearful, or out of control.

Our spiritual thoughts through souls become a small part of God's reflections and wisdom. Every absorption and reflection of light is meaningful to God. God is all integrated Light in higher integration dimensions.

We should not limit God to Man's senses and awareness. In higher dimensions, God is omniscient, omnipotent, omnipresent, and everywhere equal throughout space in spiritual time. Spiritual energy is

Spiritual Model

everywhere the same throughout the universe. Every spiritual idea we have affects each point in the universe, to some very small extent.

Human memories are imprinted within spatially complex neural membranes at many angles. Memories can be recalled fast, slow, or in reverse order. Our minds are creative and made in God's image. Picture memories are reflections of sensed environments but may be altered by current mental processes and emotions. Written words are symbols of resonating air waves that are converted to electromagnetic waves within the brain and may be elevated to consciousness.

Atoms emit and absorb light and electromagnetic radiation. Mass travels much slower than light travels. In a similar manner, light emits and absorbs spiritual waves that traverse the universe in a small fraction of a second. Light travels much slower than spiritual waves. This must be true for God to have up to date knowledge at every point in the universe. Spiritual waves pulsate between the center focal point and the boundaries of the expanding universe, absorbing and transmitting information at every point throughout the universe.

Spiritual wavelengths may extend across the universe in physical and spiritual dimensions. They have not been detected by Man's instruments. Fundamental or virgin Big Bang EMR and spiritual waves continue to expand at the speed of light along all radii creating the expanding limits of the universe. Virgin light or EMR was created by the Big Bang and have never been absorbed or emitted by mass or stars.

The universe's radius is 28 billion light years in diameter and expanding. One light year is 5.878625 trillion miles. The universe is very big. The fundamental spiritual wavelength expands very little each vibration or pulse relative to the size of the universe. However, the fundamental spiritual wavelength does expand and has near infinite harmonics for God to be omniscient and for humans to have spiritual thoughts at times.

God speaks to us through "light" and spiritual waves. Many of us have experienced expected death and strong spiritual feelings. Strong, demanding words from God changes lives. Current spiritual messages received can be as inspirational as reading traditional spiritual books.

Spiritual messages can be exciting. We need to be organized and calm before presenting spiritual truths we have received to be believed by traditional believers. Otherwise, religious and medical authorities will think we are manic and not believable. Doctors will drug us into meaningless stupors.

We must continue to develop rational, spiritual processes for guiding our lives and decisions. We must rely on trusted friends and professionals at times, and always on God. With truthful lives, spiritual rewards last longer than gold.

God's body is the physical universe and His mind is all information within light, electromagnetic radiation, and field forces traveling at the speed of light, and integrated within higher dimensions. Billions of EMR activities within our brains are integrated to form a single conscious thought. All information within EMR and field forces in the universe is integrated to form God's infinite Wisdom. Our minds and souls are very small parts of God.

In the process of dying, we may release trauma scars, sins, and become "saved" and integrated within God's Infinite Hologram. My road to salvation has been uncertain and a struggle throughout life, which I have humbly accepted. Humans need uncertainty to understand certainty. Our decisions are directed for making uncertain things certain. God and His physical laws are certain. God knows everything in the universe, but even cares about meager human lives.

God also needs certainty and uncertainty. If God had absolute knowledge of the future of the universe, He could make no decisions, have no purpose, including listening to prayers, and have nothing to look forward to.

Our Creator has created a perfect universe, but for whom? I have little idea what perfect means for human life. With a shallow human mind, I can think of many ways to improve overall human lives: perfect health and no pain, live forever, sharing perfect love, everybody loving and respecting one another, no lies or deception, everyone achieving great goals, etc. However, attaining eternal life in heaven may be worth suffering for a few years. Suffering and sacrifice have been components of spiritual leadership.

Describing something or someone as "perfect" alters thinking. Talking with or questioning someone described as "perfect" is awkward. We are afraid, she will think of us as inferior. However, she is certainly not perfect if she makes us feel inferior.

Changes occurring on earth or in heaven require energy. Spiritual energy is reflective and multiplicative. Physical energy is additive. Our souls must reflect spiritual energy upon death, or we do not attain heaven. We accumulate resonating spiritual waves in our souls by doing God's Will.

Truthful very low energy EMR harmonics are absorbed by higher dimensional spiritual integration resonances. Transitions of mental to spiritual waves occur between the right-brain and the soul. Our souls translate information back and forth between physical and spiritual dimensions. It is difficult locating our souls. Our souls are dimensionless and permeate heaven, our minds, and the universe.

Spiritual waves are created and absorbed by light. Light, or EMR, are created within our brains. Light within our minds and souls create and absorb spiritual waves.

Individual souls are comprised of unique spiritual waves and harmonics that are different from waves and harmonics of all other living things in the universe. God knows us by our unique spiritual waves and harmonics. Our eternal lives in heaven are much more real than meager physical and mental lives.

God's spiritual waves are independent of physical activities but interact with our subconscious and conscious EMR waves. EMR and light, created by physical activities, are very slow relative to spiritual waves. Spiritual waves interact with EMR waves within the brain.

Spiritual waves are perfect, omnipresent, and available for everyone. Spiritually awakened minds are prepared to receive God's pure, perfect message.

An early experience inspired a spiritual model. As a young boy scout, I, and my troop, climbed Big Mount Pleasant, in Amherst County, Virginia, early one spring morning. On the way up we heard the eerie sound of a rattle snake.

On the top of the mountain, I viewed the beautiful hills and valleys below. The clouds rose toward the top of the mountain and left my face moist and renewed as they passed through me. It gave a general, spiritual feeling. I was blessed by this beautiful experience of nature.

I do experiments envisioning my loving parents, and loved ones, who have passed on. It makes me feel spiritual and love them more. I recall their lovely images and feel like I am helping them expand their love and spirituality throughout heaven.

Everybody's crazy for not constructing their own spiritual models. My spiritual model includes science, philosophy, Christianity, and spiritual messages from God. Spiritual models must be constructed with humility and patience. Humans can only make models of the physical universe and God. Only God knows reality.

Spiritual Messages

—⚞—

When severely depressed in 1977, I could not think of, or speak, a single word. The energy of my brain and body became so low I became aware of flowing spiritual thoughts and communications without needing words. However, when regaining mental energy, I could only recall having received spiritual messages. It was similar to remembering having dreamed but not remembering dreams.

In manic episodes, spiritual messages may become so strong that manic-depressives may aggrandize themselves, but react erratically in fear of losing sanity. Reasoning limits have been broken. Thinking varies wildly. If having received messages from God, we must have patience, humility, and pray for guidance in organizing and presenting gifts.

If we have received messages of personal comfort and healing, we should praise God and tell those close to us how fortunate we are. If God's messages inspire or demand us to do His work, we should commit to His work. One brief message from God can inspire a lifetime of spiritual work. Ministers receive such callings.

In October 1994 during my last manic episode, I began believing I could reason through and solve any problem. I saw a silver lining one manic day. Dreaming while awake, I joyfully ran through my beautiful field receiving "words" from God. We became buddies that day during my worldly insanities. I would romp in the tall grass and think of something to say and clear my mind of all thoughts.

I would wait, and God's words emerged with either a comforting feeling or with a boom from the distant thunder. I was elated when God responded. His responses were deep and sometimes funnier than my questions. Surrendering without worldly cares and constraints opened my mind and soul to spiritual communication.

Manic, spiritual words were similar to dreams and difficult to recall. Here are a few examples recalled from that beautiful sunny day:

H. "Why is the sky blue?" G. "Physics."

H. "Why can't I see you?" G. "You can't?"

H. "Who are you?" G. "I am Light (EMR) through which all things are seen and done."

H. "You neglect me." G. "Who are you?"

H. "You make me laugh." [The earth shook as God laughed. I fell in the tall grass laughing.]

H. "Do you like my writing?" G. "About what?"

H. "Not making sense." G. "Makes sense."

H. "Who created the universe?" G. "Not you!"

H. "Who created me.?" G. "Me."

H. "Do you love lowly me? G. "Yes."

H. "Why?" G. "You are me."

This dream continued on and on. I was a two year old spending time with and enjoying playing a childish game with my Father. There was more reflection than response. We reflected feelings and words back and forth. Often, the simplest times are the most meaningful. I had never felt more spiritual. Observers would have thought I had lost my mind. I was learning about God. We must do things differently to expect different results.

Spiritual messages may benefit an individual, a small group, or all of humanity. If recognized, we may help God's messages benefit the world. Founding traditional religions, leaders did not seem to believe spiritual messages could be received by all who were prepared to receive.

Humble, inclusive, and loving spiritual leaders will inspire followers throughout the world. Receivers must interpret God's analogue spiritual waves into human word language for others to hear, read, and understand.

Today, spiritual leaders have advanced communication resources to bring the world together spiritually. Spiritual leaders must work to discover and maintain God's Truth. If people are truly spiritual, they would love and treat each other respectfully.

Not responding to God's message limits us, and others who would listen to us. Without humbly responding to spiritual demands, self-importance grows like a cancer, reducing caring of others. We must learn to be servants before we can learn to lead. Jesus remained a servant.

I have written for God for twenty years. His command was for me to write for Him. I have not received a command to be a spiritual leader, speaker, or evangelist. I have tried to write truthfully and spiritually.

In 1995, God's message: "Don't Leave God Out!" was so shocking that, even though feeling unworthy, I have written spiritually for twenty years and have attempted to improve spiritual communication skills for receiving healing and other blessings from God. I am unsure if I will receive another spiritual task after completing this book.

Language and communication skills are specialized for science, medicine, and other disciplines. Will scientists and medical professionals help improve spiritual communication skills? Do memorizing and repeating traditional religious dogma advance spiritual skills? This is so if believers continue of think of the meaning and purpose within repetitions. Repetitions should have deep spiritual meaning to be repeated often.

For centuries, traditional religions have had rigid spiritual beliefs and dogma in defining their relationship with God. If truthful, religions will promote worldly love and love of God. God is Holy. Followers must learn to think spiritually on their own. God made each of us with unique minds and abilities. Some may be highly spiritual without being evangelical.

Receiving spiritual communications makes us feel special, but we must keep ourselves in perspective. Receiving spiritual messages is a beginning. We have been chosen as "servants" of God and His people. It is an honor to be selected as a servant and writer for God.

Obeying spiritual communications can be demanding, but spiritual rewards are great. In depression and life threatening crises, thinking extends beyond free will into God's spiritual dimensions.

Anyone receiving powerful spiritual messages may become so excited and believe God wrote their messages on stone with lightning. That would be a miracle. We should never limit God. Spiritual messages and actions may be extremely strong at times.

God spoke to traditional religious leaders in the same way He speaks to us today when we are prepared to listen. Words in all religious books are human interpretations of God's perfect spiritual communications. Words are imperfect and fragile manmade thinking tools. Interpretations are different with different experiences, languages, and words.

Traditional religious leaders praise followers who have received spiritual messages until they conflict with their dogma. Then, they minimize conflicting influences.

In traditional religious eras, writers knew nothing about uncertainties of atoms and subatomic particles. They could only translate and interpret God's complete spiritual wave language into words they understood. We must consider history when studying spiritual books.

I have received unexpected, brief, and exciting spiritual ideas. These ideas have feelings of truth and have been better than I could have had on my own. I have had no unusual understanding what God will have others do. I am not a prophet.

Dictators have claimed having received spiritual guidance and power. However many of them have killed thousands of their own people to grow their power. Traditional spiritual leaders teach that their beliefs and dogma give followers exceptional spiritual gifts and eternal life.

God's spiritual waves and resonances contain the up to date complete history of the universe with action potentials to guide future activities.

God answers prayers and gives blessings of responsibility. Spiritual communications foster inner and world peace. True spiritual leaders do not force followers to believe as they do. They love, nurture, and gently teach spiritual reasoning.

Everybody's crazy believing they are not constrained with brainwashed thoughts and behaviors or believing they cannot receive strong spiritual messages today. Strong spiritual messages change lives. Man's greatest honor is serving God and those in need.

Spiritual Meditation

> . . . the sacred is in the ordinary, that it is to
> be found in one's daily life, in one's neighbors,
> friends, and family, in one's backyard."
>
> — Abraham H. Maslow

Our spiritual value is developed by how we do our daily tasks and how we treat our family and neighbors. We certainly cannot be spiritual and abuse anyone.

Humans are physical and spiritual beings. We are forced to spend most of our mental and physical energy engaging environments for survival, security, and for material and social fulfillment. Spiritual reflections are too often eclipsed by physical, social, and environmental struggles. Spiritual communications appear less real and must be nurtured, but sometimes we are shocked into spiritual awareness.

Brain and mental processes switch between discrete and holistic dominance. Our minds are electromagnetic activities, reflections, and resonances from neuron activities. The mind includes conscious and subconscious processes. Subconscious processes integrate to create consciousness and abilities for managing lives.

Thinking has holistic qualities. Billions of firing neurons focus to create one thought. Each thought has some influence on each nerve cell in the brain and body. Meditating and lowering the energy of the brain reduces the number of activating neurons.

The face and mind have iterative influences upon one another. Broaden and relax the face to nurture a healthier, spiritual mind. When young, faces are molded by genetics, parents, and God. As we get older, faces reflect out persistent thoughts, emotions, and attitudes. They show insecurity, control, hatred, fear, or love and caring.

I meditate to relax and set a mental atmosphere for creative and spiritual ideas. Meditation helps relieve stresses and improves facial appearance. Later, at times, new ideas flow. Creative ideas are more specific. Spiritual ideas are more general or holistic.

We must eliminate trauma, emotional, and spiritual barriers to experience God in more depth. Patience, humbleness, and reducing physical awareness increase spiritual awareness.

We do not need to go anywhere to communicate with God. He is within us as strongly as in any place in the universe. However, at times, it may be helpful to get away from distractions to experience places that give the greatest feelings of closeness to God.

If we desire to learn and benefit from, and serve, God, we need to learn His language. This may be done in many ways. One way is reading and understanding the Bible. A second way is through humble prayer. We must learn the spiritual power of patience and humbleness. We need to lower mental energy to spiritual communication levels. God responds more quickly to prayers with true need, to give us peace.

The mind must be extended beyond emotional limits briefly to become cleared of adverse effects. If Clear Minds are attained, we will be able to experience God's wisdom by synchronizing our mental waves with His spiritual waves more easily.

The brain and mind iterate back and forth creating continually changing consciousness and ideas while we are alive. Ideas are temporary and fade quickly. We can make our ideas more permanent by writing a book or building something that last for a long time. In the dying process, the brain, mind, and soul iterate to our final spiritual solution that may last forever.

The world needs warriors for Christ and His loving, peaceful ways. May God bless everyone seeking God's love and truth! My talent is patience. I, too often, fail to be humble.

Everybody's crazy not meditating to discover inner love for Christ and His loving, caring ways. When relaxed, we have freedom and ability to be creative, and experience God's presence.

Jesus

Jesus' peaceful, loving teaching is the foundation of my brand of spirituality. We should reason about our beliefs. Some religions do horrible things, in "God's Name."

From the current status, and history, of the world, rote memorizing of traditional religions has not prevented hatred or wars. Pride in memorizing skills develops egos for continuing traditions with little reason or creativity. Especially, rote memorizers believe their religions are superior to all others. I feel spiritually superior to no one.

Before His three years of teaching, Jesus' Mind had become integrated with, and was part of, God. God spoke through Him. In John Chapter 14:6 Jesus answered, "I am the way and the truth and the life. No one comes to the Father except through me." A question is: Was Jesus talking to His disciples that were present, to all of humanity, including those who will never hear of Him?

The above passage is difficult to understand. Are only Christians saved for eternal life in heaven? Are all other believers deceived and wasting their time? Other believers would disagree. Were Noah and Moses, who obeyed God but lived before Jesus' times, accepted for Eternal life?

Jesus ascended into heaven and formed a Holy Trinity with God and the Holy Spirit. Jesus' strong spiritual resonances became integrated within God's higher dimensional Eternal Resonances. All saved souls integrate within and add to God's Eternal Power and Wisdom.

In 1977, when without sleep for weeks and manic, I began believing that no human could endure so much pain and agony. The thought occurred: "I must be Jesus Christ." Later, I learned from my psychiatrist, that other manic-depressives have thought they were Jesus. Desperate confused minds reach out for Jesus and briefly internalize His identity and power.

The manic mind extends beyond reasoning limits in search of lost hope. When all hope is gone, we can only search for a spiritual reason to live or die. Jesus suffered for a reason. He suffered and died to save mankind from their sins and for their Eternal Life.

I had a momentary sense of significance in "being Jesus." During extremely high-energy with mental pain and uncertainties, manic-depressives become sensitive to spiritual communications. "Being Jesus" momentarily seemed logical, as Jesus was known for healing those suffering and receiving messages from God.

In less than a minute, I realized I did not have Jesus' love or ability and returned to being sick, weak, and uncertain of whom I was.

Without hope and sleep, I felt sure I would die but agreed for a doctor to inject a tranquilizer. Sleep came. The next morning I felt better than I had felt in months.

Jesus was not known as a scholar, but received messages and guidance from God. By lowering mental energy and feeling subservient to God, many people have received spiritual messages. Jesus did not let His spiritual abilities corrupt Truths He received from God. Many spiritual leaders have allowed spiritual excitement and pride to corrupt their messages.

Humans have an inherent need to associate with good, amazing, or "perfect" people. Jesus was amazing in His love, teaching, and spiritual influence. People were attracted to Him and His ways.

We are children of God. We could not exist without God's love. Humans have a purpose. We can reflect God's love back to Him. He needs our praises and reflections like our mothers and fathers need our love and reflections. We must love ourselves, our revered parents, and God to be complete. God and our parents made us. Loving ourselves is easier if we love God, others, and do things to be loveable. We must reflect love and respect to God as earthly mothers and fathers hope their children will reflect love and respect back to them.

Man does not have ability to completely understand perfect physical or spiritual things. The universe was built upon uncertainty. Uncertainty is always present in atoms and in humans.

If Jesus was perfect for all future times, would there be no pain or sorrow? It is difficult to define perfect lives. However, Christians believe Jesus lived a perfect three years of teaching in developing an Eternal path for those believing in Him. I believe Jesus developed a "Clear Mind" free of trauma scars, or sins to accomplish the things He has done.

Humans have little concept of "perfect" except for understanding God's perfect physical laws for creating and evolving the universe. His physical laws are always the same. Gravity and the speed of light are always the same. God has created a consistent structure to support human life.

The mind, free of trauma effects, receives spiritual communication freely. Being "saved" means surrendering lives to Jesus and God. Jesus died for those who believe in Him. Being "saved" requires a commitment to Jesus integrated within God.

Christians believe Jesus was conceived by the Holy Spirit and born of Mary, a virgin. Jesus was a Man and must have had male DNA. Does this prove that God is a Father and a Man?

My theory for there being little written about Jesus until he began teaching at thirty years of age is that He experienced severe stress and bipolar disorder due to high expectations. Jesus may have suffered bipolar disorder early in life. Certainly, to understand and heal the poor, He must have also lived through difficult and painful times. Anyone during Jesus' times with mental disorders would be put in a closet and stigmatized as demon-possessed. There is no early history.

I notice that those who have endured pain and suffering are more likely to help in hospitals and be giving. Pain and fear of dying change lives, usually, to become more spiritual.

Good political and spiritual leaders must become good servants first. Jesus told His disciples John and James that they must become servants in order to lead. How many political and spiritual leaders today think of themselves as servants to their constituents or followers?

Christian writers wrote the scriptures years after Jesus' death. Conservative Christians promote the Bible, even after many human translations, as perfect. Kings, including King James, were thought to have had spiritual powers.

King James had a Bible translation made in his name in 1611. In that time, all subjects were forced to believe as the King or Queen believed, or they sometimes faced beheading or burning at the stake. Kings and Queens forced subjects to believe that they knew the absolute spiritual truth.

Using words such as "perfect" and "genius" has prevented humans, even today, from questioning religions. Would you question someone who has been labeled as perfect or a genius?

Jesus is my spiritual leader and the Bible is valuable to me even though I do not believe it is perfect. Humans wrote and translated it. God has given us ability to question and reason about books including the Bible. Scientists and philosophers question everything.

Today, philosophers question Jesus' perfection. Ideas of "perfection" change over time. "Perfect" is difficult to define. A view of Jesus' "perfection" was that His disciples, and those who judged Him, could find no fault with, or sin in, His life.

Suffering makes humans aware of blessings we've had and upon recovery makes us humble, more thankful, and less self-centered. We search for higher spiritual meaning.

From a human viewpoint, an all-knowing, all-powerful God allows evil to occur by criminals with free wills. Spiritual perfection is difficult to define. It seems Jesus could have been more spiritual by beginning His teaching earlier and saving more lives.

People continue to suffer, die, and be killed. Life on earth is often painful. We still hope for a perfect existence or life in a perfect heaven.

What spiritual activities and purpose will we have in heaven? We must experience uncertainties, or we would have eternal boredom. There is no future or perfection without uncertainties to overcome. Without uncertainties there is no hope of doing anything new. We could only be aware of truthful, unchanging histories. We would have no future but only be aware of and mimicking, history. The future needs, and means, uncertainty.

During Jesus' life, very few people were literate. Elders told stories to pass down their way of life, for controlling their children, and for entertainment. Much of the New Testament was written sixty years after Jesus' death. After sixty years with the best of notes, it would be difficult write perfectly. Biblical writers were amazing but not perfect.

Jesus was a visionary in communicating with God! Thousands of years ago, people did not know anything about science and its logical reasoning procedures. People would more readily believe in miracles. Some of Jesus' miracles were in front of many observers.

In His era, Jesus was the modern radical preaching "radical ideas" and doing wonderful things. However, He did not speak of future inventions to make lives better. Either He did not have future science knowledge, or there were reasons only to advance lives spiritually.

Patience and servitude are needed before influencing others spiritually and sharing God's joy. Enlightened leaders must be humble but confident they have understood spiritual books and received strong truthful communications from God before influencing others. Many so-called spiritual leaders become engulfed in their own power and pride. They misrepresent God's message for their own benefit. Patience and humility are critical. Jesus waited thirty years before beginning his spiritual crusade.

Moses was a humble man chosen by God to free His people, the Jews, from bondage. However, he developed strong communication skills with God. Moses is revered as a spiritual leader for Christians and Jews.

Human life begins as God's ever present spirit and resonances are indwelled within each fertilized egg. Without God's spirit there is no life. Jesus' and all human minds were conceived with God's spirit.

Spiritual thoughts are reflected from and to God. God learns from human free wills. Humans have a purpose in this particular universe. For Eternal life, our thoughts and actions must synchronize with God's spiritual waves.

I met a lady on the way into a nursing home. She asked my name. I asked who she was. She said she was the chaplain of the nursing home. I asked her what was her purpose in visiting the nursing home that day. She said that she was going to tell residents that she loves them and that Jesus loves them. My purpose in visiting nursing homes became to tell residents that I love them and that Jesus loves them.

Everybody's crazy not believing in, and opening their minds to receiving Jesus' wisdom and love. He taught His followers to live spiritual lives. Jesus suffered and died on a cross to give everyone who believed in Him Eternal Life.

Future Spiritual Leaders

—m—

I ONLY MAKE SIMPLE SUGGESTIONS. Future spiritual leaders should have testable spiritual communication skills, and the ability to teach their skills to others. They should understand science to have broad awareness of the universe and God's relation to the universe. Their spiritual communication skills should be as certain as they recognize their own faces. A future spiritual leader should know and care about the needs of all peoples on the earth.

Future spiritual leaders should understand and relate current science facts to Man's relationship with, and responsibilities to, God. They should know and teach about God's responsibilities to man.

Scientists may become spiritual leaders. They may discover God within "virgin light." "Virgin light" comes directly from the Big Bang and God. For it to be observed on earth, it would have to be bent by numerous stars. If scientists observe and understand virgin light, they may have direct insight into God and Nothing before Time.

Normal light or EMR has been created by fusion of hydrogen atoms within the sun and stars, nuclear fission in nuclear reactors, and various chemical and friction reactions throughout the earth and universe, or heaven forbid – hydrogen or fission bombs.

Cosmic microwave background (CMB) noise appears to be the oldest light in the universe. Sensitive radio telescopes detect faint background glows that are almost the same in all directions and are not associated with any star, galaxy, or other object. This "noise" energy is strongest in the microwave region within the radio spectrum. Questions remain as to the origins of such a low intensity source that is evenly distributed throughout the universe.

My suggestions are:

1. The CMB noise may be reflections of virgin light by "Nothing" at the expanding edges of the universe billions of years ago. This reflection would be seen from all directions. In the process of expanding the universe into primordial existence and creating space, all virgin light is absorbed by "Nothing" except a small spectrum of low energy microwave EMR is reflected. All light transmits information. Reflections of CMB may have information about Creation and God.
2. The CMB noise may also be caused by spiritual waves being absorbed by and emitted from light or EMR throughout the universe. Spiritual waves are present everywhere and are consistent throughout the universe. Energy emitted from light and spiritual wave interactions would be small and undetectable. Can studying details of CMB noise help scientists discover spiritual energy and God? With sensitive tools this noise may become knowledge.

Pure Virgin Light, from the Big Bang Creation, continually interacts with "Nothing" at the expanding edges of the universe to create space and time. I am not sure if virgin light remains powerful enough to continue creating hydrogen atoms, new stars, and galaxies at the boundaries of the universe.

Since the earth is not at the center of the universe, cosmic microwave background waves, reflected from all edges of the universe, should have slightly different intensities from different directions.

Scientists may develop technology to learn of God's early development from CMB "noise." Scientists and spiritual leaders must work together to learn about and understand God. New spiritual technology will enhance communications with God in the future.

Future Spiritual Leaders

Will your future spiritual leader be serving you and God? If he is not serving you, he is not serving God. We must question motives of future spiritual leaders. However, there are many great spiritual leaders. It is very difficult to be a good, faithful spiritual leader.

With a Christian childhood, I cannot remember when I did not believe in Jesus and His teachings. If God created an entire complex universe, He certainly could have been with Jesus as He arose Easter morning. Distinguishing between science facts and beliefs is not easy.

Take your time, study, and develop your own spiritual beliefs. We have different abilities and experiences. Only follow humble spiritual leaders that invite questions. Do not let anyone convince you that their way is the only spiritual way. Learn about the universe and God through true spiritual leaders, scriptures, and science.

Everybody's crazy not believing Jesus and God care for human lives. Through love and reason, future spiritual leaders must appeal to, and inspire, all of humanity for each one to achieve their spiritual potentials

Earthly lives end at death. Spiritual lives begin at conception and may continue as spiritual waves and resonances, forever. Everybody's crazy not believing humans can work for an existence that lasts forever. We must build spiritual models to understand ourselves and God. God created man for His purpose, to serve Him. We have a spiritual purpose.

Future spiritual leaders should end sermons with a question and answer session to get to know their congregations. It is OK not to know, but get back with, answers. Too often ministers believe they must show they are smart, but they really don't get to know most of their congregation's needs.

Everybody's crazy not believing God exists in higher dimensions, which humans cannot physically sense. Humans sense God through mental and soul spiritual waves. Spiritual technology can improve spiritual communications.

Omnipresence and Omniscience

—⚅—

CHRISTIANS BELIEVE GOD IS OMNIPRESENT. We can pray anywhere, anytime and God is there to listen to our prayers and pleas. Otherwise, we would be wasting our time praying. "I can't pray today because God is on the other side of the universe." Christians do not believe this is true.

"Light," all electromagnetic waves in the universe, creates, or is, God. Extremely limited, localized light creates human minds and spiritual awareness. In prayer, we can be one with God, in a small human way.

Throughout our lives, subconscious processes have synchronized emotional memories into emotional limits, principles, and values. Our mental limits, principles, and values define who we are, and define our prayers. Either, we define who we are from experiences and our relationship with God, or others will define who we are. We must know, deep down, who we are to be true to ourselves, others, and an omnipresent and omniscient God.

This chapter/essay provides a simple model of God's omnipresence and omniscience. God is "Light," energy, information, emotions, cognizance, and purpose. His principles and reactions are as consistent as gravity. However, each person is different, and spiritually different, so God's reactions to each of us may be different.

God, or Light, does not lose energy when traveling through the vacuum of outer space, and, therefore, is independent of space, but not independent of mass. Spiritual wave and light information are exchanged with matter throughout, and at the boundaries of, the universe.

God's Virgin Light has never been absorbed, reflected, diffracted, or transmitted by matter. His Virgin Light, unspoiled by matter, continues to travel at the speed of light creating the edges of the expanding universe

God is Light and interacts with spiritual waves in spiritual dimensions, which travel much, much faster than the speed of light. Light appears nearly stationary relative to very fast spiritual integration waves necessary to explain God's omnipresence and omniscience.

God's higher dimensional spiritual waves are super relativistic to light, and resonate back and forth between the edge of the universe and the origin of the Big Bang at a rate of 10^{106} vibrations per second. Spiritual wave speed was derived in the Heisenberg Uncertainty Principle chapter using uncertainty equations and the mass of the universe. This vibration speed must be nearly infinite, or spiritually fast, for God to have information updated instantly throughout the entire universe. I estimate that the speed of universal spiritual resonances is limited by the time for light to travel one quantum of space.

Spiritual waves are reflected at the edges of the universe and capture spiritual information from all light as they are focused on, and travel toward, the origin of the universe. All incoming spiritual wave information is integrated within the Big Bang origin, or current center of the universe. Then all super relativistic spiritual waves, with updated and integrated information, are reflected outward to share complete information at each point in the universe. This spiritual resonance vibrates every 10^{-106} seconds. It is so fast God's information is updated "instantly" from a human viewpoint. Based upon the Heisenberg Uncertainty Principle and the mass of the universe, we have built a quasi-science omnipresence and omniscience model. Science may never be able prove or disprove this theory..

All science theories have assumptions. My spiritual wave theory and speed of spiritual waves are based upon the assumption that my reverse Heisenberg Uncertainty Principle held true before and at the instant of the Big Bang.

Beyond the universe is infinite homogeneous "Nothing" without space and time. There is no difference between a millimeter and a billion miles beyond the edge of the universe. One would not know if he was standing still or flying at the speed of light. Virgin light interacts with "Nothing" to create quanta of space and time as it continuously expands the universe into "Nothing."

Spiritual waves are independent of matter and interact only with light or electromagnetic radiation. Light is slow relative to spiritual waves. Light has a limited speed since it is created by the acceleration of charged matter. Virgin light travels at normal light speeds.

Spiritual waves and information are created and absorbed by Light. We should not limit God, or the universe, to human understood dimensions. Most of us do not understand general relativity, which models large processes or events in the universe. God exists throughout the universe and must be relativistic to man. Light is relativistic and communicates and interacts with fast moving stars throughout the Universe. The sun and earth are traveling at great speeds within the universe.

God's information is always complete and up-to-date at each point within the universe. We are free to pray anywhere at any time. I am unaware of philosophy or science models that attempt to explain God's omnipresence and omniscience. God consists of, and interacts with, higher dimensions while constantly traveling at the speed of light relative to matter and humans.

Scientists may never detect or measure spiritual waves with wavelengths that extend from the universe's center to its radii expanding at the speed of light. Shorter spiritual harmonic waves, carrying spiritual information, might be detected.

Everybody's crazy praying without believing God is omnipresent and omniscient. He hears our prayers wherever and whenever we are.

Structure of Heaven

—m—

THE UNIVERSE CONSISTS OF ATOMS and their nuclear, chemical, EMR, and gravity properties and structures. Space and time structures allow physical properties to exist, vary, and travel. These interrelated properties and structures have supported and nurtured human physical, mental, and spiritual freedoms.

Things remain at rest or stay in constant motion unless acted upon by a force or forces. Light transmits information that humans receive and sometimes understand. Mass includes the property of gravity and is attracted by gravity from other masses. God's non-changing, constant physical waves, including light and gravity, allow Him to control the physical aspects of the universe with some levels of certainty and uncertainty. There are always uncertainties in small atomic and human sized things.

A model of the structure of heaven may improve spiritual communications. Heaven is the higher dimensional spiritual structure supporting God's, His angels', and saved souls' existence, abilities, characteristics, activities, and freedoms. This structure supports very fast spiritual waves and resonances allowing God to share spiritual information with all spiritual entities in heaven, on earth, and throughout the universe, "instantly".

Heaven has structures for light to transmit and receive spiritual information from very fast spiritual waves and resonances in spiritual time. Its structure allows God to be omnipresent throughout the universe and heaven. Heaven's structure supports interaction between human minds, souls, and God. Its structure allows changes and communications within versatile spiritual time frames, and allows spiritual resonances and information to last forever.

Heaven's structure is holistic. Its properties are similar to hologram properties but in higher dimensions. All spiritual information is integrated into spiritual wholeness throughout the universe and heaven. God is the integration of all spiritual information with action potentials to change heaven and the universe. Human minds have action potentials to activate nerves, thoughts, muscles, and spiritual communication.

Information from each point in the universe builds a very weak overlay within God's higher dimensional spiritual hologram extending throughout heaven and the universe. Spiritual waves from all points in the universe build a very strong, bright detailed Hologram, God, in spiritual space and time. Spiritual space is integrated around and within physical space giving God His omnipresence and omniscience in heavenly dimensions.

Activities within the universe create God, and God controls the universe. Activities in the brain create the mind, and the mind controls the brain.

Let's perform a thought experiment and think of structures within heaven that are very different from those in the physical universe. With limited minds, humans can only relate spiritual dimensions to physical dimensions, in which we have some small understanding. I develop heaven models with quantum spiritual dimensions.

Let's begin by considering all spiritual information integrated within a dimensionless point in one quantum of spiritual time. In the next quantum of spiritual time, all spiritual information is transformed into infinite spiritual lines with homogenized spiritual information oriented in all spiritual quantum angles. Identical information along each spiritual line would be viewed differently from different positions.

In a third quantum of spiritual time, all spiritual information is transformed into infinite planes with homogenized spiritual information oriented in all spiritual quantum angles. A virtual observer would observe each hologram plane at different angles.

In a fourth quantum of spiritual time, all spiritual information is transformed into an infinite homogenized sphere with identical quanta of spiritual information, however, observed differently from different quantum angles and distances.

In an additional quantum of spiritual time, all spiritual information is transformed into higher infinite dimensions of homogenized spiritual information in "all higher spiritual quantum angles." These steps continue to an infinite number of spiritual dimensions, or God. This model is meant to promote thoughts that spiritual time and the structure of heaven as very different from physical time and structure. Spiritual dimensions are beyond comparison to physical dimensions.

A spiritual milestone would be if all people and countries on earth were trustworthy, trusted, loved one another, and worked for peace and mutual fulfillment. As a spiritual achievement, physical beings would learn to transform between spiritual and physical dimensions. There must be benefits of physical and spiritual forms.

Heavenly and physical structures interact according to "physical and spiritual relativity laws." God's Will and human free wills can become united for spiritual unity, at times. Everybody's crazy not thinking about the structures of heaven and the universe that support God, and human spiritual abilities and activities.

Heaven Model

In earlier mind models, subconscious tools for manipulating sub-thoughts to construct thoughts were mental holograms. Mental hologram scenarios become evident in dreams.

Upon physical death, spiritual waves resonate within our souls to become integrated, complete, and prefect in everlasting spiritual dimensions. Our spiritual hologram scenario resonances can be "seen" by all spirits in heaven and more easily by our deceased loved ones with shared images and similar DNA.

God is continually aware of earthly and heavenly activities. In severe stress, we may receive images of our beloved spirits guiding our thoughts. Spiritual holograms with similar DNA and coordinated resonances while on earth have greater mutual awareness. Heavenly activities increase mutual hologram resonances that broaden heavenly communications.

If from some tragedy a dying process extends for some time, spiritual hologram images may linger and be seen by the living. This intermediate process between mental and spiritual transition is the source of paranormal occurrences and may provide insight into existence after death.

Models of heaven began during my expected death occurrences. When alone and expecting death, only God matters. We grasp for God's attention, understanding, and our redemption.

Everlasting spirits in heaven are independent of physical bodies and space. Our spiritual awareness, spiritual holograms, extend holistically throughout the universe and heaven for God's understanding in spiritual dimensions.

Physical information integrated into spiritual waves travel throughout the universe in spiritual dimensions trillions of times faster than the speed of light. This must be true for God to be constantly and holistically aware of, and controlling, His universe. I cannot believe God would create a universe He was not continually aware of and could not control.

Upon death, our souls, spiritual wave resonances, are integrated throughout God's Complete Hologram. As spiritual beings, we will assist God by sharing spiritual activities on earth and in heaven. Our spirits will receive God's Blessings and grow spiritually. As we grow, we will learn more of God's Wisdom and receive greater spiritual responsibility. Our purpose will be to serve God. Heaven would not be blissful without pleasant meaningful things to do.

Our spiritual purpose will be to assist God's Complete Hologram reflect and control the universe as it evolves. Holograms are always complete but can become more detailed with more information. We will holistically assist the living throughout the universe become closer to God. We may have some focus on loved ones on earth.

God's reflections control the universe in a similar manner as the mind reflects control to the brain. Human spiritual holograms are integrated as faint spiritual shadows within God's Infinite Hologram making it a very tiny bit brighter and continually more detailed. God's Heavenly Hologram includes infinite integrated resonances or spiritual holograms.

In 1977 when depressed and expecting death, I received images of my beloved parents, aunts and uncles, in heaven working together to help me communicate with God. Distressed high-energy mental resonances integrate and dwell at the edges of spiritual dimensions.

God is holy. He does not only listen our prayers. He is aware of our whole lives when we pray to Him. The spiritually accomplished and faithful have power in heaven. The arrogant deceased were not seen in my expected death visions.

God is aware of all things in the universe including human prayers. He continually integrates their light and spiritual resonances into His Complete Spiritual Hologram each quantum of spiritual time. God's higher dimensional Hologram details are the same throughout the universe. God is Light and continually travels at the speed of light relative to matter and humans in physical time and space. His spiritual information travels trillions of times faster than the speed of light in spiritual time independent of spatial dimensions. Spiritual speeds and time are not limited by matter and physical activities.

After death, our soul's vague, weak, yet complete spiritual holograms are integrated within God's powerful, bright, and infinitely detailed Hologram, in heaven. God's Spiritual Hologram reflects and multiplies spiritual information in higher dimensions. We shouldn't limit God to Man's awareness and abilities. With spiritual lives, each of us can make God's Hologram a tiny bit brighter and more detailed. Death frees our souls from brain and body responsibilities.

Spiritual waves resonate between the center of the universe and its expanding boundaries. The point of the Big Bang and the universe's current center may differ depending upon the uniformity of the universe. Mass bends light but not spiritual waves.

God's Wisdom of the universe and heaven is the same at each point in the universe. Spiritual waves reflected from all boundaries of the universe absorb information from each "hologram" point in the universe and focus it toward the center of the universe. The center focal point of the universe absorbs, integrates and reflects all updated spiritual wave information back to all points in the universe as God's Infinite, Conscious Hologram. Spiritual information is identical at each point in the universe but is reflected differently depending upon various mental and spiritual perspectives, or "angles."

God, an Infinite Spiritual Hologram, judges us strongly by those we have treated the worst. If a husband is cruel to his wife but treats everyone else well, he is judged primarily by decisions about and behaviors toward his wife. Evaluations of thoughts and actions are multiplied to construct spiritual worth. Small fractions of evil thoughts and actions reduce effects of good spiritual factors. Neutral interactions have a value of one.

If asking for forgiveness, God may adjust spiritual values. Christians believe Jesus had perfect spiritual values. I pray for forgiveness for not understanding or being insensitive to others.

Jesus described heaven to His disciples in John 14:2: "In my Father's house are many rooms; . . ." Jesus spoke so his disciples could understand Him. With science backgrounds, today, we might interpret this to mean that there are many resonances in heaven for our spiritual holograms to live within forever and ever. God prepares a place for our spiritual resonances or souls in heaven.

Upon death, our mental holograms become transformed and integrated spiritual holograms independent of space and time. Spiritual holograms are more real and lasting than the physical bodies and environments from which they were experienced. Our awareness becomes free of the physical to exist in heaven forever.

Christians sing praises to Jesus and God hoping for spiritual rewards on earth and anticipating eternal bliss. What could eternal bliss be? Spiritual bliss includes awareness of, and "living," exciting activities in heaven. There is unity of purpose in heaven making it a spiritual place. Heaven would be boredom and Hell without uncertainties and expecting spiritual victories throughout the universe and in heaven.

God is omnipresent and His spiritual dimensions surround each atom and all physical dimensions. Heaven's dimensions are the spiritual structures allowing God to exist. Heaven is to God as EMR within the brain is to the mind.

For some of us, special places that make us feel spiritually relaxed, or even in awe of, Jesus and God, enhance spiritual communication. I love the idea that "God cuddles us." Spiritual communications are greater with low or very high mental energy beyond that of normal daily activities.

Only our love and concern for God and others elevate our spirits for acceptance into heaven. I do not think God entirely separates souls in heaven from our lives, memories, and awareness on earth. Otherwise, our earthly work would have been meaningless.

We will share our love, interests, and concerns throughout the universe in greater spiritual detail with those we cared about on earth. Others and I have experienced images of loved ones as they died. This gives reason for believing we will remain close to those we loved on earth when received in Heaven. When near death, I became aware of my beloved parents and deceased Aunts and Uncles. God reflects and multiplies our love for all beloved spiritual beings when we meet them in heaven.

There is more versatility in thought and activities in heaven than on earth. Heavenly time is different. Our souls are independent of gravity and physical space. In heaven, our spirits will always have time to do everything God asks and all the spiritual things we wish to do. Spiritual and physical times are very different but there is a connection.

Upon death, souls separate from human bodies. Souls become spirits and will have different freedoms and challenges in heaven. They will have access to all spiritual wisdom and will perfectly understand and love one another. Spiritual activities will be integrated toward God's completeness. Only souls that are able to love all souls and spirits in heaven will be accepted. I don't think it is so easy to attain heaven. Practice loving!

Our souls or spirits will extend evenly throughout the universe in spiritual dimensions. Everything our spirits do will affect the entire universe and heaven to some small extent.

We understand how intricate and detailed electricity can be in computers and within the internet. Spiritual space is trillions of times more intricate than the internet in physical space. All spiritual wisdom exists at each point of physical space in spiritual space.

God and humans continue to learn. God has perfect awareness of all universal and spiritual history but increases His perfect awareness and wisdom every second. This must be true since God gives humans free will.

We may say God's wisdom is infinite. In math if we add to infinite, we still get infinite. From a human viewpoint adding our souls to God's infinite wisdom is still infinite. Humans have little concept of infinite. Infinite goes on and on without end.

Each minute' change of EMR within the mind changes awareness and meaning. Refined EMR within the brain has more spiritual importance than a lightning bolt. Heaven is the same throughout the universe and beyond.

Christians believe in the Holy Trinity, the Father, Son, and Holy Spirit. Jesus is integrated within God's Completeness. All accepted souls are integrated within God as part of God. Jesus was an example of being accepted into heaven. Accepted souls may have greater or lesser influence in heaven.

Christian denominations interpret the Bible differently. Each seems to give different emphases on different parts of the Bible.

Oligarchies are governed by religious leaders and by their strict interpretations of their religious books. Words, including words in spiritual books, are never perfect. Imperfect human words can only interpret the meaning of God's perfect spiritual waves. Words are manmade and never perfect. God's perfect Light and gravity waves have consistent properties for transmitting energy and meaning throughout the universe.

Written words can share somewhat consistent and lasting messages that may be interpreted similarly by readers. Unchanging written words relate to God's consistent spiritual waves, in some small respect.

God's spiritual wave language is constant throughout the universe. I don't think anyone believes that God communicates in English throughout the universe.

Socrates was a wise philosopher; however, he did not fully believe in the state religion. At that time, 399 BC, government leaders dictated beliefs. The Greeks believed in many gods. Socrates was executed because the jurors convicted him of corrupting the youth with non-accepted ideas and beliefs. In oligarchies, citizens were and are brainwashed to believe in the government's strict religion, or they must lie to avoid execution.

Socrates asked whether it is better to live or die. In court, he said that an afterlife of nothingness is better than an untruthful life. So many wonderful, intelligent, and forward looking people have been executed by strict religious zealots.

Christians believe not every soul passes the Bar to receive Eternal Life. Christian leaders go to great lengths to nurture and control follower lives for them to be accepted for Eternal Life, sometimes, to the detriment of their lives on earth.

The Muslim religion is an oligarchy. Imams rule and make government decisions. Muslim women may be killed if they are raped through no fault of their own, and severely punished if they go out alone without a family male escort. Strict interpretation of the Koran gives Muslims the "right" to kill anyone who will not convert to Islam. Even today, Muslims have strict punishments similar to that the Greeks had in 400 BC. In earlier times, Christians had strict punishments for not accepting their beliefs.

Anyone killing another who has done no evil to them but looks or believes differently will certainly have no possibility of Eternity. Some spiritual leaders have misinterpreted God's spiritual communications or twisted them for their and their people's benefit.

If religions interpreted and accepted God's holistic spiritual truth, believers would strive for peace and brotherly love throughout the world. God made each of us differently to understand and love one another.

Heaven is the structure supporting spiritual waves and resonances that record and maintain the history of events in the universe and are reflected to and integrated within God. God is holistically aware of, reflects, and integrates all spiritual waves into His Complete Spiritual Hologram.

All physical things deteriorate over time. Spiritual waves and memories in spiritual dimensions are constant and never deteriorate. God's spiritual information is trillions, trillions, and trillions times more than that on the internet.

Everybody's crazy not believing there are higher dimensions in heaven. Most of us do not understand general relativity and certainly not all of God's dimensions. Anyone claiming to know God in detail must understand general relativity. God was the first physicist and engineer and made the laws for governing activities in the universe.

Proof of God's Existence

PROVING THAT GOD EXISTS AND has great wisdom and powers over a great big universe is difficult but may be accomplished in our or future generations. The world will become more spiritual. God needs our spiritual ideas and reflections to make Him more perfect and Holy. Love, from our children and other loved ones, makes us more complete and spiritual.

Some philosophers infer that only the physical exists. The mind is spiritual beyond the physical. If activities in the brain can produce worldly and spiritual thoughts, Activities throughout the universe can produce spiritual wisdom, God. Both the mind and God depend upon physical activities for existence.

God and the universe are recursive. After God created the universe, the activities in the universe create God and He controls the universe with His spiritual and physical laws and forces.

Let's consider ways the mind can be spiritual. A scientist thinks of a painful toe and in the next moment thinks of a star he observed through a telescope hundreds of light years away. Light cannot travel as fast as the human thought. The mind is spiritual beyond the physical observations and processes that created it. Humans share abstract ideas, mathematics, and relationships beyond physical experiences.

Some philosophers believe that only the physical provides an understanding of reality. To some extent, this seems to be true.

However, we should not limit God to human sensed and understood dimensions. Scientists are only beginning to understand the universe, God's physical reality. Today's science understanding relates to a few pieces of sand. God's wisdom relates to the entire universe.

Some philosophers, and atheists, argue that everything in the universe, including humans, was created by random chance. However, humans and other things in the universe become more organized. My belief is that if the universe began randomly there would be no organizing forces. God and humans organize.

The Second Law of Thermodynamics states that physical systems become more random and disorganized over time. Crystals and living things appear to violate this law. Our minds become more organized with memories as we experience, grow, and live. However, the brain and body need outside energy to organize and control bodies and thoughts.

Nuclear reactor engineers and operators cannot predict individual neutron paths and interactions with uranium and other reactor core materials but, with physics and probability, can predict detailed neutron distributions and interactions to safely control reactors. On a much larger scale, God controls the universe with His physics, chemistry, and probability laws.

With physics, biology, and probability laws, God created man and living things through natural selection. According to today's science creation models of the universe, Genesis writers in the Bible were unable to describe the order of creation. However in their era, writers of Genesis made an amazing model of Creation. Man has always had an interest in understanding where he came from. Cosmologists make models of creation, but must make assumptions before constructing their models.

God designed and constructed probability laws for atoms throughout the universe. Probability laws give the universe uncertainties for God's and Man's exciting futures. Without probability, everything in the universe would be predictable. There would be nothing exciting to look forward to. Humans and God continue to learn.

If God knew the entire future of the universe, He and man would be predestined and all decisions in the universe would be imaginary or fake. Human observed randomness and probability may not be the same as God's observed randomness and probability in higher spiritual dimensions. God and humans observe each other relativistically. General relativity proves that the universe does not always adhere to human observed realities and reason.

Biblical writers wrote with knowledge and words they understood. It is difficult to believe in perfect biblical writing and perfect understanding of those words thousands of years later. I believe in the spiritual intent of the Bible as my spiritual standard. Proclaiming the Bible as perfect makes it easier to indoctrinate and control followers. People like to associate with powerful and "perfect" leaders and activities.

God communicates to us by influencing our minds and souls through His perfect spiritual waves. Humans can only interpret and translate God's spiritual waves into imperfect manmade words. Human words are never perfect. Identical spiritual waves are interpreted differently by different receivers depending upon their backgrounds and the words they know and understand. Humans are never perfect.

Aspiring to be perfect accelerates both good and bad behaviors. Thinking, of oneself as spiritually superior, twists minds toward selfish control and evil. Anyone believing he is spiritually perfect is spiritually inferior.

In any argument for or against the existence of God, we must develop and understand our assumptions. Without assumptions, we must model the entire universe and God. Many scientists and philosophers are unaware of, do not know, or do not define their assumptions, in their physical and spiritual models.

Human vision and mental skills have been constructed through genetics and cultured by reactions to physical and social environments over generations. Human history has been molded by human reactions to images, environments, and actions. Human reality depends upon the developmental history of our senses and brains. We sense God's existence with inner sensitivities to spiritual waves and by observing His creation with the skills we have. Six thousand years ago human understanding of reality was much different than that of today.

The past cannot be changed. We live in an uncertain present. The future can sometimes be influenced by the past and present but is never entirely predictable. Time changes all things.

Man can predict his future to some extent. God predicts the future of the universe to a larger extent. God limited His ability to predict to probability laws. Without probability laws, God would not be able, to judge humans, other living things, and physical occurrences. Existence would have no purpose if God and Man knew everything about the future. Man and God are not predestined.

Human decisions would be "fake" decisions. God would not create Man to live fake lives. God is the Truth and nurtures Truth for the future.

Our souls transform mental resonances into spiritual resonances extending throughout the universe. Spiritual dimensions are very different from the physical spatial, time, and energy dimensions. Spiritual waves and energy are the same everywhere, they are independent of space, and cannot be measured by man's instruments. Science measuring devices can only measure differences in physical space and energy.

When stimulated, atoms emit light and EMR that always travel through space at constant speed independent of the speed of atoms that emitted that light. Observers moving at very different speeds will also observe that light as having the same speed. Relativity has proven that light has these unusual properties. Light properties seem unreasonable without relativity. God's observations of earthly activities are very different than our observations. Our understanding of God's activities can only be relativistic and limited.

Light emits and absorbs very, very fast spiritual waves that are independent of space. Scientists cannot detect spiritual waves because their frequencies are so fast and their information is so refined. Differences are too small to be measured. Spiritual waves are so fast relative to light that light moves only one quantum of space during each spiritual vibration between the center and edges of the universe.

Spiritual wave vibrations are perfectly reflected between the Big Bang origin and the expanding edge of the universe. Spiritual energy is never lost.

Virgin light continually interacts with and is reflected by "Nothing" at the edge of the expanding universe. "Nothing," beyond the edge of the universe, remains independent of physical space. In "Nothing," zero and infinite space are the same.

With each spiritual wave vibration, it imparts and receives spiritual information to and from each quantum of light, or EMR in the universe. Spiritual vibrations influence all light quanta in the universe "instantly" in spiritual time.

General relativity is difficult for most of us to understand but is an intermediate step toward understanding God. Our souls have access to God's complete, holy, wisdom wherever we may be. Our minds receive only spiritual wisdom we are prepared to understand and not eclipsed by trauma distortions. Clear minds, freed of all trauma effects, may be able to access all spiritual wisdom they are prepared to understand.

Jesus received spiritual wisdom from God He was prepared to understand. Jesus never spoke of having knowledge of future scientific inventions, or, possibly, he taught only what the people of His time could understand.

Humans should never be so arrogant to believe they can sense or detect all dimensions of reality. There is no reality without God's awareness. He is the Alpha and Omega of all things. This model of God is my intuitive reality.

These ideas begin a proof that God and His abilities exist:

1. Jesus performed miracles and healed the sick and lame. He was seen by many people after He arose from the dead. He is proof of God for Christians.
2. From a distance, I sensed an emotional inner message from my son, when he expected a traumatic car crash. This message was beyond physical explanations.
3. I awoke from dreaming and receiving a shocking vision of a friend as he died, several miles from me. Emotional, spiritual messages and visions are sent by God through spiritual waves.
4. Others, having knowledge of events with no ordinary way of knowing such events, proves God has shared wisdom through spiritual waves.
5. Anyone sharing information with others at the same time without normal or electronic communication channels will prove that God shares wisdom through spiritual waves.
6. A person or scientist who proves unusual physical facts or predicts unusual events beyond what scientists could expect has received wisdom through God's spiritual waves. I believe God shared spiritual wisdom with Einstein.
7. We cannot directly prove our minds exist. However we can prove our minds exist through controlling our bodies and organizing our environments and lives. We cannot directly prove God exists, but we can observe Him controlling and organizing the universe.
8. If we praise God and share spiritually during life, upon death, we will prove God exists.

Readers may think of other ways to prove God exists. Humans prove they have minds only by physically expressing thoughts, motions, or actions. Doctors measure electricity on surfaces of the scalp through EEGs. They measure EMR patterns that create the mind.

They may eventually relate certain EEG patterns to distinct conscious thought.

God proves He exists by organizing and controlling physical activities throughout the universe so humans can live. But He gives us freedom of physical and spiritual choices. The mind recursively organizes the brain and body with freedom of choices.

Everybody's crazy not believing God exists in very different spiritual dimensions. Humans can only make models of God and His dimensions. We cannot directly detect our minds or God. However, we can detect the body being controlled by the mind, and the universe being controlled by God.

Quantizing God

—⚡—

SPEED, AND ABILITY TO OBSERVE and comprehend speed, is important in everyday and spiritual life. Movies are a series of still picture frames some projected at 24 frames every second. Due to visual limits of our eyes and integration characteristics of our minds, we comprehend seeing smoothly changing activities in movies and in life. In reality many things happen too quickly for our vision.

Human vision and thoughts are limited. We cannot see a bullet flying through our vision. It does not stay in one place long enough for our eyes and mind to see it. Some cameras take pictures at 5000 frames per second. We can view these videos later at slower rates to "view" and understand very fast changing events such as explosions beyond normal comprehension. Technology allows us to learn about and "see" very fast, small, or distant things.

Altering video speeds can deceive viewers' senses of reality and energy. Understanding speed and timing variations is important in engaging and surviving environments, and in spiritual communications. False speeds falsify physics.

Scientists and engineers have digitized or quantized music on CDs. Digitized music is so refined that again we sense continuous sounds. By digitizing sound, music can be perfectly reproduced without loss of fidelity.

Physical space and time are very, very, finely digitized, or quantized. Scientists model space and time with quantum mechanics.

For practical purposes, space and time are modeled as continuous. Scientists are able to measure the quantum energy of very small electron spins, but can only calculate quanta of time and space.

For God to be modeled as perfectly omnipresent and omniscient, His knowledge of the universe's history cannot degrade. As introduced in my "Nothing before Time" essay, spiritual waves vibrate between the origin and the edges of the expanding universe 10^{106} times every second. Spiritual waves traverse space and time quanta throughout the universe every 10^{-106} seconds, recording quantum changes throughout the universe. God's awareness of the entire universe is down to the quantum level and updated every 10^{-106} seconds.

His historical wisdom is permanent but is continually integrated with current events as time progresses. God integrates all physical activities in the universe each quantum of time into spiritual completeness for His understanding. The universe changes each quantum of time. The configuration of everything in the universe and heaven is the foundation of God's omniscience. The configuration of imprints on complex neural membranes is the foundation of human memory as the basis of thought.

Spiritual waves interact and share information with light field forces in space. Spiritual waves do not interact with matter, or confined energy. If space is quantized, field force and spiritual waves must also be quantized.

Spiritual waves are God's communication tools that may somewhat relate to human subconscious processes. God may not need to be constantly aware of these very fast processes, but be aware of their results. Human consciousness is not aware of all activities in the brain but only needs to be aware of the results.

Light, electromagnetic waves, construct God's consciousness. Very fast spiritual waves may be God's subconscious processes. Humans do not need to be aware of all the subconscious iterations constructing conscious thoughts.

Everlasting spiritual waves, in higher dimensions, transmit spiritual knowledge throughout the universe allowing God to manage spiritual actions and laws that globally affect the entire universe. Human subconscious processes within the mind and soul enable humans to interact spiritually with God. Much of human spiritual activities remain on subconscious levels.

Spiritual models must include relationships and reactions on the earth, in black holes, and throughout the universe. It is illogical to believe God's influence is stronger on earth than in other areas of the universe. God must be aware of and equally influence galaxies that are billions of light years away.

God is holy. When He reacts to our prayers, His reactions, actions, and solutions extend throughout the universe and heaven. However, each of us may have unique spiritual resonances, and be the only person or entity receiving His message directed to us.

God would only create a universe that he could monitor and control. The diameter of the universe is approximately 28 billion light years across. It takes light about eight minutes to travel the 93 million miles from the sun to the earth. The universe is big!

Spiritual quantum waves are so fast that they appear to present continuous analog information to God – All Light in the universe. We are able to mathematically write a number for the speed of God's spiritual wave but mentally we can only think of spiritual waves as traveling "infinitely" fast.

Spiritual quantum mechanics models explain how God has spiritual time and energy to know the position and energy of every atom in the universe.

God is continuously updated with current, complete physical and spiritual information. This is the simplest model I could make to satisfy God's omniscience and omnipresence characteristics.

Everybody's crazy not believing God senses, and understands the purpose of every small atom and every big Galaxy. Atoms are quantized. To understand activities and probabilities of atoms and the entire universe, God must be quantized and relativistic.

Model of God

"The whole problem with the world is that fools and fanatics are always so certain of themselves and wiser people so full of doubts."

— Bertrand Russell, Philosopher

1 John, Chapter 1 Verse 5: "God is light; in Him there is no darkness at all."

Life is a matter of perspective. My cat sees me as the elephant, in the room, who feeds him. We humans have some perspective of ourselves, our environments, and God. Christians believe we are God's children. In reality, we have little idea how an infinite God perceives brief, fragile human lives relative to a long lasting, great big universe.

After expecting immediate death and surviving, we learn more about our inner selves and God in a flash than we have learned throughout earlier lives. It takes the rest of our lives to recall and interpret God's perfect wisdom at normal conscious speeds. We can only use imprecise human made words to communicate God's perfect spiritual information.

Biblical writers had some understanding of light. Its communication properties are perfectly consistent and truthful.

Today, scientists understand much more about light and electromagnetic radiation. God lets us use Him – light and electromagnetic radiation, for our purposes when we understand Him and His properties. We continue to understand more about Light and God. Information shared over the internet reaches us through controlled electricity and electromagnetic waves.

God is omnipresent, omniscient, and controls the universe with His field forces. He must include, or interact with, very fast spiritual waves to be aware of and control a great big universe. I believe Apostle John's statement in this epistle but expand upon concepts of light and spiritual waves. Scientists and the enlightened will discover more about spiritual waves in the future.

John Chapter 1 Verse 1: "In the beginning was the Word, the Word was with God, and the Word was God." Writers of the bible used "The Word" to describe God. The written word was the best constant, non-changing communication biblical writers were aware of for sharing "Perfect" spiritual information. Enlightened believers could not see or touch God but could "hear" Him within their inner minds.

Biblical writers may have been aware of the constant wave properties of light and gravity. God is Light, with constant, truthful communication properties that interact with very fast spiritual information waves. Spiritual waves must exist for God to be omnipresent and omniscient. The sun and earth speed through space. God must keep up with the moving earth where we happen to be.

God gives us seeds for nurturing ideas. We must work to develop them into words as simply as possible. The best ideas in this book have been inspired by God.

God is the Hologram reflection of all integrated forms throughout the universe. From a human viewpoint He is relativistically infinite.

Humans only sense three spatial and one time dimensions and can only make theories about models of God. Our physical bodies are confined to exist, move, and interact within these dimensions. Human minds can imagine additional dimensions with their spiritual abilities. God and His spiritual dimensions interface with the light within man's minds and souls.

I have experimented, made theories of, modeled, and written to discover God. Humans will never be able to detect or measure God since He is the same throughout the universe. Humans can only measure differences. Some philosophical reasoning leads to proven science to benefit mankind physically and spiritually.

Human physical and spiritual sense abilities are very different. Spiritual and physical space and energy are very different. God's awareness and influence over a great big universe must be much faster than the speed of light

We should be mindful in claiming we know God. Humans know little of God's activities and abilities. No one should claim he is spiritually superior to another.

The misguided arrogant distort God's communications for their purposes and aggrandizement. Unbelievably, some even feel empowered to destroy and kill in God's name. They are brainwashed and brainwash, deceived and deceive. I can only present my life and spiritual perspectives.

God's principles are based on deep, fundamental truths with exactness, consistency, symmetry, consistent overall probability, and universal purpose. Atom uncertainties and human free will thinking and actions may be part of God's consistent overall probability. Nuclear engineers cannot predict decay of individual uranium atoms, but can predict overall decay of a large number of uranium atoms. In some sense we may be like atoms to God.

God's communication and wisdom nurture lives toward His truths. Spiritual individuals aspire to learn and adhere to God's principles.

God perfectly communicates through light, electromagnetic radiation, gravity, and spiritual waves. "The Word" was a reasonable term to describe God since people of that time knew the written word was unchanging and constant.

Words and translations of words are manmade and never perfect. Words are interpreted differently by listeners and readers. Meanings of words change over time as human experiences and knowledge advance.

Spiritual communication includes the "Written Word," Light, electromagnetic radiation, gravity, and spiritual waves. A word is a vibration in the air or a selected group of letters on some medium, including paper. The purpose of any human communication medium is to transmit meaningful electromagnetic mental and spiritual resonances from within one mind to within another mind or minds.

With modeling, I attempt to understand who and what God is. If we do not understand Einstein's general relativity, how can we understand God?

God was created as the beginning of time from "Nothing." With free will, He created the universe as His body with a Big Bang, exploding space, matter, energy, and time into existence. God is to the universe as the mind is to the brain. God is the universe's mind with consciousness of all history of the universe and heaven.

God needed a plan or blueprint, materials, skills and energy to construct the universe. Builders need similar things to build buildings. God developed skills to create or design and build the universe from "Nothing." The word "create" is a term for building something new but omitting thought and details on the building process. Scientists study how God designed and built the universe but have not begun to study how He designed and built heaven.

Most of us think of God as constant throughout the universe. We can pray anywhere and God is there to listen to our prayers. God has extraordinary abilities to keep up with us on the earth:

1. 1.3 million miles/hour - speed the Milky Way center is traveling relative to the extra galactic frame of reference
2. 450,000 miles/hour - speed the sun is revolving around the center of the Milky Way

3. 67,000 miles/hour - speed the earth is revolving around the sun
4. 1,000 miles/hour - speed the surface of the earth rotates at the equator

God keeps up with us as we fly through the universe at great speed and varying directions. God travels at the speed of light relative to each galaxy, star, planet, and human. In our galaxy alone, there are 100 to 400 billion stars. God has infinite abilities to keep up with His universe including us.

Christians believe God makes judgments about the universe and mankind. He integrates increasingly diverging histories of physical and mental activities within the universe into His spiritual omniscient dimensions. God absorbs our thoughts and wishes within His Infinite Hologram. Communicating with God is a fundamental purpose of human subconscious and conscious minds. Those meekly surrendering to God are more likely to receive strong spiritual messages and blessings.

Cosmology extends my physics based models of God. Cosmology calculations require additional dimensions for modeling and integrating very small and very big things into one consistent mathematical system. I model these additional dimensions as spiritual dimensions. Higher integrating and converging spiritual dimensions have a physical beginning and a spiritual conclusion or ending. God exists as Light within reflective spiritual space and time dimensions.

Spiritual space and time are very different than physical time and space. God, in spiritual space, heaven, reflects meaning throughout the universe.

When we learn about our inner selves, we learn about God, within us. The better we understand ourselves the more directly we can praise God and receive His blessings. God receives and integrates all spiritual waves and resonances to love all who worship and praise Him. God is somewhat similar to earthly fathers and mothers. His good "children" throughout the universe make Him feel and be more complete.

Creating life, including Man, is a source of satisfaction for God. We are God's children. Our good children reflect their raising and are sources of pride and satisfaction for us.

Genesis 1:24, reads: "And God said, 'let us make man in our image, in our likeness.'" I do not believe God is a big Man in outer space. This description does not make sense to me. This spiritual translation may have been the best biblical writers could do at that time. I believe God made Man's mind, including higher spiritual dimensions, in His image. The same EMR, gravity, and spiritual waves that construct human minds construct God and His spiritual abilities.

God is infinite relative to Man. If we learn about His universe, we learn about God. I can only develop science based philosophical models to better understand God and my own mind.

After near death experiences, I have become aware that loving and being truthful add to God's wisdom and happiness in spiritual dimensions at each point in the universe and in each dimension in heaven. Discovering a physical or spiritual truth is as emotionally important as finding a true love. The more we learn about the universe the more truthful we can be for God.

Traditional religions include suffering and healing toward spiritual enlightenment. Jesus healed the sick and suffered to spiritually save lives. At emotional limits, the brain breaks through trauma and emotional barriers to sense spiritual resonances for physical and mental healing. I would not have been chosen to write spiritually without having suffered so deeply at the hands of others.

God is omnipresent. His presence is just below mental energy levels in spiritual dimensions. When praying, we pray to God within us. We do no need to go anywhere to pray. God and heaven are consistent throughout the universe. The better our models of God; the better we can communicate with, learn from, and praise Him.

Christians think of God as our Father in heaven. As we get older, we praise our good parents more for raising and teaching us. When we were young, we assumed things would always be the way they were without question. We should praise God for a world and universe that allows us to live, and sometimes love.

From a non-mathematical view, God and the universe are infinite. Current mathematics structures can represent extremely large numbers even greater than the size and energy of the universe and heaven.

Fundamental Christians claim the Bible is everything anyone needs to know about God. It is unbelievable that one book could contain everything believers need to know about an infinite God. Earlier Christian leaders must have promoted the idea that: "They knew everything important about God" to control believers.

If the Bible is everything we need to know spiritually, we would not need manmade laws. In traditional religious eras, the Bible may have been everything societies needed to build and live spiritual lives. The Bible is the Word of God as "translated" by fragile, biased, human writers. If we analyzed our lives relative to everyone in the world, we would realize how biased we and our writings are toward our ways of life.

Meanings of human words are never perfect. There are "God's Perfect Spiritual Waves," but there is no perfect "Word of God." God is biased toward goodness, love, mercy, and truth. Light and gravity have constant properties and always transmit true and perfect meaning and actions.

Before creation of the universe, there was only spiritual existence: God. His awareness is infinitely faster and more detailed than human awareness. Anything traveling at the speed of light is different than things that can be observed by humans. God is always traveling at the speed of light relative to everything physical, including humans.

A well-known law of relativity states that light is observed as having the same speed if an observer is stationary on the earth or traveling toward that same light at 0.9 times the speed of light. Normal reasoning does not apply to relativity, light, and God.

Light, EMR, provides information through our eyes and skin to our brains. Our minds are constructed by EMR from nerve and neuron activities and by spiritual waves from God. Our thoughts provide information to God through electromagnetic resonances that activate spiritual waves. Our brains and minds have recursive relationships with God. He provides information to us and we are free to react to or ignore His nurturing.

James Clerk Maxwell explained the behaviors of electricity and electromagnetic radiation, light, with a set of four equations. These equations support that the speed of light is measured the same independent of an observer's velocity toward or away from the direction of that observed light. Maxwell did not initially get the recognition he deserved for his brilliant discoveries. He died in 1879 at the age of 48.

Einstein studied Maxwell's work while developing relativity. From relativity, God, Light, observes physical reality as a point independent space or physical speeds from different perspectives throughout the universe. God interacts with energy and space very differently than humans.

Humans and matter are dependent upon space and relative differences in speed. Without space humans would not be able to think, move, or go places. If space is observed to contract to zero when traveling at the speed of light, God observes the universe as a physical point and all universal information is converged within a spiritual "point" that is uniformly reflected throughout the universe. Relativity explains God's omnipresence and omniscience. Access to God's wisdom depends upon direction of light and perspective of observers. God has a very different perspective of physical space, time, and energy.

With interwoven spiritual and physical dimensions, God understands and controls an evolving universe. In listening and responding to prayers, God nurtures our lives in His relativistic time. We must be open-minded to learn about the physical universe and God's spiritual dimensions.

No one surrendering to God degrades or destroys others. Espousing spiritual superiority is rejecting God. It is thrilling to be on a humble path toward acceptance by God. He understands we are not perfect, and we lose sight of spiritual paths at times. Anyone loses spiritual purpose if bragging about being spiritually saved and spiritually superior.

If God knew the entire future of the universe and heaven, existence and man would be predestined without purpose. God and humans could make no "real" decisions. God would only be a recorder of physical and spiritual events. My God is greater than that. God observes and judges all activities in the universe with His higher dimensions, in spiritual time.

Heaven is the structure that supports spiritual waves and resonances including those of everlasting spirits and angels. Together the physical universe and heaven support Light. Light exists between the physical and the spiritual. God communicates with man and controls the universe.

God has a recursive relationship with the universe and heaven and has consistent values and purpose. His judgments change human lives. Man's purpose may be, to help God observe and judge slow human size things and events on earth. Man influences God. If man progresses spiritually, God progresses.

God needs feedback and praise from human perspectives. As parents grow older, they need praises and reflections from their children to confirm successful spiritual lives. Children are delayed reflections of parents. Humans are delayed reflections of God.

Scientists study God's precise, unchanging physical laws that humans must obey. Spiritual laws allow human decisions and choices. Humans learn more from God during spiritual surrender and during emotional and stressful pleas for help. God learns more about humans during their quiet and their stressful times.

The universe was created from uncertainty of existence. Integrating small uncertain physical things into large things increases overall certainty. God integrates information, including uncertainties, from all activities within the universe into His Complete Spiritual Hologram creating absolute certainty in spiritual time, and space.

God's probability laws develop uncertainty for physical and spiritual futures. Without uncertainty there is no purpose to observe or do anything. There is no future. The future means uncertainty.

God's light and field force laws are precise and perfect. Scientists can mathematically understand and predict God' constant probability laws on a large scale. For example, it is uncertain when any one uranium atom will decay and release neutrons. However, with large numbers of uranium atoms, the probably rate of decay is constant. In understanding probabilities and uncertainties, nuclear engineers have built paradigms to design and operate nuclear reactors.

Paradigms are principles for developing models, theories, or blueprints for doing things or guiding life decisions. Successful habits develop paradigms. Organized wordless thoughts on riding a bike construct a paradigm. Many of us have developed paradigms for communicating with God

Uncertainties during near-death events change our most important paradigms. God made uncertainties in the universe to give us freedom to make decisions. Life is nothing without uncertainties, options, and decisions.

There is always uncertainty in atom activities. God knew quantum mechanics and relativity when designing the universe. In most cases, bigger things have greater certainty. God used spiritual integration over the entire universe when designing heaven to record His paradigms and perfect certain history. God has perfect certainty of the universe's history and can predict the overall future of the universe into the long term future.

Scientists develop mathematical models to predict activities within the universe for man's purposes. Man's interpretations and predictions of God's perfect "spiritual waves" are not as well understood.

God gave humans free will. They can be spiritual one minute and evil the next. We can hate one person who has tried to destroy us and love another who treats us well in the next moment.

I thank God for His love and for those who treat me well and love me. We should ask God for justice of those who have harmed, or done evil, to us. God does not want anyone degraded or suffer by the evil of others.

Giving humans and other living entities free will gives God uncertainties allowing decisions and judgments. Without uncertainty, God would be merely a recorder of known events.

Humans see through a small spectrum of electromagnetic radiation, light, and hear with limited air frequencies. God "sees" through and is all electromagnetic spectra.

Rigid, dogmatic people think they know reality. Intelligent people understand they know very little of reality. Humans can only make limited models of reality. Only God knows reality. God knows every atom in instruments we use to do work. We can see, feel, and experience feedback when using a hammer.

Humans are spiritual beings within physical bodies in a physical world intricately integrated within higher spiritual dimensions. Spiritual dimensions are more real than physical dimensions. No person understands God without understanding his inner self.

In practicing mental reconstruction, inner "spiritual" processes become more conscious. Spiritual leaders may guide us toward experiencing God's love and spiritual rewards, but only we can feel His presence within us. God communicates through relativistic spiritual channels, and waits for us to be prepared to receive. Patience is my best virtue.

God has consistent, complete wisdom. His message is the same to everyone. However, each of us receives only spiritual information we are able to understand through our unique mental and spiritual resonances. We receive God's wisdom through our personal spiritual "radio" channels.

God is constant and communicates with us today as strongly as in traditional religious times. He has not run away. We must be prepared to receive His blessings. Being aware of spiritual feelings and messages began in 1977 when helpless, near death, and surrendering to God.

I have done research and worked to understand and heal my overstressed mind. Extreme stress overrides or corrupts mental limit structure. With added stress, minds go out of control.

We must learn new paradigms and construct new limits to navigate a new future. Developing spiritual lifestyles and integrating them into spiritual beliefs is important in life and preparing for after life.

To be accepted by God, we must surrender as a small child surrenders and looks up to parents for acceptance and protection when hurting or in trouble. Low mental energy is best when searching for God's acceptance.

God's spiritual waves are more detailed and precise than Man's best science and mathematics. Each point of the universe contains God's perfect spiritual wisdom. If we do not believe God is everywhere, we would be wasting time praying wherever we happen to be.

I use "perfect" to describe God. Otherwise, I only use "perfect" to describe things and actions which are exciting and better than I had imagined.

Throughout history, God has revealed His Purposes and Himself to His Chosen Disciples. God told Moses: "I am that I am." He could not tell Moses in more detailed or scientific terms because Moses would not have understood. God only gives us Wisdom we can understand. With current science, we may understand more about Light, Higher Dimensions, and God.

In a science sense, there is no such thing as the "Perfect Word of God." There are perfect Spiritual Waves, everywhere, throughout the universe. Humans can only interpret God's perfect waves into fragile manmade words, with various shades of meaning, which may be interpreted differently by readers and listeners. Who would believe God communicates throughout the universe in manmade English? Christians believe biblical writers were inspired by God, perfectly, truthfully, unselfishly, and were unbiased in their writing. Knowledge at that time was less than that of today. Biblical writers may have done the best they could.

My theory is that spiritual waves interact only with or within light in higher dimensions. Spiritual waves transmit perfect, truthful information throughout the universe and heaven and are not slowed by interacting with matter.

God integrates relationship histories for complete understanding of lives for His judgments. He responds to integrated whole life experiences. Scientists and engineers divide things into components to analyze them. After understanding all parts, they integrate individual components to understand functionality of some devise or aspect of nature.

Mankind's ultimate frontiers are between minds and souls, and souls and God. Science will find that each of us is an important child of God with inborn and developed spiritual value and potential.

God's higher dimensions in developing, integrating, and dispersing spiritual information throughout the universe have similarities to brain and mental activities creating consciousness. Human minds are made in God's image. The brain is physical, and the mind is spiritual. The universe is physical, and God is spiritual.

My model of spiritual waves vibrating between the center and the edges of the universe creating God's omniscience and omnipresence has similarities to human experience. Our minds integrate our sense information creating consciousness enabling our voices and bodies to control environments for our purposes.

Our minds are designed to learn about physical and psychological environments. Our spiritual purpose is to learn about and serve God beyond "normal mental limits." Spiritual environments become more apparent during emotional and physical illnesses, especially so, when near death. Beyond mental limits, we can only trust in God.

Albert Einstein discovered the relationship between mass, energy, and light, $E = MC^2$. With future technologies, scientists will learn more about interfaces between physical, light, and spiritual energy.

If we learn more about spiritual resonances, God will give us greater access to His infinite spiritual wisdom and energy. To be all powerful, God must consist of all field forces in the universe, including electromagnetic, gravity, strong- and weak-nuclear, electroweak, Higgs, and higher spiritual field forces. We will learn about what is and isn't God through science. If we develop spiritual technology, we will receive greater spiritual guidance and, possibly, experience heaven on earth.

Spiritual waves and time are independent of matter and interact only with "Light" in higher dimensions. Scientists may never directly detect spiritual dimensions. God's integrated Holy Hologram consists of "images" of all physical things and mental holograms throughout the universe, in spiritual dimensions.

Laser holograms become more detailed as more coherent light is focused on photographic media from different angles. Mental holograms, or memories, become more detailed with continued coherent EMR absorbed by neural membranes oriented at many angles throughout the brain.

We sometimes see our own images in dreams. At emotional limits, we sometimes see images of our beloved angels in heaven. When stimulated, our minds can recall all of life's experiences.

Our genes construct unique higher dimensional spiritual resonances that make spiritual communication unique. Parents and relatives have similar genes with similar spiritual resonances. Our higher dimensional spiritual waves from our souls create resonances within our blessed angels in heaven and within God. God integrates an "infinite" diversity of higher dimensional spiritual waves and resonances into His Oneness as a bright detailed "Universal Spiritual Hologram."

Model of God

This thought is similar to subsets of 80 billion neurons firing to construct one conscious idea.

Each deceased human spirit may exist in specific higher dimensions or resonances. God's integrated, detailed Hologram may consist of near infinite dimensions and resonances. We know so little about spiritual dimensions. We can only make simple models of spiritual dimensions.

On the earth, humans are only a speck in the universe. God's view of size is much different than ours. There is little reason to believe God only communicates with humans.

DNA not only has strong influences in our physical and mental lives but also in spiritual lives. I and Dr. Eban Alexander (*Proof of Heaven*, 2012, Simon & Schuster), in expected death experiences, experienced images of relatives' spirits in heaven, with emotional attachments, being instrumental in saving our lives. We and relatives' spirits, with similar DNA, communicate with similar spiritual waves.

God's spiritual waves consist of nearly infinite frequencies and dimensions in spiritual space. Each atom may have different spiritual resonances for God to know and keep track of. Spiritual waves integrate to form God's complete awareness of the universe.

Light waves travel in one physical direction with its energy alternating within traverse electric and magnetic fields in two perpendicular spatial directions. Scientists have measured that light and physical space is curved by mass and expands at large distances from galaxies. Gravity is within and affects space. Relativity and God's higher physical and spiritual dimensions are not easy to understand. Future scientists may relate light to spiritual waves in greater detail.

In spiritual space, spiritual dimensions may curve back on themselves and be very different from physical spatial dimensions. Spiritual and physical dimensions are intertwined. God is integrated "Light" from all physical and spiritual directions. We should not limit God to our three spatial and one time dimensions.

Human eyes and minds are sensitive to a small spectrum of light. God is sensitive to all EMR and spiritual waves to understand, control, and reason about the universe.

God's spiritual waves have infinite frequencies in many spiritual dimensions. Human minds receive only specific spiritual waves they can comprehend. Spiritual frequencies from our souls are immediately received by God. God receives our prayers. We have some small influence throughout the universe. My models of the universe and God may help scientists and spiritual leaders to discover more of God's Truths.

Our minds and souls are sensitive to specific spiritual wave frequencies similar to radios receiving specific frequencies. Similar DNA resonances receive similar spiritual frequencies.

Our minds develop protocols to integrate sensations and understand relationships to environments. If it were not so we would see all atoms through vision or feel all atoms we touch. Instead we see and feel integrations of atoms. We do not need to see or feel very small details to engage our levels of environments. Human senses integrate details of views to best fit our purposes. Our sensitivities and thoughts are size adjusted.

At the speed of light, God integrates, observed physical space, to a point with infinite time to observe physical activities. What spiritual traits could be more helpful in observing and controlling a great big universe?

Cosmologists have proven that the universe exploded from a point or very small volume. Space was very different immediately after the Big Bang than it is today. Space was highly energized.

If God is all powerful, the universe could have come into existence as some large, near infinite volume with more or less energy and mass. Rather than constantly expanding, the universe and matter might be contracting or remaining fixed in space. The universe could have been very different.

Why is the universe not bigger or smaller? Why are atoms not heavier or lighter, or bigger or smaller? Atoms integrate to build molecules, compounds, and stars. Why is chemistry the way it is? Cosmologists study physical parameters and have theories explaining why the universe had to be the way it is for it to exist.

Spirituality is sharing with God and others. I have often isolated myself to concentrate on understanding my unusual feelings and ideas. If I would have shared with and listened to others early on, they would have told me I shouldn't think and write the way I do. Writing became part of my healing and spiritual process.

For inner healing, I have extended thinking below and above routine energy levels to engage God's spiritual healing powers. Words cannot describe spiritual enlightenment. Spiritual thoughts extend beyond the physical world.

Christians believe in the Father (God,) the Son (Jesus,) and the Holy Spirit integrated into spiritual oneness. This model may also be the Father (God - all spiritual resonances into oneness,) all saved spiritual resonances (all souls accepted in heaven,) and the Holy Spirit (communicating with heaven and human minds.)

Jesus' spiritual resonances, absorbed within God's Infinite Hologram, are powerful enough to attract truthful human souls to higher spiritual dimensions. Jesus' spiritual resonances continue to save Christians for eternal spiritual existence.

God shares mental and physical abilities with Man. He has given Man a small amount of free will and power. For this reason, God is not omnipotent but is very, very, very nearly omnipotent.

Models help us think about complex things – such as the universe and God. Our souls are a tiny part of God. A reason to love ourselves is that God is within us.

Our bodies are confined within physical dimensions. Human minds sense meaning in God's spiritual dimensions.

The arrogantly misguided distort their spiritual communications for their aggrandizement. I can only give my humble perspective of life and spiritual understanding.

Intuitive models are meant to inspire controversy and discovery. It has been heartwarming and exciting to receive spiritual messages, and feel close to God. I conclude this intuitive model of God with feelings of hope and love.

Expected death, bipolar disorder, and healing successes promoted a rebounding spiritual life. God reveals Himself in mysterious ways. Jesus is God's gift to all who believe in Him.

I pray for deceased loved ones' happiness and fulfillment in heaven. Everlasting spiritual existence is more real and stable in spiritual time than physical lives are in physical time.

Everybody's crazy not learning about God through spiritual books, science, prayer, and spiritual communications. If we nurture spiritual communication skills, we can receive directly from God. God gives us goals and freedom to accomplish them with the skills we have and can develop along the way. He continually nurtures us.

Conclusion Section

Conclusion

—⚍—

"Love, hate, read, write, live, and die, I see heaven in the sky!

— H. Fulcher

Crossing the Bar

"Sunset and evening star, And one clear call for me.
And may there be no moaning of the
bar when I put out to sea.
But such a tide as moving seems asleep, too full for sound or foam.
When that which drew from out the
boundless deep, turns again
home.
Twilight and evening bell, And after that the dark!
And may there be no sadness of farewell when I embark.
For though from out our bourne of time and place, the flood may
bear me far,
I hope to see my Pilot's face to face When I have crossed the bar...."

— Alfred Tennyson

A Philosophy of Healing and Spirituality

IDEAS WITHIN THIS BOOK ARE incomplete, independent, and were without encouragement from others. I have been unable to recall and nurture so many seeds, that God has given me, into words. However, he has given me patience and confidence to write for twenty years.

Writing this book has been under duress. I have frequently had an unusual criminal breaking into my home. Only on a few occasions has he stolen or vandalized expensive things. In the last year or so, his goal seems to be to hide things to harass and bully me. This uncertainty may have helped creativity.

I have survived severe sibling abuse during childhood and severe emotional spousal abuse, depression, bipolar disorder, and expected death. In this book, I have shared emotional mind healing and spiritual challenges.

This work has been successful for me. I originally wrote for my family in case they needed help in healing. Later, I refined writing in hopes readers will also benefit from my theories, successes, and failures. Difficulties required development of alternative healing and mind expansion models, and models for aspiring to experience God's presence.

I have spent 20 years experimenting and writing to develop alternative healing success. Psychological and psychiatric models and exercises require briefly stressing the mind to limits for releasing repressed trauma memory energy toward inner healing. We learn most about our minds at emotional limits. Models, theories and exercises are provocative, promote creative thinking, and were presented truthfully. Philosophy models often begin with science and continue with reason.

Emotional, spiritual writing began locked in a psychiatric cell in 1977 that restored my sanity. In depression, the mind is less than normal but later can become a higher normal. A once lost mind and soul has discovered a path of healing, sanity, and spiritual awakening.

Early models included baby and childhood learning, brainwashing, school bullying, psychology, and predicting. With poor childhoods, brainwashed adults control in fear of being controlled.

Religions and societies brainwash young minds to mold them for continuing their lifestyles, goals, and beliefs. My work is creative, controversial and simple relative to science text books.

Inner psychiatric sensations were presented truthfully. Healing explanations are based on science but extend into philosophy. Healing and faith are foundations of religions.

Models of the brain and mind have explained subconscious activities and conscious abilities. Physics models have explained consciousness. Spiritual communication models are based upon inner feelings and sensations, physics and cosmology, Christianity, and philosophy. Spiritual models explain God's omnipresence and omniscience in higher spiritual dimensions. Christianity, physics, cosmology, and philosophy were integrated into one spiritual model. Through expected death experiences and inner spiritual communications, we learn about who we and God are. Father, Son, and the Holy Spirit, integrated within one Complete Infinite Hologram, were explained.

In need and near death, we receive strong messages from God. Models have developed alternative spiritual foundations to ponder. I believe in Jesus, God, and science and have attempted to understand similarities in purpose.

With healthy brains and positive, spiritual environments all children can become geniuses. With psychiatry advances, children will be able to purge repressive trauma and emotional scars early using mental reconstruction and psychiatry. Clearing minds of trauma effects requires psychiatric effort over a long period of time.

We work for short and long term completion in things we do. We talk and write in complete sentences. Successfully completing long and difficult goals are the most rewarding. Attaining eternal life is our last goal to complete on earth.

We must develop mental, work, and spiritual principles to feel complete. Healing my bipolar disorder and completing this book have been long term goals. This work is intuitive. Some ideas and principles may be proven later through science. Albert Einstein's theoretical discoveries were intuitive and proven later by science experiments.

In 1995, God demanded that I write for Him. I have been blessed to write spiritually for over twenty years. I have performed this healing and spiritual work independently. Doctors and those close to me would have discouraged me from this rather different and long endeavor.

In mania, I lost worldly reason; did unreasonable things, but gained spiritual insight. Briefly stressing the mind to limits at times has prevented manic episodes. Since practicing alternative exercises and making creative mind models, I have not had a manic episode since 1994. My personal cure, a monumental success! What could be better proof than this?

My work is so different that psychiatrists, doctors, and scientists would discredit it without scrutiny. This has historically been true for new creative works, by so called "authorities."

Dan Shechtman discovered pentagonal quasi-crystals over twenty years ago. He was ridiculed, and even lost a job, over his commitment to his discovery. In 2011, he was awarded the Nobel Prize in chemistry for his work now used to convert low temperature heat to electricity. Many scientists have been ridiculed for their creative work. A few are listed.

- Galileo – Used the telescope and agreed with the Copernicus theory – **He** was **imprisoned by the Church** for discovering the earth rotated about the sun. Religions have consistently opposed science advances over established dogma.
- Louis Pasteur – For germ theory of disease and father of microbiology – authorities did not believe very small things such as germs could cause human diseases.
- C.J. Doppler – Opposed the accepted "Aether" theory, and discovered stellar light shifts.
- Wright brothers – American government authorities refused to come to demonstrations – they did not believe machines could fly.

- Gregor Mendel – Genetics
- Cricket and Watson – DNA – the double helix

Without understanding some will ridicule and discredit my work. Mental reconstruction has not been easy. If it were easy, my alternative healing processes would have been discovered and practiced earlier. My best characteristic has been patience to recognize and study sensations and continue exercises that release repressed energy from overstressed neural networks.

Future psychiatrists should assist patients in understanding and releasing inner stresses rather than flooding their brains with mind numbing drugs. Unfortunately, everyone is looking for a quick fix and dollar. It takes time and dedication to clear brains and minds of trauma effects. With mental reconstruction, my brain and mind has developed a consistent, principled structure. There were no shortcuts.

Brains and minds are complex. Many may benefit from this new mind healing technology. Psychiatrists can't do everything to heal minds. Only we can truly heal and control our own thinking and minds. We must develop a mindset to surrender, who we have been, to become who we want to be. Many close to us will try to keep us in "their minds" place.

Our minds have been compartmentalized to lesser or greater extents by traumas and senses of failure. Splintered, compartmentalized minds can be reunited into whole, complete spiritual minds with mental reconstruction and for developing personal spiritual models. Personal models need to begin with spiritual and logical structures found in established religions.

Continued research will refine healing processes in shorter times. Adults have lived with repressed trauma effects for so long they do not recognize their restrictions.

Chiropractic nerve healing may occur quickly. Muscle and limb control can be quickly healed. The brain is more complex and healing takes much longer than nerve healing. Thinking improvement is slow and difficult to measure. Those of us, who have had difficulties, recognize our most important possession is our minds.

My ultimate healing goal: "The Clear Mind," has been elusive but I feel is attainable. Progress continues. Healing sensations have been amazingly pleasant and progressive over twenty years of experimentation and practice. My long-range goal has been elusive but steps along the way have been exciting and rewarding.

After surviving near-death experiences, many of us believe God has saved us for some spiritual mission. The purpose of that mission may not be clear for some while. My mission was to heal and write about my bipolar disorder, integrate science and spirituality, and share ideas with God and readers.

We learn about God and His Creation through spiritual books, spiritual leaders, personal spiritual communications, one another, and through science. Science discovery is the understanding and praising of God.

We can only interpret God's prefect spiritual waves with imperfect manmade words. We must interpret spiritual waves and refine writing into our best, truthful words before sharing them. Writing gives spiritual ideas a constant nature and increases importance to readers and God. It takes considerable effort to select the best words to represent spiritual communications.

Spiritual waves travel much, much faster than, and interact with, light as they vibrate between the Big Bang origin and the expanding boundaries of the universe. Spiritual waves absorb and integrate spiritual wisdom from all light, electromagnetic radiation, and other field forces throughout the universe. Spiritual waves do not interact with matter. The speed of light is slower and limited by its creation and absorption by, and interaction with, matter.

Spiritual waves in higher dimensions may be too long and too fast for humans to measure. From a human viewpoint, spiritual waves may be considered infinitely fast and independent of space and mass. We should not limit God to human sensed and understood dimensions.

For the world to advance peacefully, philosophers, scientists, and religious leaders must "interpret" current spiritual messages and historical spiritual documents and relate them to science facts. Spiritual judgments should be made on historical and current interpretations and on science facts.

Religions should teach, not brainwash children. Brainwashing breeds fanatics who become void of love, caring, and reason. Hitler killed to gain power over everyone he could. Evil dictators masquerade as spiritual leaders. False religions teach that God is only for their group or race. Any religion that attempts to gain influence through threats and killing is a false religion and should be abandoned.

Until now, I have considered brainwashing as negative and limiting. Even though limiting, some childhood brainwashing is good. Eat properly. Go to school. Don't walk in front of a moving car. I "must" wash my hands after using the bathroom, or I have an uneasy feeling of forgetting something important. Brainwashing is necessary for training soldiers to put the interests of their country above their own comforts and interests.

As a Christian, it is important to teach children in a gentle way to love and believe in Jesus and God, so they can culture their own spiritual beliefs as adults. Religion like normal life is a compromise between conformity and creativity. Jesus and other great leaders did not conform to current standards.

Christians believe Jesus indwells within our minds and souls and invites us to become spiritually complete and accepted in heaven for Eternity. Jesus and saved souls are integrated within God's higher dimensions. Spirits, resonating spiritual waves, in heaven are more real than human minds and bodies on earth.

In public and religious education, we must teach our youth how to think and not what to think. Great discoveries and organizations were made by people who have learned how to think. Spiritual discoveries will be made by spiritual leaders who have learned how to think and communicate with God.

A Philosophy of Healing and Spirituality

Using the Large Hadron Collider in CERN, Switzerland, physicists have recently discovered the, high energy, 120 GEV Higgs Boson, or "God" particle for understanding God's creation of matter and gravity. Understanding building blocks of the universe will provide greater understanding of God. It took fifty years to design and construct the Large Hadron Collider and the experiments and sensors to prove Higgs's and Englert's impressive theory. I love connecting science with God.

Traditional spiritual models describe few details of life after death. Christians believe there are many mansions or rooms in heaven for our Eternity. With the understanding people had in traditional religious times, this was a reasonable interpretation.

With the current science, we may be able to improve on models of heaven. Heaven and God consist of infinite spiritual waves and resonances. Upon death, saved humans become harmonics within God's infinite waves and Hologram. If prayers influence God, spiritual humans will have influence on God's activities and decisions.

This model has implications. If angels influence God, it is idiotic for young people to abuse or steal from older people. Heaven will be lost. Respecting elders is an age old spiritual tradition.

Christians are blessed when following God's suggestions or commands even in difficult at times. We are most spiritual when bearing God's burdens. Each of us has opportunities to be spiritual, even in unexpected times. The best of times is overcoming long, difficult challenges.

While writing this book, I have developed principles to enhance my own and others lives. My peoples of all nationalities and races love and nurture peoples of all nationalities and races. They never unnecessarily control, or feel and act superior to, anyone. They do not believe their religions are superior or perfect. I frequently pray to nurture my people. Spiritual relationships are with God, but truthful spiritual leaders can help us develop unique spiritual paths. Humans are unique with unique experiences.

Evil people are not my people. Some believe their religions are superior and perfect. They do not mind hurting, controlling, acting superior to, bullying, stealing from, lying to, or killing, others. I mostly avoid these lost souls but sometimes pray they will discover God's purpose for their lives.

I am thankful for being able to obey God's calling. In a world with so much brainwashing and hate, please keep truth, creativity, and love alive. May God bless everyone working to heal their minds and to discover their spiritual destinies. Without thinking of the future, we are nothing.

At times, I have had intuitive, spiritual ideas, which seemed so original that words have not been defined to describe them. Too often, ideas are lost. If we work towards God's needs of completion, we are meeting our own needs of completion.

Evil schemes to make and makes dishonest incompleteness. Subconscious processes iterate and converge to complete, truthful consciousness for each moment. The soul integrates each moment in life to converge toward a complete spiritual life. Saying, "Bless my soul," means to bless an entire life. God integrates all souls to assist Him converge to complete understanding and control, of the universe and heaven.

The mind, soul, and God always search for completeness. Untruthful, evil lives do not assist God in His Holy Completeness. Overcoming the greatest obstacles to completeness provides the greatest rewards of completeness.

Thank you for being a part of this mind and spiritual adventure. Expect to love everyone, but we may choose not to love those abusing us. You may lose your health if you do! To the best of my ability, I have been truthful. I could not have had so many ideas without God's guidance. This is my story; this is my song, praising my Savior all the day long. Amen.

Everybody's crazy but you and me! You have read this book and may add to, or create new, models. We have taken a mental and spiritual path less traveled. Readers must dream and pursue their own healing and spiritual adventures. Together we must have great expectations for the future!

I have written about unusual, serious, and difficult ideas and occurrences. Let's keep our sense of humor. I conclude with two humorous sing-a-long songs I have written. Enjoy!

All About JACK ©
by
Hugh Drummond Fulcher - Physicist

A sing along song – for audience participation!

Instrumental theme –Jack's our man if he can't do it, nobody can!

It's a little ditty about an old friend, - Jack *instrumental theme*
If you don't know him you don't know, - Jack! - *instrumental*
Who's in love with the Queen of Hearts? - Jack! - *instrumental*
She's queen and fate's mean, don't go back, - Jack! - *instrumental*

Who ate no-fat but licked the platter clean? - Jack! - *Instrumental*
Who bought magic beans for the bean stalk? - Jack! - *Instrumental*
Who is nimble - and who is quick? - Jack! - *Instrumental*
And who jumped over the candle stick? - Jack! - *Instrumental*

Who works all trades, but master of none? - Jack! - *Instrumental*
Who built his house and kept on building? - Jack! - *Instrumental*
Who sat in a corner eating plumb pie? - Jack! - *Instrumental*
When the frost is on the pumpkin, there's - Jack! - *Instrumental*

Her tire is flat, and yes she needs, - Jack!   - *Instrumental*
Who went to fetch a pail of water? - Jack!   - *Instrumental*
And who fell down and broke his crown? - Jack! - *Instrumental*
Who still loves Jill on that steep hill? - Jack!   - *Instrumental*

Who still loves Jill on that steep hill? - Jack!   - Slow *Instrumental*

Instrumental

Repeat

Say Cheese ©
by
Hugh Drummond Fulcher - Physicist

A sing along song – for audience participation!

Instrumental - *This little ditty begins and ends with, Cheese*

This little ditty begins and ends with, - Cheese – *Instrumental*
Sing this song with me if you, - please – *Instrumental*
That girl over there is just a, - tease - *Instrumental*
There's nothing to do but shoot the, - breeze - *Instrumental*

We can go no where without our, - keys – *Instrumental*
Sit down with me and feel at, - ease - *Instrumental*
Babe, let's dream to sail the seven, - seas - *Instrumental*
Now let's talk 'bout the birds and, - bees - *Instrumental*

It's cold out side and we might, - freeze - Ins*trumenta*l
The snow is falling, let's grab our, - skis - *Instrumental*
Going down hill we must bend our, - knees - *Instrumental*
If we get too wet, we might, - sneeze! - *Instrumental*

Now babe don't boast 'bout your smart, - degrees - *Instrumental*
Come along with me and be my, - squeeze - *Instrumental*
Now is the moment that we must, - seize - *Instrumental*
Smile at the camera and just say, - cheese - *Instrumental*

Smile at the camera and just say, - cheese – "Slow" *Instrumental*

Slow Instrumental - *This little ditty begins and ends with, Cheese*

www.ingramcontent.com/pod-product-compliance
Lightning Source LLC
Chambersburg PA
CBHW070159240426

43671CB00007B/493